Ringgummimatte
Micha Zweifel

A note on captions:
Matthew Stadler composed the captions by visiting Micha Zweifel's library many times and selecting a dozen or so books from which to take quotations. Each quotation is identified by author and book title. Following each quotation, the captions also identify the artworks or scenes pictured.

Anmerkung zu den Bildlegenden:
Matthew Stadler hat die Bibliothek von Micha Zweifel mehrmals besucht und sich rund ein Dutzend Bücher ausgesucht, um die Bildlegenden in Zitatform zu verfassen. Die Herkunft jedes Zitats ist durch Autor und Buchtitel gekennzeichnet. Im Anschluss werden die abgebildeten Kunstwerke oder Szenen genannt.
(Deutsche Übersetzung ab Seite 79)

Dodie Bellamy
Crimes Against Genre in *Academonia*

Walter Benjamin
Arcades Project (translated from German by Howard Eiland and Kevin McLaughlin)
Das Passagen-Werk

Walter Benjamin
One Way Street in *Illuminations* (translated from German by Harry Zohn)
Einbahnstraße

Walter Benjamin
What is Epic Theater? in *Illuminations* (translated from German by Harry Zohn)
Was ist episches Theater?

Michael Camille
Image on the Edge

T. J. Clark
Painting at Ground Level

Tove Jansson
The Summer Book (translated from Swedish by Thomas Teal)
Das Sommerbuch (Übersetzung aus dem Schwedischen von Birgitta Kicherer)

Siegfried Kracauer
Ginster (translated from German by Carl Skoggard)
Ginster

Siegfried Kracauer
The Salaried Masses (translated from German by Quintin Hoare)
Die Angestellten

Agnes Martin
Writings
Schriften (Übersetzung aus dem Englischen durch das Kunstmuseum Winterthur)

Eileen Myles
Afterglow (a dog memoir)

Michael Polanyi
Personal Knowledge

Gertrude Stein
Composition as Explanation in *What Are Masterpieces?*

1 “Sophia had no flashlight, and it was dark. The path was an endless, empty street in the moonlight between shaggy houses. At the end of the street was the window with its moon-white sky, and beneath the window lay the robe, a pile of stiff folds, coal-black in its own shadow. Sophia had slammed the trapdoor with such a bang that she couldn’t retreat. And so she crept over and sat down in her cardboard box.” Tove Jansson, *The Summer Book.* THE TALK, 2014, exhibition view, TENT Rotterdam, photo: Ghislain Amar

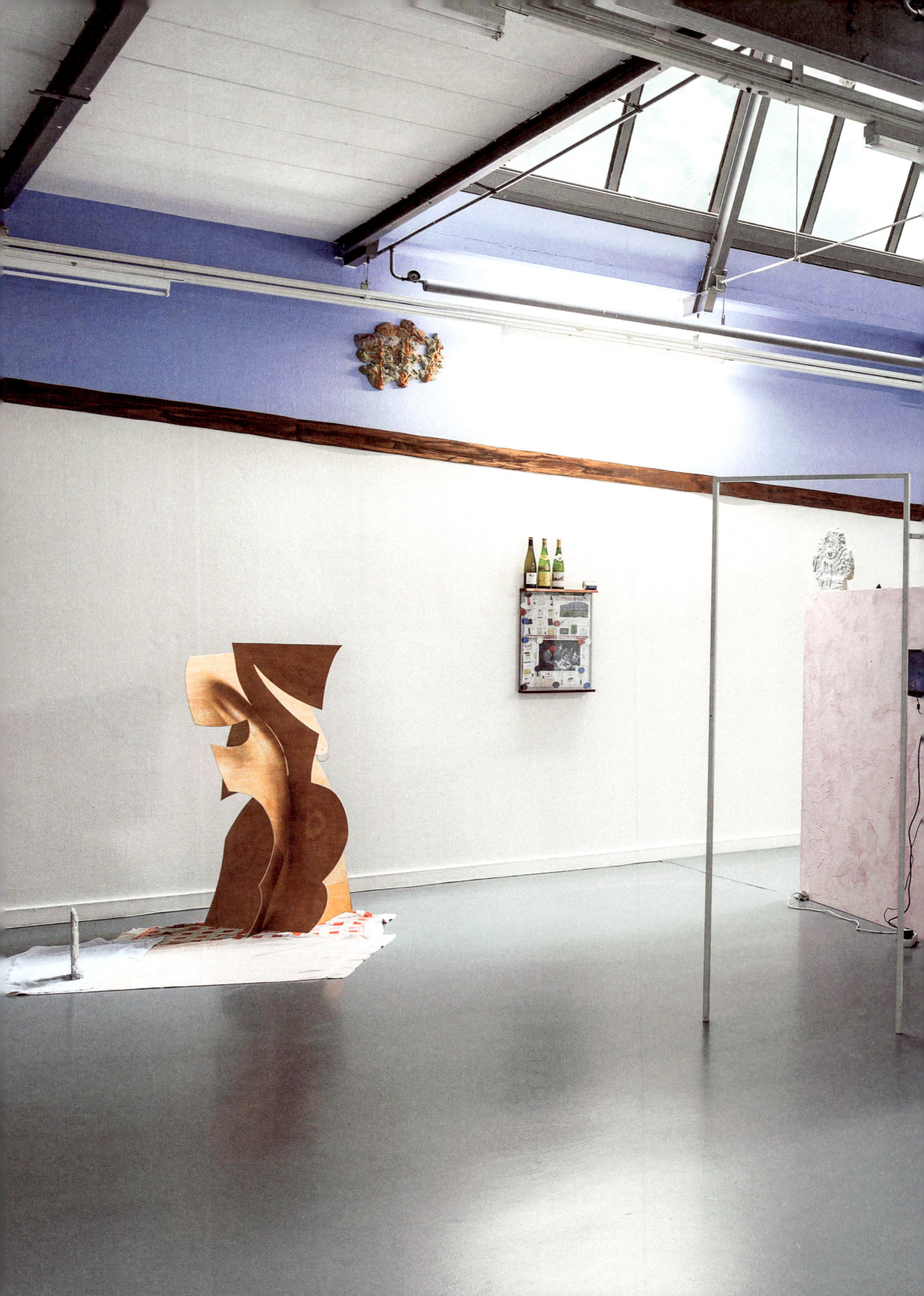

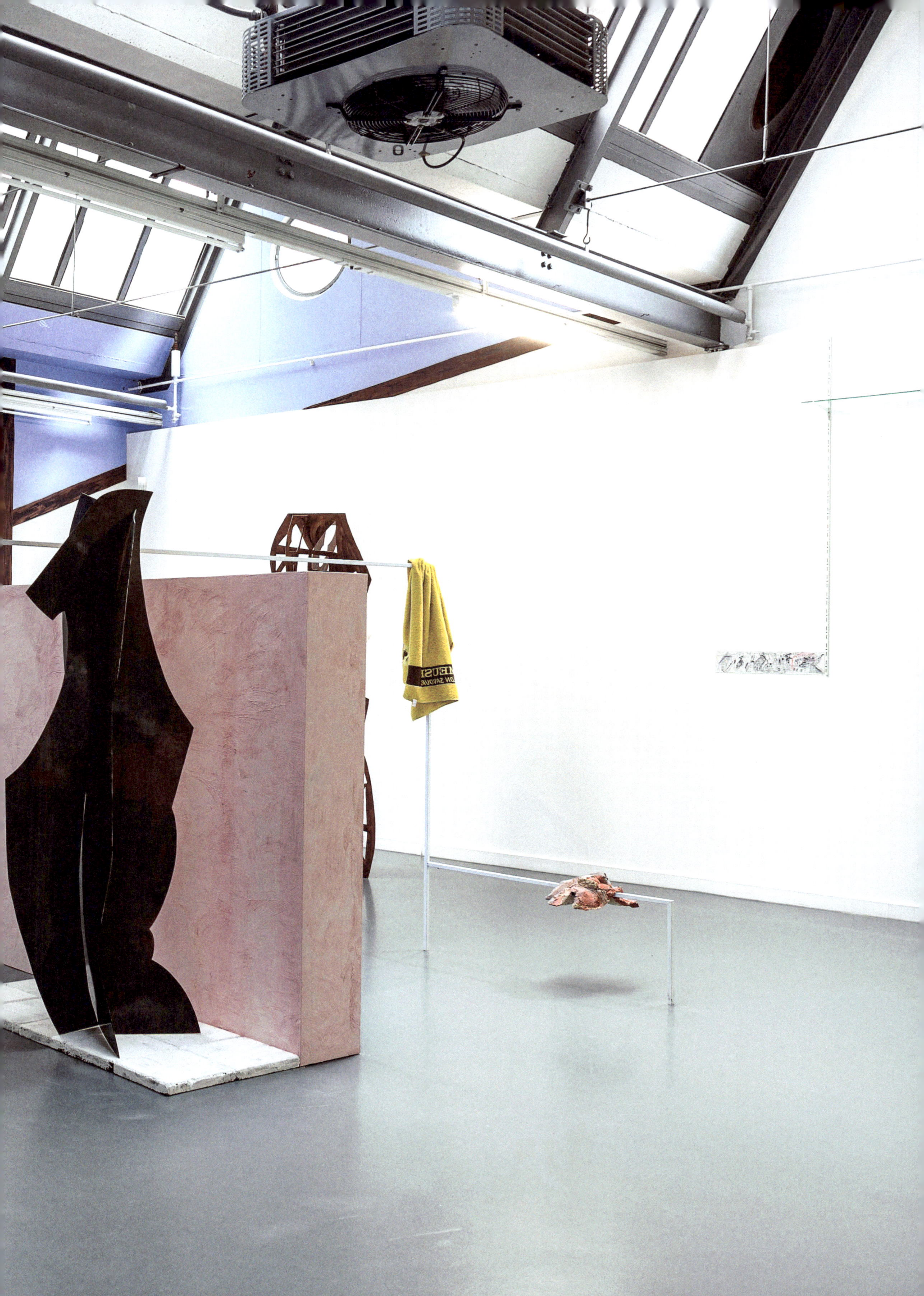

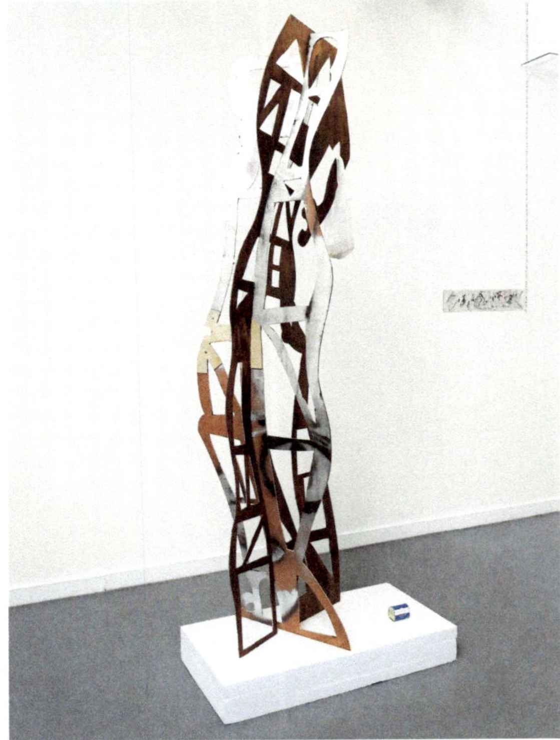

2 "The legs were by themselves in the world. They tore the ground to shreds and pressed on with nothing beneath them. Often they marched across the clouds, wading through the blue holes." Siegfried Kracauer, *Ginster.* FAIRE DES COMMISSIONS, 2014, plywood, spray paint, stain, styrofoam, foie gras, TENT Rotterdam, photo: Ghislain Amar

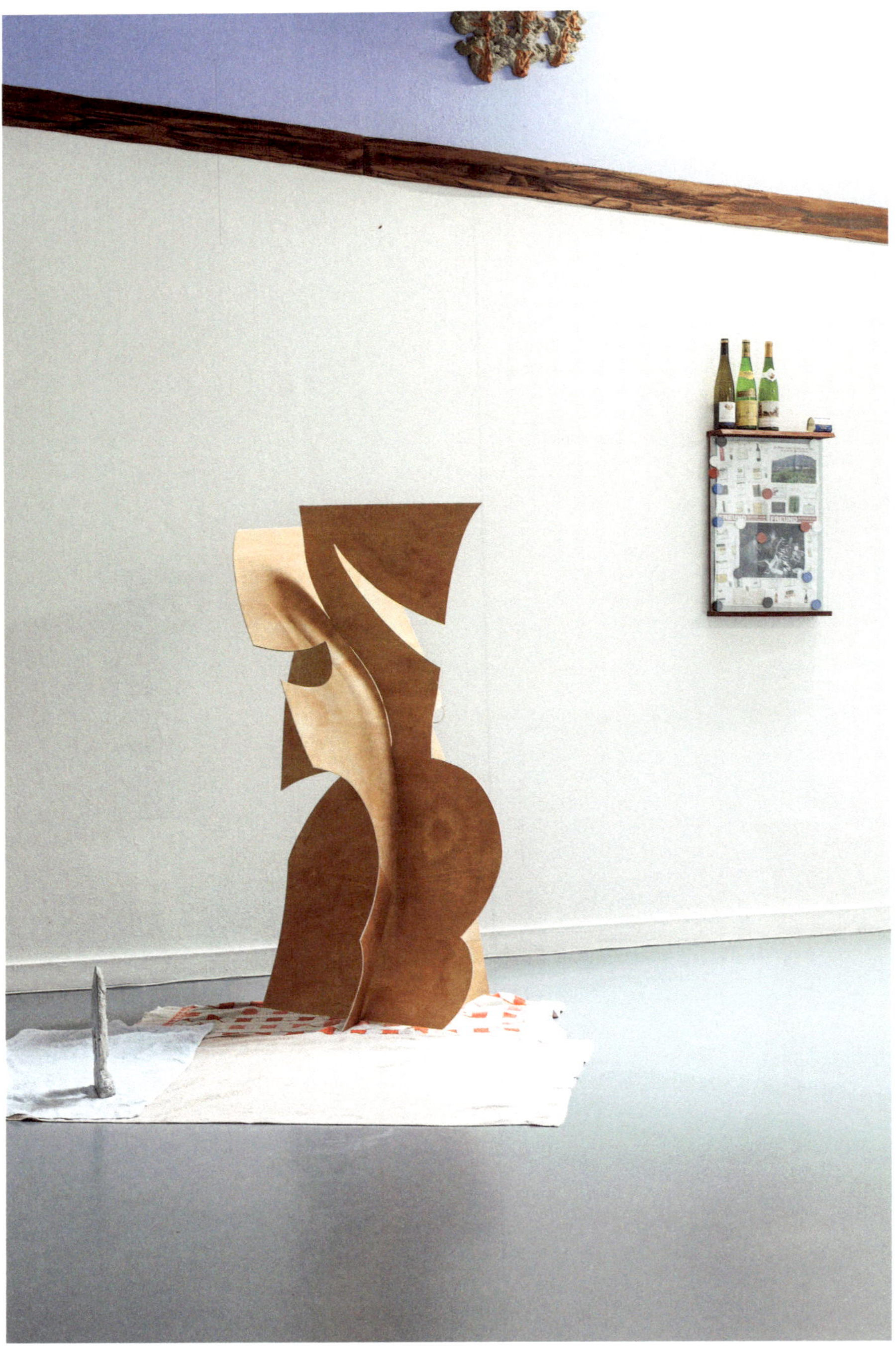

3 "The pretense of children is not a dream. They are playing and they know it." Agnes Martin, *Writings*. BAIGNEUR, 2014, Stained plywood, earring, towels, TENT Rotterdam, photo: Ghislain Amar

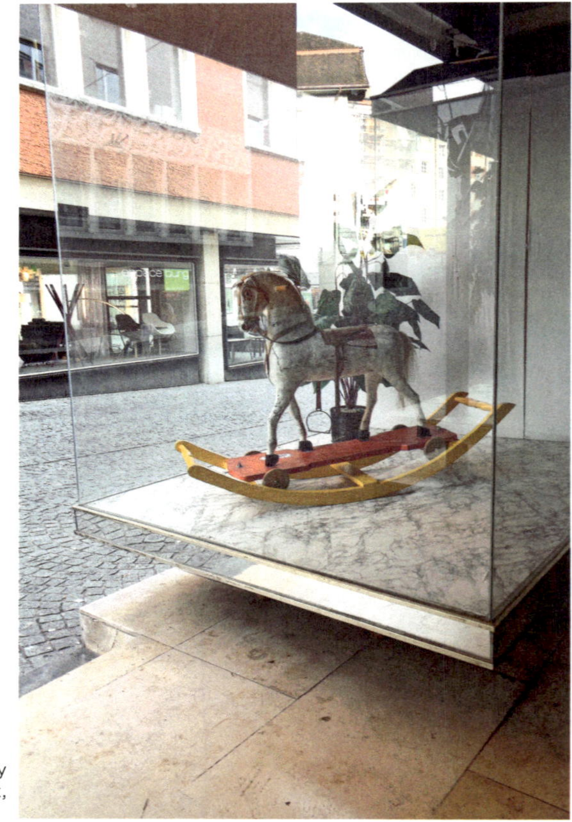

4 "For even here, in the land of the fallen, the memory of bipedalism lives on. The egg is the evolutionary cycle beginning again. The first cell sprouts legs, steadies itself, and sets off up Darwin's hill." T.J. Clark, *Painting at Ground Level.* Shop window, Biel/Bienne, 2016

Art does not emerge in a vacuum. It is always located in space and time. After all, we are shaped by where we come from, what culture we live in, which language(s) we speak or what education we have had. Through their works artists respond, albeit in very different ways, to society, to their environment, to the time they live in. But, vice versa, does art enable us to draw conclusions about the world? For example, what world would extra-terrestrials who landed by chance in Micha Zweifel's exhibition see? What would they tell their loved one on their far-distant home planet?

From a window the gaze falls on undergrowth or the full moon (fig. 96), a chalet stands in the deep snow (fig. 97), Sam's car is parked by the edge of the forest (fig. 100), swans swim on a pond (fig. 58), animals graze on an alp (fig. 84), perhaps there's a bakery, but there's certainly enough to eat where the journeymen lie on the ground with bloated bellies (fig. 87, 88). The architecture consists mainly of brick walls, street lamps glow in numerous places, pets lie or sit around the place, solitary flies appear. It is a simple world with simple furnishings, apart from several tall, fragile, modernist sculptures (fig. 1–3), which also seem to be ageing a bit. Not much is earned here. This world is more suburb or working class neighborhood than fashionable centre.

And the people? Teenagers slouching on chairs and window sills (fig. 5, 6, 120), travelling on the bus or sitting on steps dangling a ciggie in their mouth (fig. 23, 24). In addition to these almost or actually life-size juveniles, three smaller, stocky figures populate this world combining infirmity and mischievousness in a wayward alliance.

Micha Zweifel is interested in how the world is shaped, how buildings, logos, ads, workplaces and the many inconspicuous little things we often do not perceive consciously, impact our bodies and our psyche. On his way through the city, the artist photographs masonry, doormats, architectural details, façade decorations, advertising signs, sculptures in the public domain, attempts at all kinds of improvements, and animals, again and again: swans, chickens, dogs, donkeys. The collection of images is not systematic, instead Micha Zweifel captures things that strike him *en passant*. The details and situations are mostly rather ordinary and sometimes quite ugly. Micha Zweifel does not evaluate, however. He turns his attention to, and a curious, affectionate gaze on the more or less deficient banalities and inadequate solutions, whereby his snapshots are as unpretentious as his motifs. The, at first sight, arbitrary frames are precisely focussed on a situation or a structure that Micha Zweifel translates directly or indirectly into plaster reliefs, sculptures or installations.

This interest in the simple combined with figurative representation recalls the work of Peter Fischli and David Weiss, that famous artist-duo with whom Micha Zweifel shares the loving gaze at the ordinary, the unadorned everyday, the work with simple materials and the lapidary nature of the titles. But Micha Zweifel does not offer us SUDDENLY THIS OVERVIEW or the whole VISIBLE WORLD (titles of works by Fischli / Weiss). His works are instantaneous takes, fragile and precarious. There may well be an inherent narrative, but its frays at the edges or leads nowhere. Series tend not to be complete, but rather to incline towards slow change. His latest series of white plaster reliefs (fig. 84, 91, 119) therefore is based on a casting model that changes slightly from image to image. First, the mountain landscape turns up in an alp. Then that landscape slowly becomes urban, the Swiss Alps become a Dutch city so that the artist's two current lifeworlds intermingle. CALENDAR—the tile of the series—is thus also a three-dimensional expression of time.

In addition to his everyday living environment, Micha Zweifel's work is also replete with references from art history and folk art, whereby here too simple everyday life is to the fore, as in the Dutch peasant genre founded by Pieter Bruegel the Elder (1525–1569). Micha Zweifel cites his paintings TWO MONKEYS (1562) and THE LAND OF COCKAIGNE (1567), reversed, due to the casting technique (fig. 81, 87–88). The CALENDAR series recalls cattle drives up to the Appenzell alpine pastures due to the repetition and partly due to the motif. Modernist sculptures similar to those by Antoine Pevsner seem to have inspired a series of thin plywood sculptures that play with concepts of statics, verticality and fragility (fig. 1, 3), while the bronze sculptures take up themes from classical sculpture or else the fragmentation and dynamics of Cubism and Futurism. Like the statue THE DESTROYED CITY (1951–1953, fig. 56) by Ossip Zadkine (1890–1967), Micha Zweifel's bronze figures also seem to be simultaneously powerful and wounded. The vulnerability they exude results essentially from the technique and the concomitant surface finish. When making these bronze sculptures (fig. 25, 29, 37, 39) the artist forms the casting model by welding the wax slabs together directly; these normally only serve to transfer a model. Because he leaves out the intermediary step, there is always only just one single cast; the model is lost during casting. The seams, the openings and the view inside seem to speak of hard times, but the mischievous faces contrast with this, as does the dancing pose in the case of LIFT. Micha Zweifel's works have a characteristic haptic quality and workmanlike finish. For this reason he believes it is important to master techniques himself and explore how they can be employed even in a way that is contrary to the traditional methods. In his case, "banal motifs" serve to direct the eye to the "problems of making something", as he writes to his father in an email exchange reproduced in this publication.

Just like one relief can emerge from the previous one, so too different works combine in his exhibitions to create situations, only to then turn up again a few years later in different connections. For example, the little dog HÜNDLI (fig. 5) has a master at his side (FREUND ET FILS, 2013–2018, fig. 113, 117) in a later exhibition. The point of departure for Micha Zweifel's work is the heterogeneity of the world, the simultaneity of different perceptions. Thus the gaze at the world, inspiration, and the artwork are constantly interacting, like the pictorial worlds in this publication. Micha Zweifel shows that works do not emerge in isolation, that art and life intermingle and proceed in a field of references. That is certainly much more obvious when seen from outer space.

5 "The peasants luxuriate in the temporary city." T.J. Clark, *Painting at Ground Level*. THE TALK, 2014, exhibition view, TENT Rotterdam, photo: Ghislain Amar

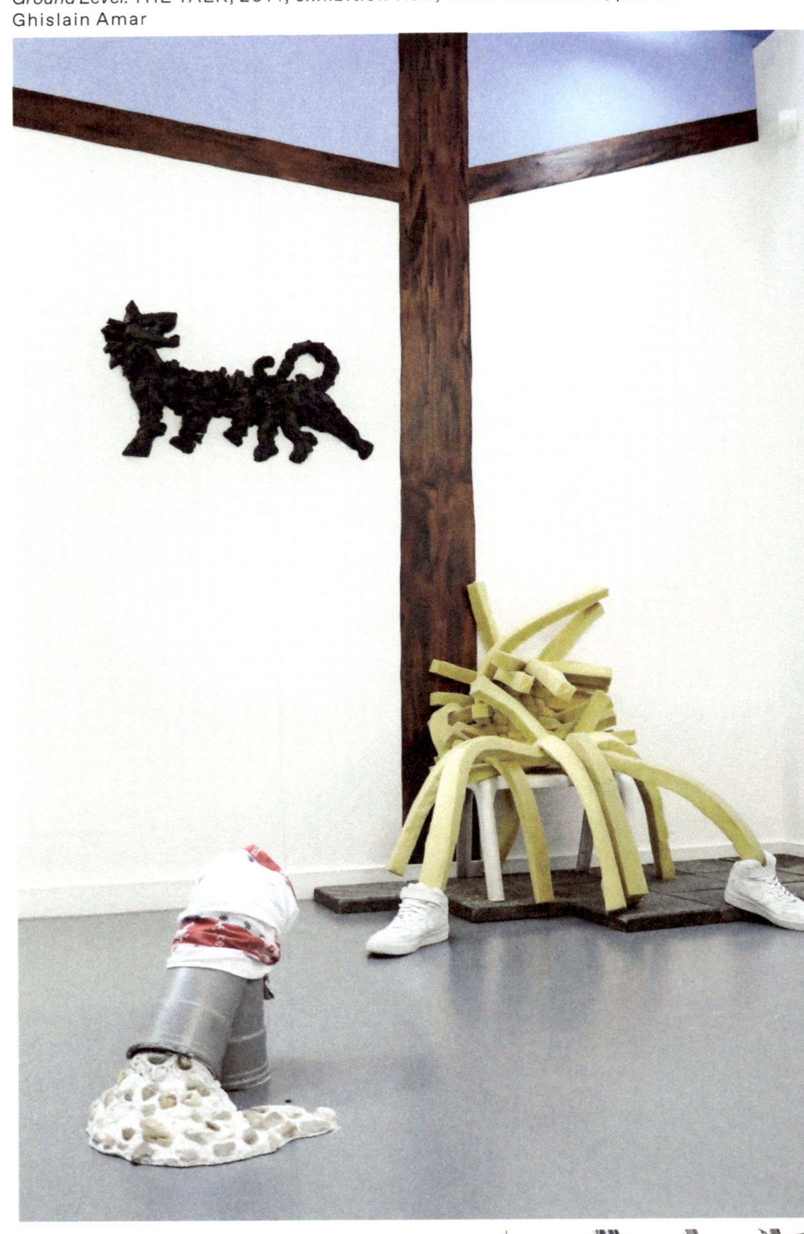

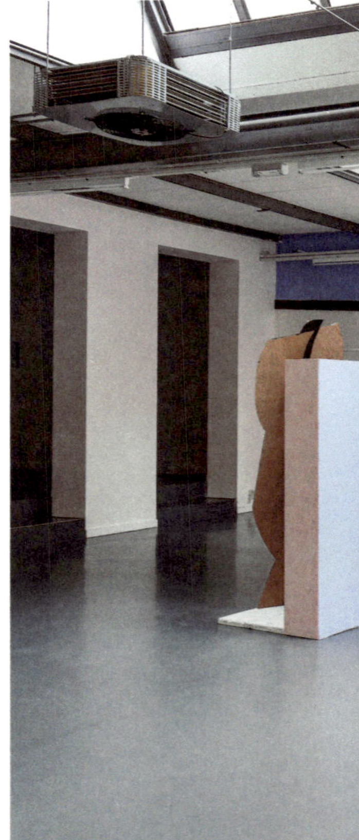

Kunst entsteht nicht im luftleeren Raum. Sie ist immer zeitlich und geografisch verortet. Denn wo wir herkommen, in welcher Kultur wir leben, welche Sprache(n) wir sprechen oder welche Ausbildung wir haben, prägt uns. Künstlerinnen und Künstler reagieren mit ihren Werken auf die Gesellschaft, auf die Umgebung, auf die Zeit, in der sie leben, wenn auch auf sehr vielfältige Weise. Doch ermöglicht umgekehrt die Kunst Rückschlüsse auf die Welt? Welche Welt würden beispielsweise zufällig in Micha Zweifels Ausstellung gelandete Außerirdische sehen? Was würden sie den Lieben auf dem fernen Heimatplaneten berichten?

Aus dem Fenster fällt der Blick auf Gestrüpp oder den Vollmond (Abb. 96), ein Chalet steht tief verschneit im Schnee (Abb. 97), Sams Auto ist am Waldrand geparkt (Abb. 100), auf einem Weiher schwimmen Schwäne (Abb. 58), Vieh weidet auf der Alp (Abb. 84), vielleicht gibt es eine Bäckerei, sicher aber genug zu essen, so wie die Gesellen mit geblähten Bäuchen am Boden liegen (Abb. 87, 88). Die Architektur besteht hauptsächlich aus Backsteinmauern, vielerorts leuchten Straßenlampen, Haustiere liegen oder sitzen herum, vereinzelt tauchen Fliegen auf. Es ist eine einfache Welt mit simpler Möblierung, mit Ausnahme von einigen hohen, fragilen, modernistischen Skulpturen (Abb. 1–3), die aber auch schon etwas in die Jahre gekommen zu sein scheinen. Hier wird nicht allzu viel verdient. Diese Welt ist mehr Vorstadt oder Arbeiterquartier als schickes Zentrum.

Und die Menschen? Da lümmeln Teenager cool auf Stühlen und Fenstersimsen (Abb. 5, 6, 120), fahren Bus oder sitzen mit einem Stängel im Mund auf der Treppe (Abb. 23, 24). Neben diesen fast oder tatsächlich lebensgroßen Jugendlichen bevölkern diese Welt drei kleinere, gedrungene Figuren, in denen Versehrtheit und Schalk eine eigenwillige Verbindung eingehen.

Micha Zweifel interessiert sich für die Gestaltung der Welt, dafür wie Architekturen, Logos, Reklame, der Arbeitsplatz und die vielen kleinen unscheinbaren Dinge, die wir oft nicht bewusst wahrnehmen, auf Körper und Psyche wirken. Unterwegs in der Stadt fotografiert der Künstler Mauerwerk, Fußabstreifer, architektonische Details, Fassadendekorationen, Reklameschilder, Skulpturen im öffentlichen Raum, Verschönerungsversuche aller Art und immer wieder Tiere: Schwäne, Hühner, Hunde, Esel. Die Bildersammlung ist nicht systematisch angelegt, vielmehr erfasst Micha Zweifel Dinge, die ihm en passant auffallen. Die festgehaltenen Details und Situationen sind meist von ausgesprochener Gewöhnlichkeit und manchmal eher hässlich. Doch Micha Zweifel wertet nicht, vielmehr wendet er sich aufmerksam, mit neugierig-liebevollem Blick den mehr oder weniger mangelhaften Alltäglichkeiten und unzulänglichen Lösungen zu. Seine Schnappschüsse sind dabei so unprätentiös wie die Motive. Die auf den ersten Blick willkürlichen Ausschnitte fokussieren jedoch präzise auf eine Situation oder Struktur, die Micha Zweifel direkt oder indirekt in Gipsreliefs, Skulpturen oder Installationen übersetzt.

Das Interesse am Simplen, verbunden mit gegenständlicher Darstellung, erinnert an die Werke von Peter Fischli und David Weiss. Mit dem berühmten Künstlerduo teilt Micha Zweifel den liebevollen Blick auf das Gewöhnliche, den ungeschönten Alltag, das Schaffen mit einfachen Materialien und das Lapidare der Titel. Micha Zweifel bietet jedoch weder PLÖTZLICH DIESE ÜBERSICHT noch die ganze SICHTBARE WELT (so zwei Werktitel von Fischli/Weiss). Seine Arbeiten sind

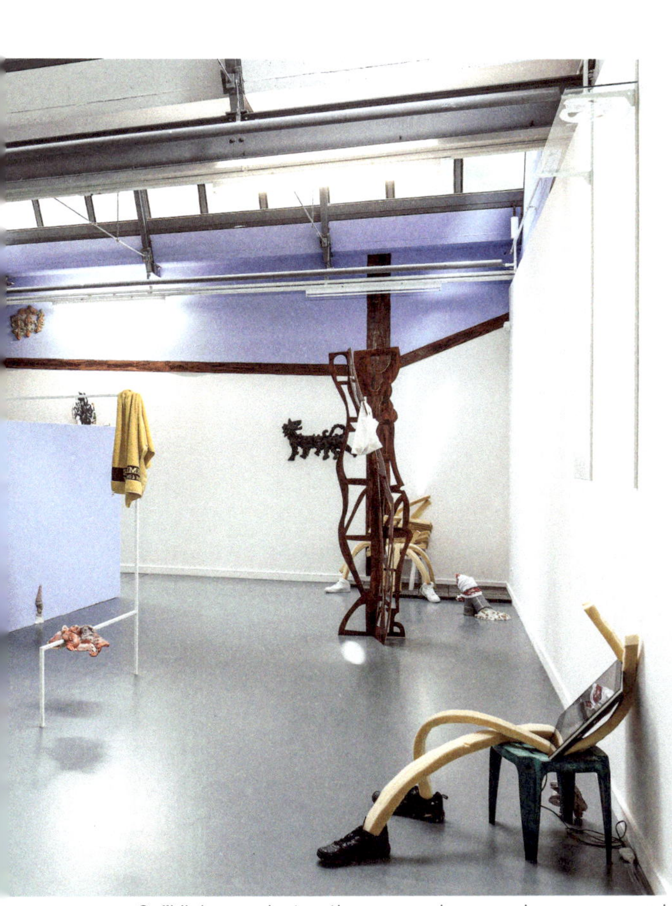

6 "Violence, destructiveness and possessiveness are an integral part of response to the concrete. This distresses some people very much and they would like to escape from response to the concrete in order to avoid them. But there is no escape." Agnes Martin, *Writings*. THE TALK, 2014, exhibition view, TENT Rotterdam, photo: Ghislain Amar

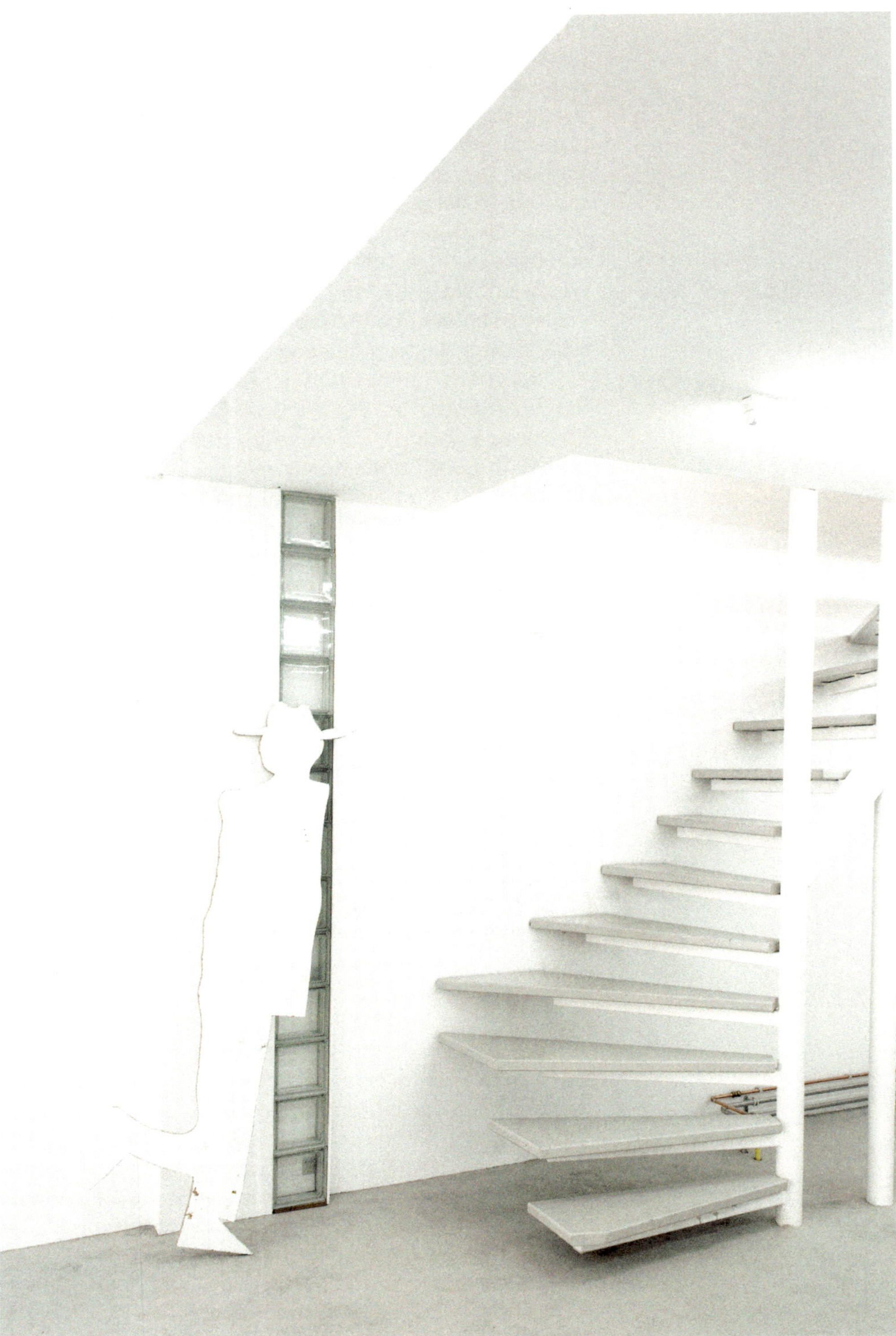

7 “He was long and expressionless, like a mark of punctuation which sets off nothing. After the war it was his intention to go on growing, straight into his father’s business.” Siegfried Kracauer, *Ginster*. LEANING FIGURE, 2016, coated chip board, glass bricks, Rib Rotterdam, photo: Sabrina Chou

Momentaufnahmen, fragil und prekär. Narration ist in ihnen zwar angelegt, franst aber aus oder führt ins Leere. Serien tendieren nicht zur Vollständigkeit, sondern zur langsamen Veränderung. So basiert die neueste Serie weißer Gipsreliefs (Abb. 84, 91, 119) auf einer Gussvorlage, die sich von Bild zu Bild ein wenig wandelt. Zuerst taucht in der Berglandschaft eine Alp auf. Nach und nach wird die Landschaft urban, werden die Schweizer Alpen zur niederländischen Stadt, so dass die beiden aktuellen Lebenswelten des Künstlers ineinander übergehen. KALENDER – so der Titel der Serie – ist insofern auch ein plastischer Ausdruck von Zeit.

Nebst dem alltäglichen Lebensraum fließen Referenzen aus Kunstgeschichte und Volkskunst in Micha Zweifels Arbeit ein, wobei auch hier das einfache, alltägliche Leben im Vordergrund steht, wie in den niederländischen Bauernszenen von Pieter Bruegel dem Älteren (1525–1569). Micha Zweifel zitiert dessen Gemälde ZWEI AFFEN (1562) und DAS SCHLARAFFENLAND (1567) aufgrund der Gusstechnik seitenverkehrt (Abb. 81, 87–88). KALENDER wiederum erinnert in Bezug auf Repetition und teilweise aufgrund des Motivs an Appenzeller Alpaufzüge (Abb. 84, 91). Modernistische Plastiken wie von Antoine Pevsner scheinen Paten gestanden zu haben für ein Serie Skulpturen aus dünnem Sperrholz, die mit Statik, Vertikalität und Fragilität spielen (Abb. 1, 3), während die Bronzeskulpturen eher Themen der klassischen Skulptur oder die Fragmentierung und Dynamik von Kubismus und Futurismus aufgreifen. Wie Ossip Zadkines (1890–1967) Plastik DIE ZERSTÖRTE STADT (1951–1953, Abb. 56) wirken auch Micha Zweifels Bronzefiguren kraftvoll und verwundet zugleich. Die Verletzlichkeit, die sie ausstrahlen, kommt wesentlich aufgrund der Technik und der damit einhergehenden Oberflächenbeschaffenheit zustande. Für die Bronzeskulpturen (Abb. 25, 29, 37, 39) schweißt der Künstler die Gussvorlage direkt aus den Wachsplatten, die normalerweise nur der Übertragung eines Modells dienen. Weil er den Zwischenschritt auslässt, gibt es immer nur einen einzigen Abguss. Die Vorlage geht beim Guss verloren. Die Nähte, die offenen Stellen und der Blick ins Innere scheinen von schweren Zeiten zu erzählen. Die schalkhaften Gesichter kontrastieren jedoch damit und bei LIFT auch die tänzerische Haltung. Haptik und handwerkliche Fertigung prägen Micha Zweifels Arbeiten. Daher ist ihm wichtig, sich selbst Techniken anzueignen und auszuloten, wie sie auch entgegen ihrer traditionellen Methoden eingesetzt werden können. »Banale Motive« dienen ihm dabei, den Blick auf »Probleme des Machens« zu lenken, wie er im E-Mail-Austausch mit seinem Vater in dieser Publikation festhält.

Ähnlich wie ein Relief aus dem vorhergehenden entstehen kann, verbinden sich verschiedene Arbeiten in seinen Ausstellungen zu Situationen, um ein paar Jahre später wieder in anderen Beziehungen aufzutauchen. So erhält beispielsweise das HÜNDLI (Abb. 5) in einer späteren Ausstellung ein Herrchen zur Seite (FREUND ET FILS, 2013–2018, Abb. 113, 117). Ausgangspunkt von Micha Zweifels Arbeit ist die Heterogenität der Welt, die Gleichzeitigkeit unterschiedlicher Wahrnehmungen. So stehen der Blick in die Welt, Inspiration und Kunstwerk in einer steten Wechselbeziehung wie die Bildwelten in dieser Publikation. Micha Zweifel legt offen, dass Werke nie isoliert entstehen, dass Kunst und Leben ineinander gehen und in einem Bezugsfeld stattfinden. Aus dem Weltall gesehen ist das bestimmt noch viel offensichtlicher.

8 "Ground level, then, is, among other things, regression. It is where bodies sink back into sleep or death or disintegration; where fat babies dream." T.J. Clark, *Painting at Ground Level.* Corbel of Limestone French Aquitaine, ca 1150–1200, 2018, The Metropolitan Museum of Art, New York

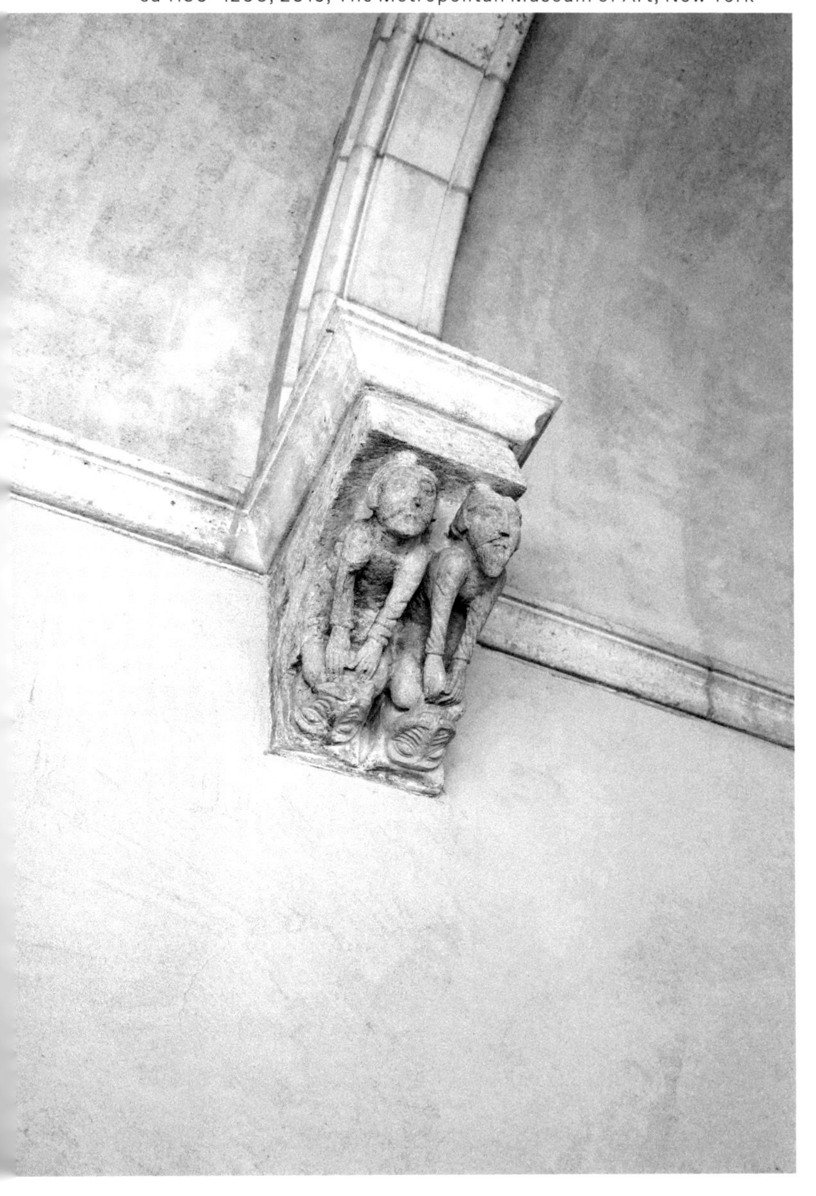

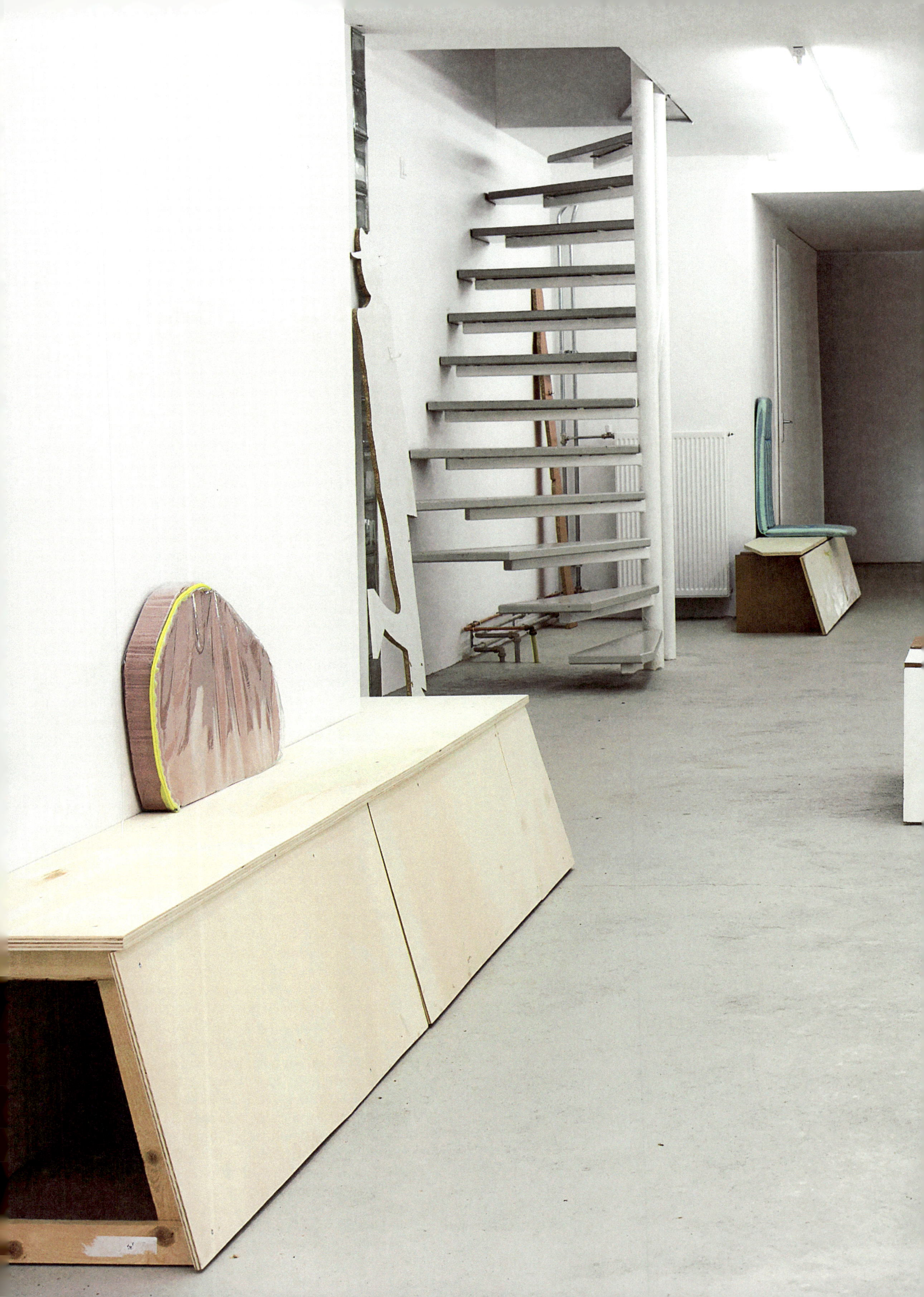

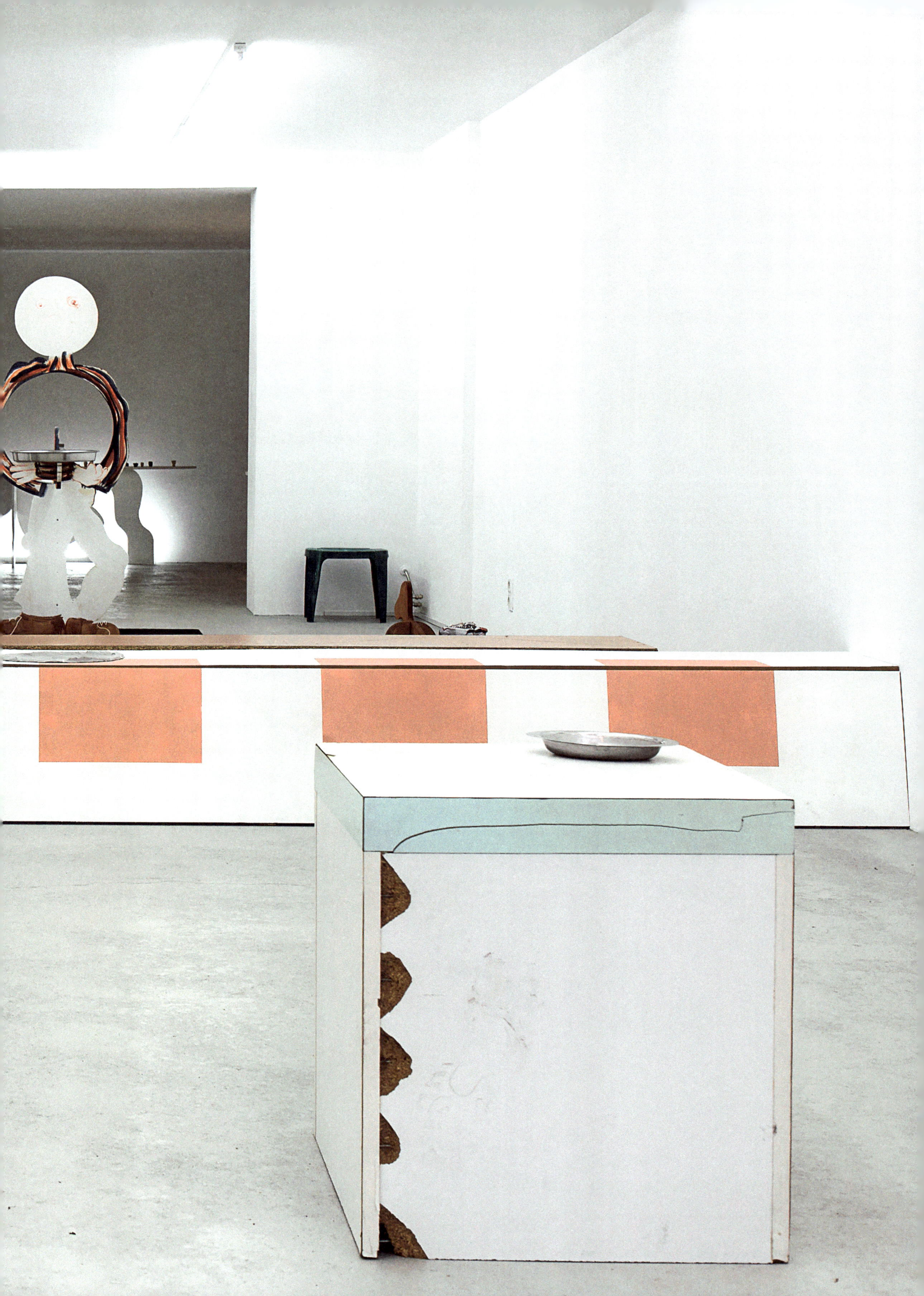

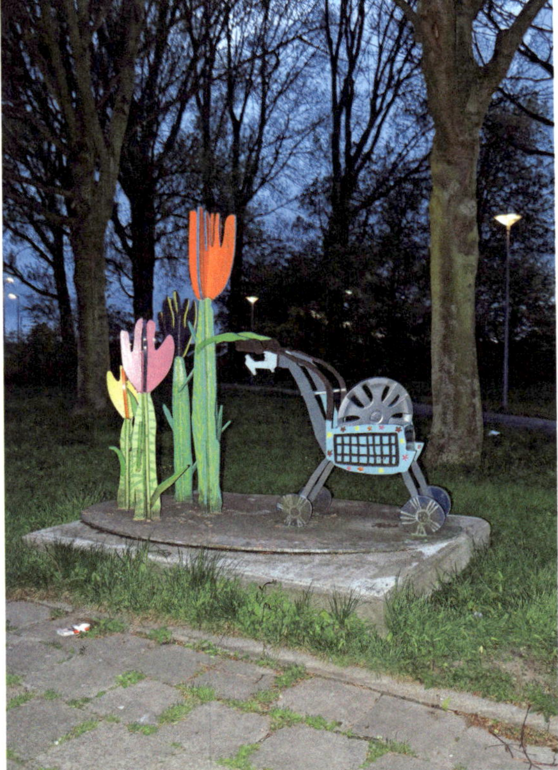

10 “Along toward morning the makeshift fleet split up. The boats floated farther and farther apart, each one setting off by itself to its own home. By dawn, the sea was empty. The wind died. The rain stopped. A clear and lovely midsummer morning arranged its colors in the sky, and it was very cold.” Tove Jansson, *The Summer Book.* Unknown artist, Tulip family with walker, Schulpweg, Rotterdam, 2016

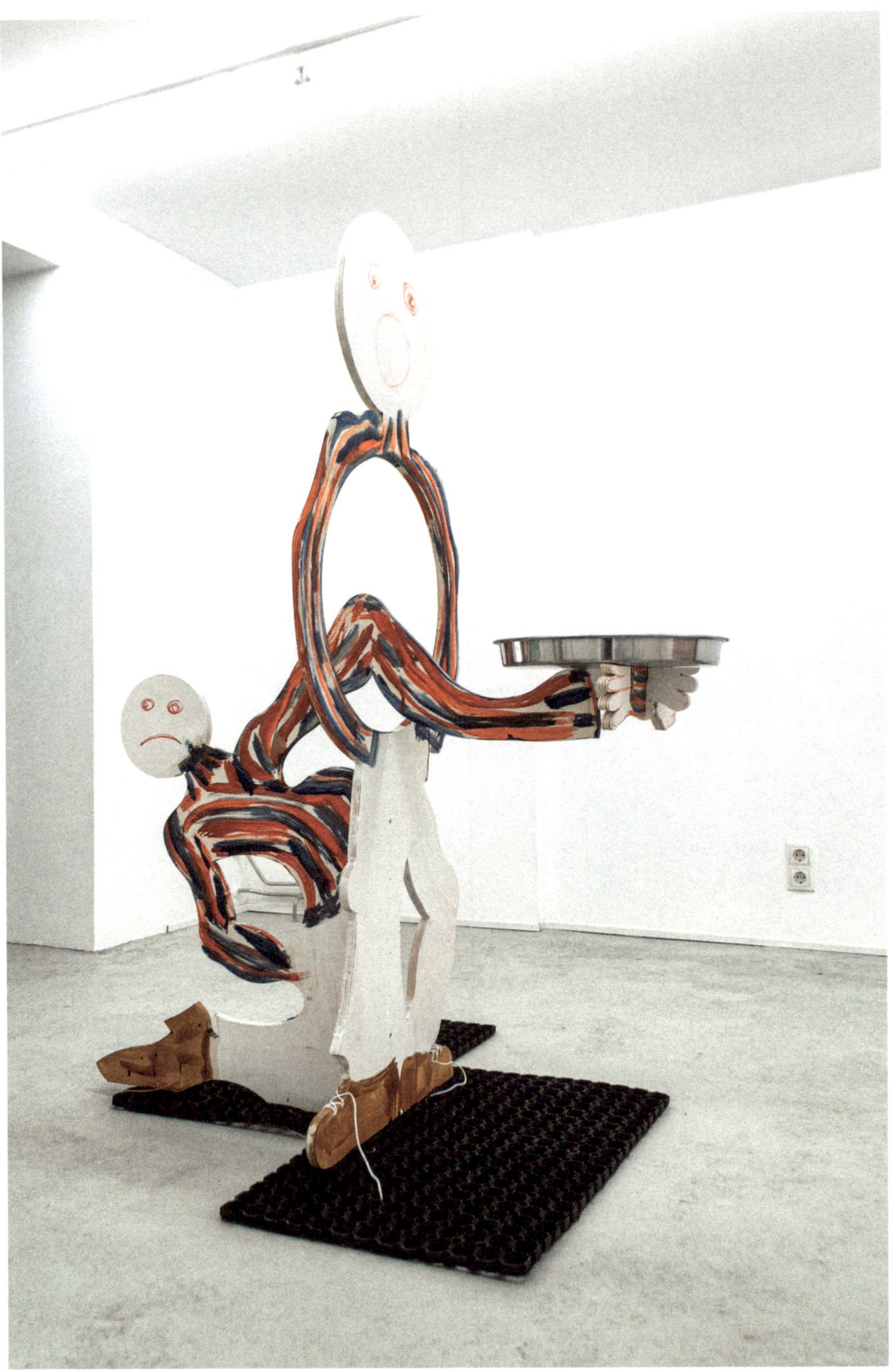

11 “The way we use a hammer or a blind man uses his stick, shows in fact that in both cases we shift outwards the points at which we make contact with the things that we observe as objects outside ourselves. While we rely on a tool or a probe, these are not handled as external objects. We may test the tool for its effectiveness or the probe for its suitability, e.g. in discovering the hidden details of a cavity, but the tool and the probe can never lie in the field of these operations; they remain necessarily on our side of it, forming part of ourselves, the operating persons. We pour ourselves out into them and assimilate them as parts of our own existence. We accept them existentially by dwelling in them.” Michael Polanyi, *Personal Knowledge.* BUTLER (A SERVING SCULPTURE), 2016, plywood, paint, marker, tray, door mat, shoe laces, Rib Rotterdam, photo: Sabrina Chou

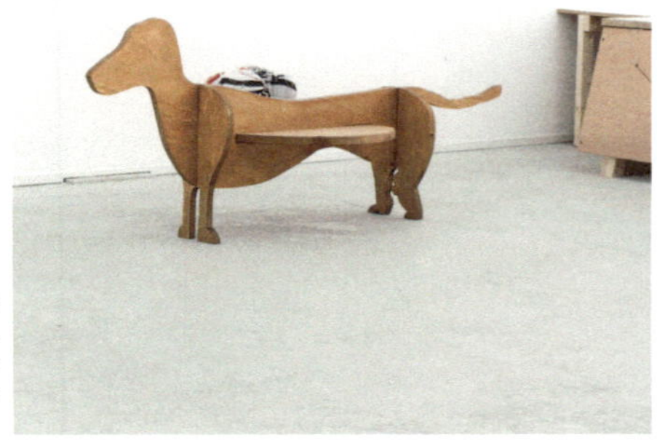

12 “Sophia and Grandmother sat down by the shore to discuss the matter further. It was a pretty day, and the sea was running a long, windless swell. It was on days just like this—dog days—that boats went sailing off all by themselves. Large, alien objects made their way in from the sea, certain things sank and others rose, milk soured, and dragonflies danced in desperation. Lizards were not afraid.” Tove Jansson, *The Summer Book.* DACKEL, 2016, stained plywood, Rib Rotterdam, photo: Sabrina Chou

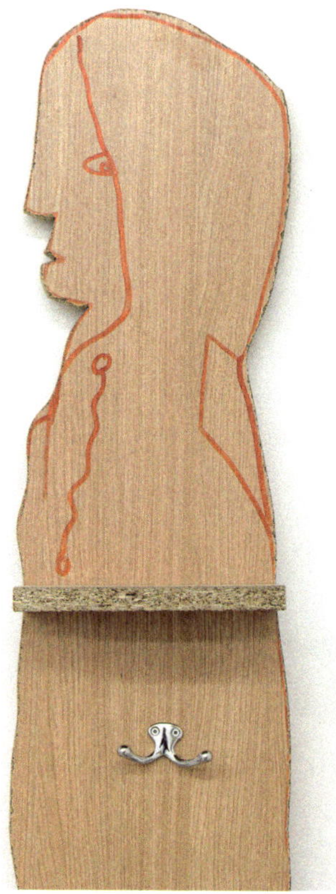

13 "Before the abjection of a blurred genre the traditionalist feels faint. As when death infects life, when poetry infects fiction, identity, system, order is disturbed. The rest stretches out before us, spasming and bleeding." Dodie Bellamy, *Crimes Against Genre* in *Academonia*. SCULPTURE FOR BAGS, JACKETS AND KEYS (LEANING), 2016, chip board with plastic laminate, double hook, marker, Rib Rotterdam, photo: Job Willems

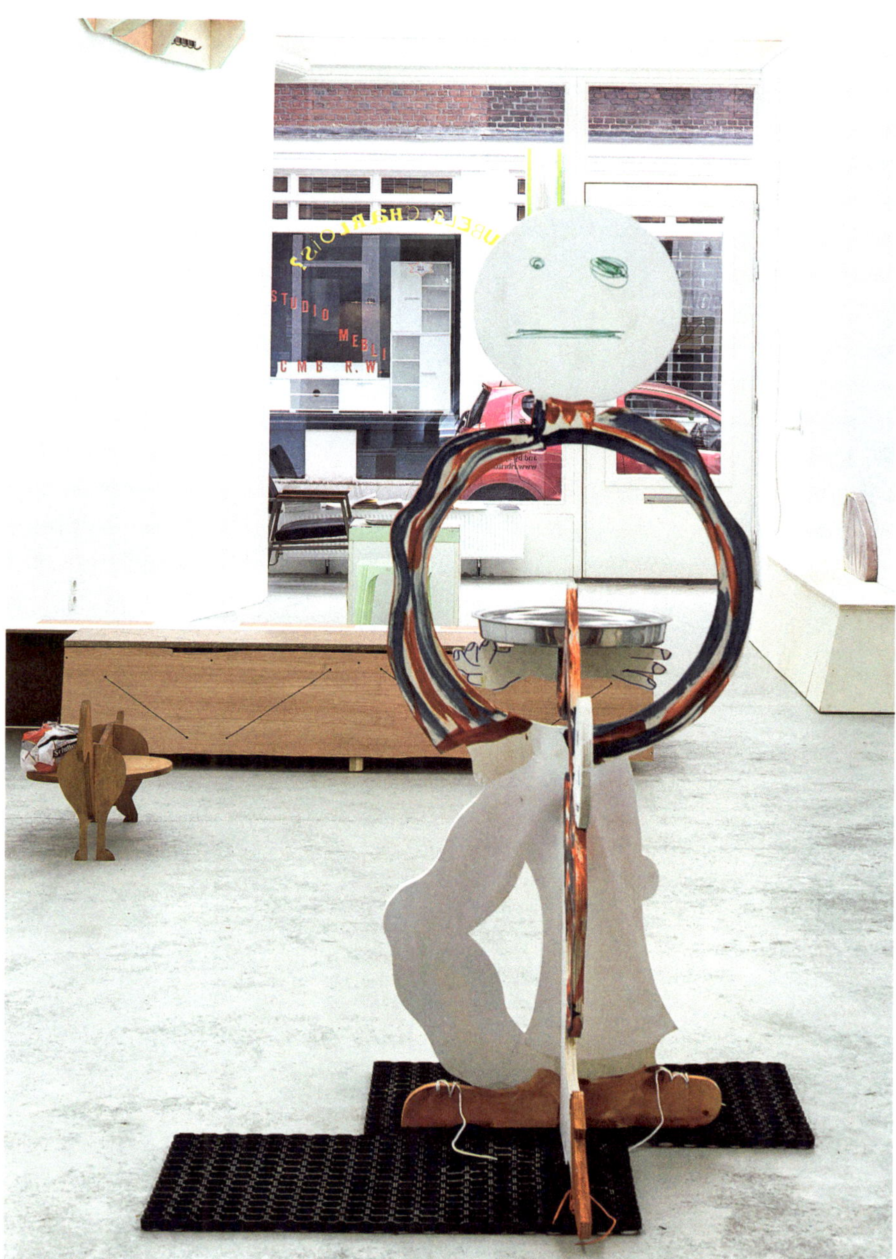

14 "One learns that the tormentor frequently compelled his victim to work according to wrong instructions; described him—humiliated as he already was anyway—as a malingerer; incited him against the departmental manager and the latter against him. As can be seen from the documents of the case, the office monster tormented the petitioner's colleagues too. If one of them made a move to complain, he would at once declare: 'I deny everything.' And people kept quiet out of fear. In despair the petitioner then began to drink and came to work irregularly." Siegfried Kracauer, *The Salaried Masses*. MEUBELS, CHARLOIS?, 2016, exhibition view, Rib Rotterdam, photo: Job Willems

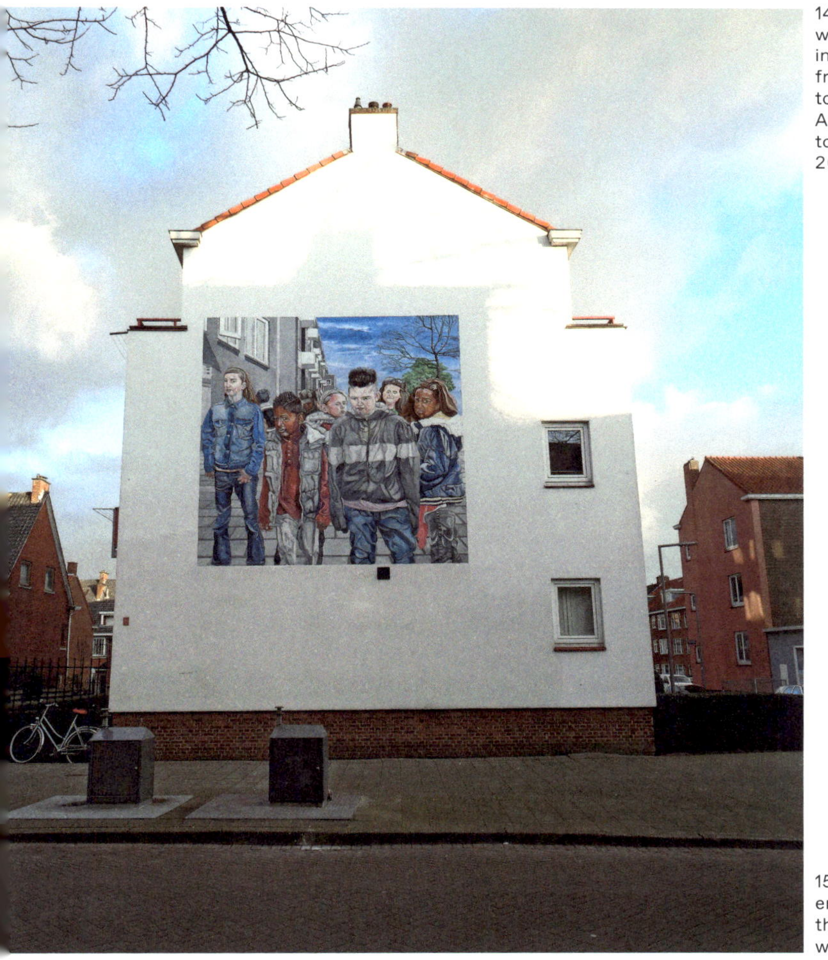

15 "We are in the midst of reality responding with joy. It is an absolutely satisfying experience but extremely elusive. It is elusive because we must recognize so many other things at the same time." Agnes Martin, *Writings*. Jupiterfab, *Community Human Identiy*, 2010, wallpainting, Verboomstraat, Rotterdam, 2016

16 "In charms and riddles, things that were neither this nor that bore, in their defiance of classification, strong magic. Openings, entrances and doorways, both of buildings and the human body (in one Middle English medical text there is mention of a medicine corroding 'the margynes of the skynne'), were especially important liminal zones that had to be protected." Michael Camille, *Image on the Edge.* UNTITLED / PISTACHIO FLOOR, 2016, foam pillow with vinyl cover (Collaboration with Sabrina Chou) / Portland cement, pistachio shells, Rib Rotterdam, photo: Job Willems

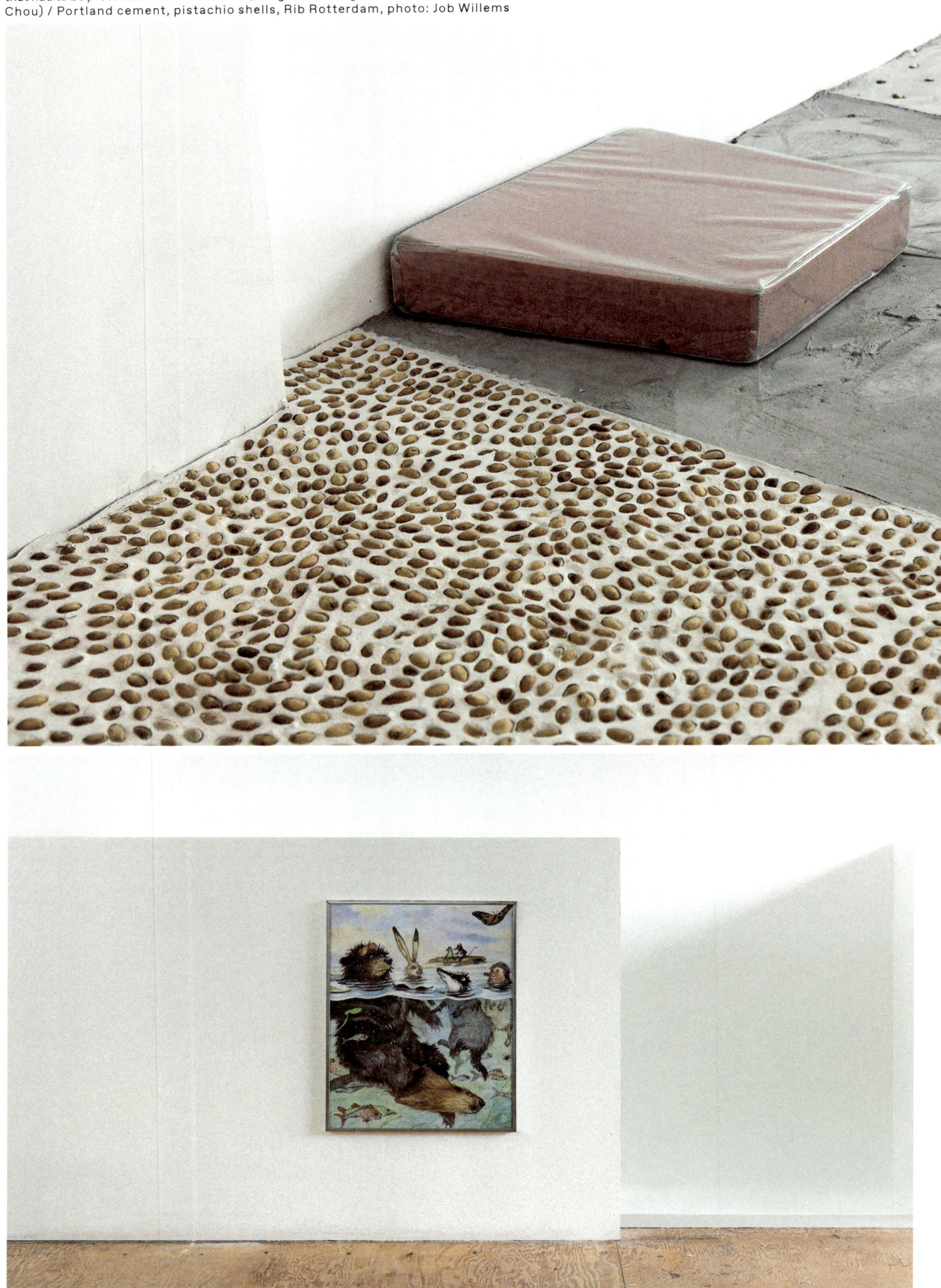

17 "Dragons, humans, mermaids, fishes eat all kinds of things; vegetables and animals are not simply jumbled together but actually bite and digest one another, sometimes even themselves, in spiraling orgies of autophagia." Michael Camille, *Image on the Edge.* LEVEL (FOUND IMAGE), 2016, framed color print, Rib Rotterdam, photo: Job Willems

The Sculpture of Everyday Life
Vivian Sky Rehberg

I have a sculpture by Micha Zweifel in my home. Or rather, there is a sculpture by Micha Zweifel, which is not mine, in my home, which is also not mine. This sculpture hangs on a pristine wall in the newly renovated apartment I've just rented in Brussels. Formerly it hung on a blemished, also rented, wall in Rotterdam, the city where I first met Micha in 2012.

It's unlikely you've seen this sculpture "for real", and unlikely you ever will. If you are among the few people who have ever visited one of these homes, you may have seen it. Maybe, after a dinner once, or over tea, you saw it. Maybe you didn't notice it or didn't know Micha made it. I haven't spoken about it with anyone. The sculpture is not a secret, but it is untitled.

Soon, in these pages, a photographic reproduction will transmute the material of Micha's untitled sculpture into information for you, while in the meantime I try to capture in words what its material presence in my home represents to me.

Now is when I wish I could be a songwriter or a poet, or even a philosopher, why not? A writer who can get the closest to things, feel how to express the lyric, the elusive, the obstinate.

Well, I studied art history instead, and for quite a long time. Through that study I acquired a perceptual reflex that has ever since conditioned how I have experienced and communicated about art. Years spent on expensive, diligent training, making repeat visits to museums and galleries to discover, identify, and examine increasingly familiar objects I would no longer need a label to identify, dispersed over floorplans I could eventually navigate without a map. These museums and galleries were located in small towns and big cities; the location didn't really matter once you understood the format of periodization or curation. Ultimately, I could, on an initial visit to a museum or gallery in Chicago or Bern, Krakow or Ithaca, scan a room and instantly identify whatever might hold my interest, hence merit a closer look. I became very efficient at looking and at not looking, expedient at adjusting and according my preferences.

This efficiency of mine evolved into a comportment, a distinct way of holding my body and moving through anywhere art is exhibited. Except for at art fairs, which I scurry around at a tilt, as if pushing myself through a strong wind. And except for in an artist's studio, or at home.

At one point, I realized that I had developed such a prying way of seeing! One fully instrumentalized by a need to know, and worse, by a need to prove that knowledge. This is a way of seeing predicated on the fear of appearing to not know, rather than on curiosity, chance or desire. My single viewpoint beamed from me, overdetermined by an uneasy, unreliable, one-point perspective.

I came to that realization a few years ago, when I started looking at Micha's untitled sculpture. It occurs to me now, as my senses shift and, it must be acknowledged, deteriorate, that my horrible eyesight also contributed to my inquisitive, prying and peering, way of seeing. These days I need two pairs of lenses, crystal barnacles clinging to my corneas and perching on my nose, to be able to see anything at all.

My man, who is an artist like Micha, and also his good friend, purchased the untitled sculpture from Micha in 2017. Since then, daily, I have stared at it or gazed at it or watched it out of the corner of my eye. It has never been indifferent to me, nor I to it.

It left for Brussels in the same box in which it first entered, a box labelled "Micha's Sculpture" which I had apparently saved and stored in the cellar. There are few proud moments in moving house—one of them can be finding the fitting box you had forgotten. For some time after arriving in Brussels my man kept comparing the move from the old apartment to the new one to time travel: "it's like leaving the nineteenth century and entering the twentieth," he'd repeat. He arranged both the old and new wall displays, including the placement of Micha's untitled sculpture, without my guidance. As it had previously, Micha's sculpture now hangs, surrounded by some decorative objects and other artworks, mostly paintings and drawings, either purchased from friends or gifted, or found on the street or in flea-markets. Except now it hangs in the twentieth century.

When you picture an untitled sculpture hanging on a wall surrounded by found objects and gifts, what do you picture? Leave the words on the page and take a moment to picture it. I would like it if you could briefly call to mind how you live with sculpture, before you read a bit more about how I live with this particular one.

Close your eyes for a second. Take a breath.

It feels like I've been lying for eons on either of the couches facing the wall, with my barnacled head shipwrecked on pillows, looking at Micha's untitled sculpture. Just marking the flow of a day of travelling time. From a supine or lateral position, adopted not out of laziness or leisure but out of necessity, I've discovered, obliquely, how it's such an ordinary thing: living with a sculpture. I also discovered that the value of living with this sculpture has been anything but ordinary, for me. It's not easy for me to convey that value, the everyday-life value of a sculpture, without lapsing into the appropriate and accommodating discourse that became so familiar to me, and from which my daily life estranges. The simplest, most benign way to put it is to say that Micha's untitled sculpture repeatedly gains and holds my attention. Again and again and again. Day after day, we keep making time for each other, making space for each other. That time and space between us, silently, keeps expanding and retracting.

But why? But how? This sounds like a mystification!

I should show you now. Or offer a description: Micha's untitled sculpture is a landscape format, relief sculpture cast in plaster. Reliefs are common architectural features. Images or decorative patterns protrude, more or less prominently, from sculpted, engraved or flat backgrounds. It occurs to me how I too protrude from a surface, like a relief bulging from the blanketed surface of the couch. Through mimicry and identification, I too have become a common architectural feature, in the home.

Right now, Micha's untitled relief sculpture faces west. It hangs near a north wall made entirely of windows and a sliding glass door that opens onto a balcony almost too narrow for any purpose. The couch sits next to the windows, facing east. The apartment is on a low floor, so the wall often sits in shadow. Hypothetically, my neighbor told me, in the night a person could climb onto the car (not mine) that is always parked in the building driveway, leap onto the ledge and in through the sliding glass door in order to rob the apartment. They could even steal Micha's untitled relief sculpture. I just took it down from the wall to measure it: 29 × 40 × 3 cm, and it weighs only three kilograms.

Up until just the other day I didn't even know what Micha's untitled sculpture is meant to be a sculpture *of*. I had never considered asking because it wasn't a puzzle to me. I didn't need to know for the sculpture to do its work of repeatedly gathering my senses, day after day. Now that I do know its subject, I can assure you that, coincidental with its form, its content is enlivening.

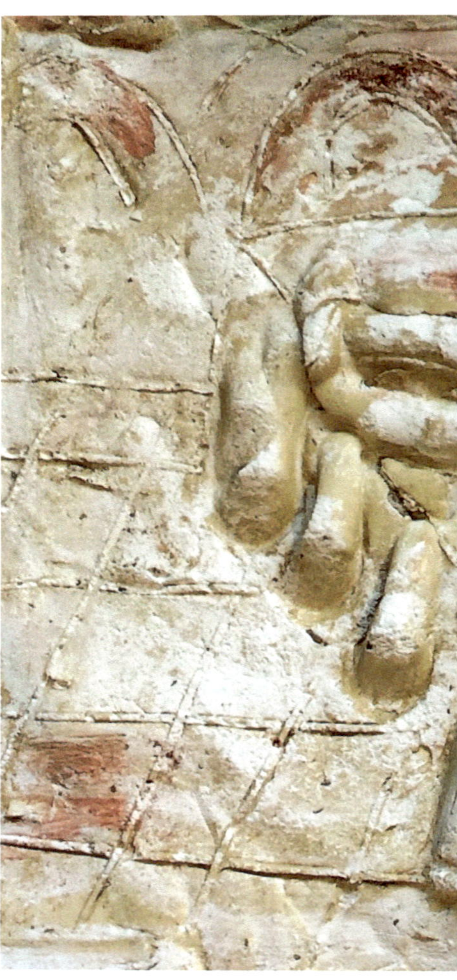

Bei mir zu Hause habe ich eine Skulptur von Micha Zweifel. Genauer gesagt: Es gibt eine Skulptur von Micha Zweifel, die mir nicht gehört, in meinem Zuhause, das mir ebenfalls nicht gehört. Diese Skulptur hängt an einer makellosen Wand in der frisch renovierten Brüsseler Wohnung, die ich seit Kurzem gemietet habe. Davor hing sie an einer schäbigen, ebenfalls gemieteten Wand in Rotterdam, jener Stadt, in der ich Micha im Jahr 2012 zum ersten Mal getroffen habe.

Es ist eher unwahrscheinlich, dass Sie diese Skulptur »in echt« gesehen haben, unwahrscheinlich auch, dass Sie sie jemals sehen werden. Wenn sie zu den wenigen Leuten gehören, die einmal in der einen oder der anderen Wohnung zu Besuch waren, könnten Sie sie gesehen haben. Vielleicht haben Sie sie einmal bei einem Abendessen gesehen oder beim Tee. Vielleicht ist sie Ihnen gar nicht aufgefallen oder Sie hatten keine Ahnung, dass sie von Micha stammt. Ich habe nie mit jemandem über sie gesprochen. Die Skulptur ist kein Geheimnis, aber sie hat keinen Titel.

Schon bald – auf diesen Seiten – wird Michas Skulptur OHNE TITEL durch eine fotografische Reproduktion für Sie in Informationen übersetzt sein. In der Zwischenzeit versuche ich aber, in Worte zu fassen, was ihre materielle Gegenwart in meinem Zuhause für mich bedeutet. Das ist der Moment, da ich mir wünsche, ich wäre eine Liedermacherin, eine Dichterin, vielleicht sogar eine Philosophin, warum nicht? Eine Schreibende, die den Dingen möglichst nah kommt, die ein Gespür dafür hat, das Lyrische, das Flüchtige, das Eigensinnige auszudrücken.

Stattdessen habe ich Kunstgeschichte studiert, sogar ziemlich lange. In diesem Studium habe ich mir einen Wahrnehmungsreflex zugelegt, der seitdem konditioniert, wie ich Kunst wahrnehme und darüber kommuniziere. Jahrelanges, teuer bezahltes, eifriges Lernen, wiederholte Besuche in Museen und Galerien, um zunehmend vertraute Gegenstände zu entdecken, zu identifizieren, bis ich keine Schilder mehr brauchte, um sie zu identifizieren, und keine Karte, um meinen Weg durch die Räume zu finden, in denen die Werke planvoll verteilt sind. Diese Museen und Galerien befanden sich in kleinen und großen Städten; auf den Ort kam es eigentlich nicht an, solange man das Format der Periodisierung oder Präsentation verstand. Schließlich war ich so weit, dass ich, wenn ich zum ersten Mal ein Museum oder eine Galerie in Chicago oder Bern, Krakau oder Ithaca betrat, den Raum scannen und sofort ausmachen konnte, was mich interessieren, was einen genaueren Blick verdienen könnte. Ich bin sehr effizient darin geworden, zu schauen oder eben nicht zu schauen, zielsicher den Blick anzupassen, gemäß meinen Vorlieben.

Diese Effizienz entwickelte sich bei mir zu einem fixen Verhalten, einer spezifischen Körperhaltung, einer bestimmten Art, mich durch Orte zu bewegen, an denen Kunst ausgestellt wird. Mit der Ausnahme von Kunstmessen, über die ich in gebeugter Haltung husche, als müsste ich meinen Weg durch einen Sturm bahnen. Und mit der Ausnahme von Ateliers oder eben zu Hause.

Irgendwann wurde mir klar, dass sich meine Art des Sehens zu einem Spähen entwickelt hatte. Es stand gänzlich im Dienst der Aufgabe, Wissen zu erlangen, schlimmer noch, Wissen unter Beweis zu stellen. Es ist eine Art des Sehens, die mehr von der Furcht bestimmt ist als von Neugier, von Zufall oder Verlangen; man könnte den Anschein erwecken, dass man etwas nicht weiß. Ich strahlte eine einzige Sichtweise aus,

18 “What would a world be like—this seems to me Bruegel’s question—in which all human activities slowed to the pace of the large intestine?” T.J. Clark, *Painting at Ground Level.* UNTITLED, 2015, plaster pigments, photo: Vivian Sky Rehberg

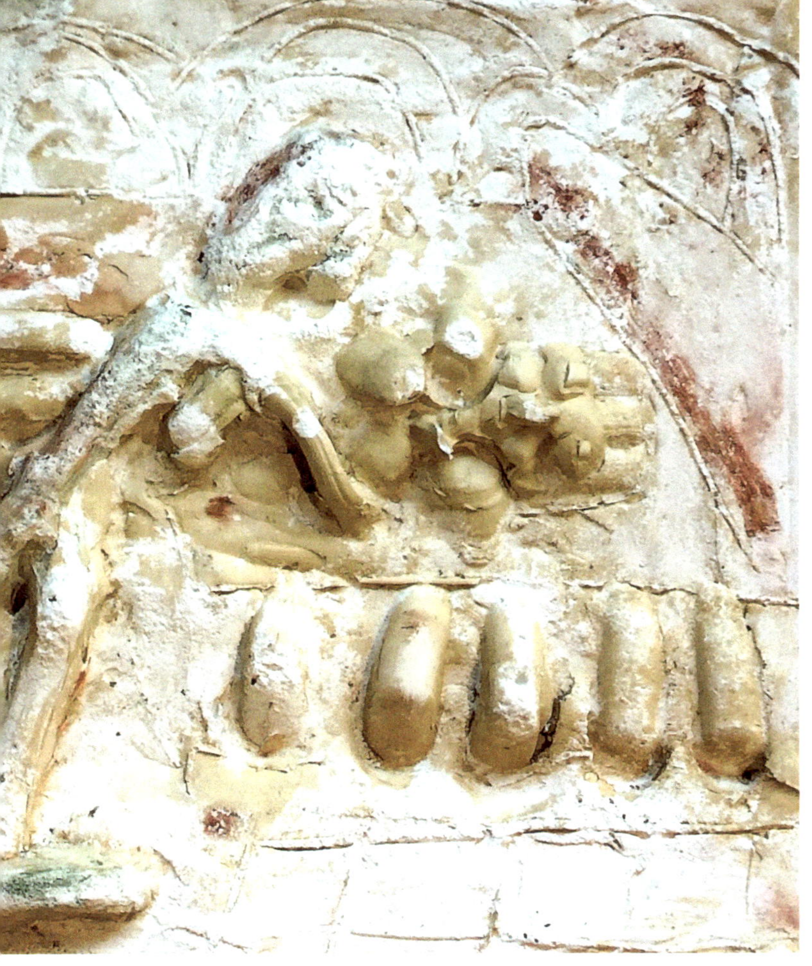

überdeterminiert durch eine unheimliche, unzuverlässige, einäugige Perspektive.

All das wurde mir vor einigen Jahren klar, als ich anfing, Michas Skulptur zu betrachten. Jetzt, da sich meine Sinne verändern und, wie ich einräumen muss, verschlechtern, scheint es mir, als hätte auch meine entsetzlich schlechte Sehkraft dazu beigetragen, dass meine Art des Sehens ein solches Ausschauhalten, ein solches prüfendes Spähen war. Inzwischen brauche ich zwei verschiedene Linsen, um überhaupt etwas zu sehen, kristalline Seepocken, die an meiner Hornhaut haften und auf meiner Nase sitzen.

Mein Mann ist wie Micha Künstler und eng mit ihm befreundet. 2017 hat er Micha die Skulptur OHNE TITEL abgekauft. Seitdem habe ich sie täglich angestarrt, angeschaut, aus den Augenwinkeln betrachtet. Sie war mir niemals gleichgültig, ich war ihr niemals gleichgültig.

Nach Brüssel ist sie in derselben Schachtel gelangt, in der wir sie bekommen haben, einer Schachtel mit der Aufschrift »Michas Skulptur«, die ich offensichtlich aufbewahrt und im Keller verstaut hatte. Es gibt wenige Momente beim Umziehen, die einen stolz machen – einer davon kann die Entdeckung einer passenden Schachtel sein, die man ganz vergessen hatte. In der ersten Zeit nach unserer Ankunft in Brüssel verglich mein Mann den Umzug von unserer alten in die neue Wohnung mit einer Zeitreise: »Es ist, als hätten wir das 19. Jahrhundert verlassen und das 20. betreten«, sagte er wiederholt. Wie in der alten Wohnung arrangierte er in der neuen die Werke an der Wand, einschließlich der Skulptur von Micha, ohne meinen Rat einzuholen. Wie schon zuvor ist Michas Skulptur nun von dekorativen Gegenständen und weiteren Kunstwerken umgeben, größtenteils von Gemälden und Zeichnungen, die wir entweder von Freunden gekauft oder geschenkt bekommen oder aber auf der Straße oder auf Flohmärkten entdeckt haben. Nur dass sie jetzt im 20. Jahrhundert hängt.

Wenn Sie sich eine Skulptur ohne Titel vorstellen, die an der Wand hängt, umgeben von Fundstücken und Geschenken, was sehen Sie dann? Lassen Sie die Wörter kurz Wörter sein und nehmen Sie sich einen Augenblick, um sie sich vorzustellen. Ich fände es schön, wenn Sie sich kurz in Erinnerung rufen würden, wie Sie mit einer Skulptur leben, bevor Sie noch etwas mehr darüber lesen, wie ich mit dieser einen, bestimmten lebe.

Schließen Sie Ihre Augen eine Sekunde lang. Atmen Sie ein.

Ich habe das Gefühl, als hätte ich Ewigkeiten auf einem der Sofas gelegen, die dieser Wand gegenüberstehen, mein kristallbesetzter Kopf in den Kissen gestrandet, und Michas Skulptur angesehen. Nur registrierend, wie die Zeit über den Tag verstrich. In Rücken- oder Seitenlage, die ich nicht aus Faulheit, nicht zur Entspannung eingenommen hatte, sondern aus Notwendigkeit, habe ich nebenbei entdeckt, dass das eine ganz gewöhnliche Sache ist: mit einer Skulptur leben. Ich habe auch entdeckt, dass der Wert, mit dieser Skulptur zu leben, für mich alles andere als ein gewöhnlicher ist. Es fällt mir nicht leicht, diesen Wert zu vermitteln, den Alltagswert des Lebens mit einer Skulptur, ohne in den so angemessen scheinenden, sich bereitwillig anbietenden Diskurs abzurutschen, der mir so geläufig geworden ist und von dem sich mein Alltagsleben entfremdet. Die einfachste, liebevollste Art, dies auszudrücken, wäre wohl zu sagen,

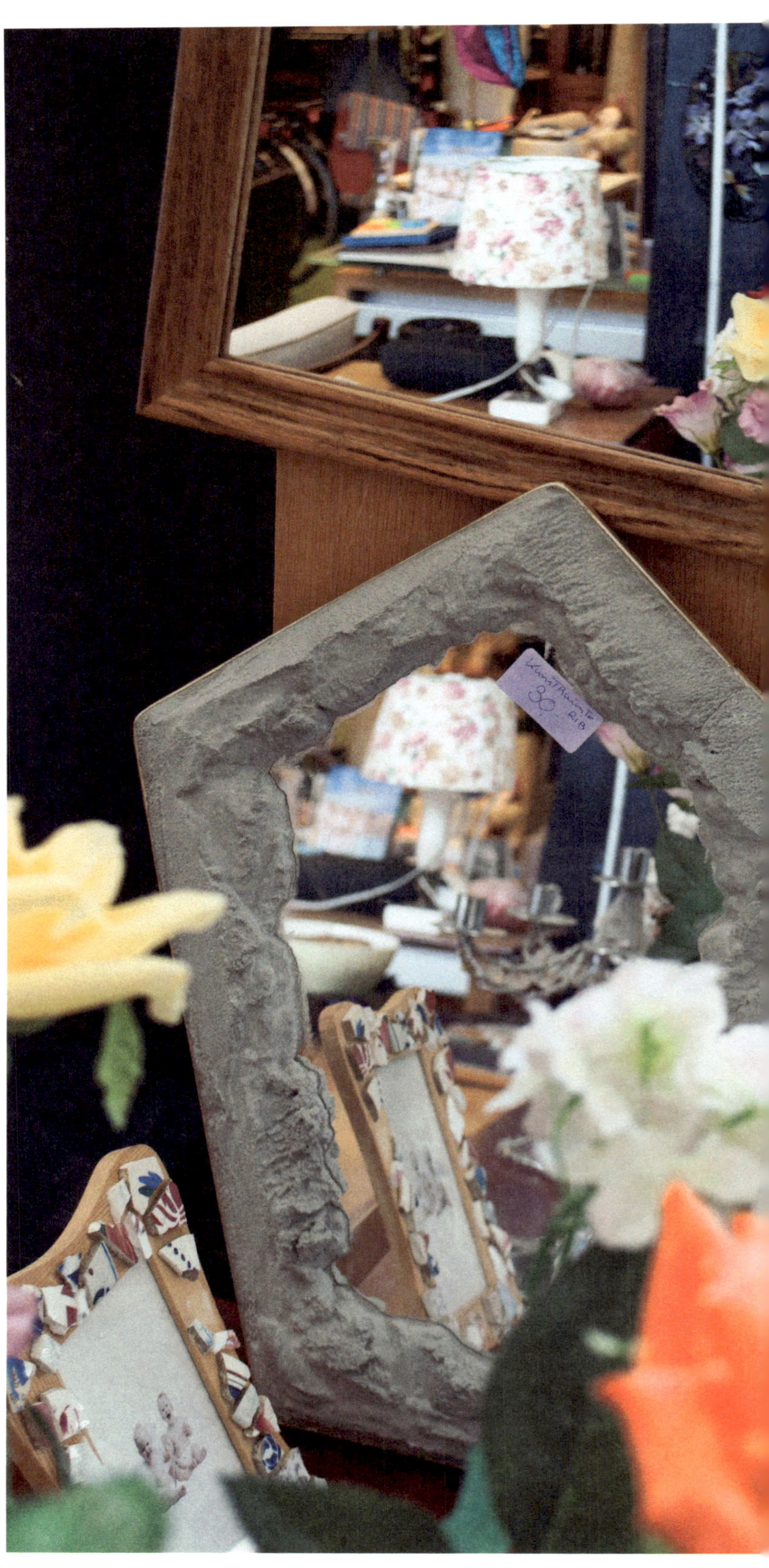

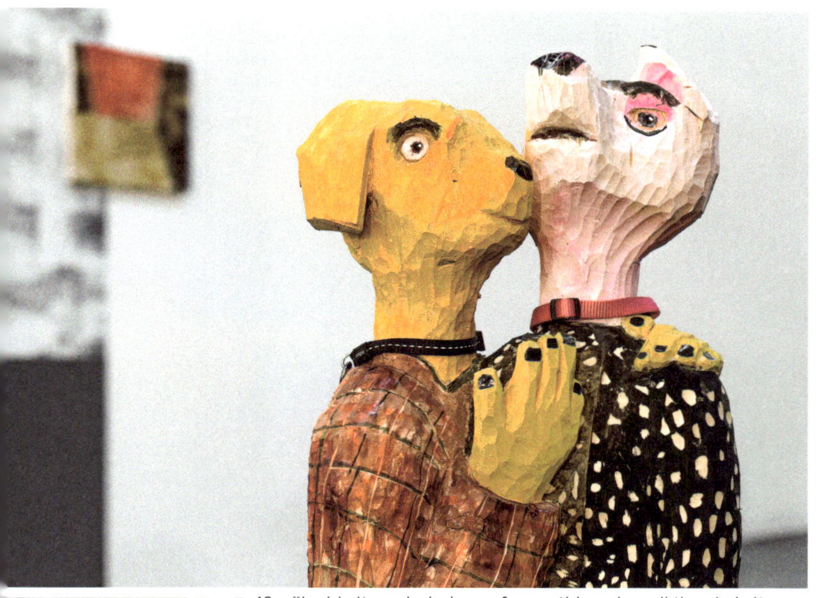

19 “Inside it reminded me of something else, all the air. Is it necessary for there to be a first air—an air that simply is yours? A place supremely young and old where you've spent your whole life. Growing up dying, going down to the beach, drinking, kissing. Are there people who have never lived in their air. Is this mine. I have never been one of a pair of young lovers, a young couple—but this air is mine. I know my air.” Eileen Myles, *Afterglow (a dog memoir)*. DIE ZWEI FREUNDE, 2020, Swiss stone pine, acrylic paint, nail polish, dog leashes, Kunstmuseum Luzern, photo: Marc Latzel

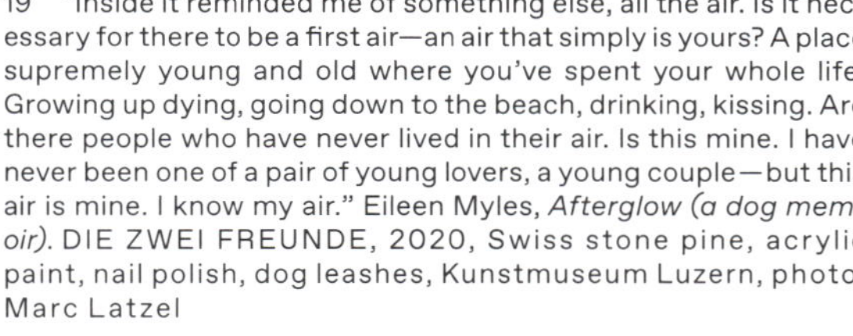

dass Michas Skulptur immer wieder meine Aufmerksamkeit auf sich zieht und zu halten weiß. Wieder und wieder und wieder. Tag für Tag geben wir einander Zeit, schaffen wir einander Raum. Diese Zeit und dieser Raum zwischen uns dehnt sich stumm aus und zieht sich wieder zusammen.

Aber warum? Aber wie? Es klingt nach einer Sinnestäuschung!

Jetzt sollte ich sie Ihnen zeigen. Oder eine Beschreibung liefern: Michas Skulptur OHNE TITEL ist eine Reliefskulptur im Querformat, die aus Gips gegossen ist. Reliefs sind ein gebräuchliches Architekturelement. Bildliche Darstellungen oder dekorative Muster ragen, mehr oder minder weit, aus einer geformten, geprägten oder flachen Oberfläche heraus. Es kommt mir vor, als ragte auch ich aus einer Oberfläche heraus, wie ein Relief, das sich aus der mit Decken versehenen Oberfläche des Sofas hervorwölbt. Durch Mimikry und Identifikation bin ich selbst zu einem architektonischen Element in meinem Zuhause geworden.

Im Moment ist Michas titellose Reliefskulptur nach Westen ausgerichtet. Sie hängt in der Nähe einer Nordwand, die nur aus Fenstern und einer Schiebetür aus Glas besteht, die auf einen Balkon führt, der fast für jeden Gebrauch zu klein ist. Das Sofa steht neben den Fenstern und ist nach Osten ausgerichtet. Die Wohnung befindet sich in einem der unteren Stockwerke, deshalb liegt die Wand oft im Schatten. Theoretisch könnte, wie mein Nachbar mir sagte, ein Einbrecher in der Nacht auf das Auto (nicht meins) klettern, das immer in der Einfahrt geparkt ist, auf den Sims springen und dann durch die Schiebetür in die Wohnung eindringen. Er könnte sogar Michas Reliefskulptur stehlen. Ich habe sie jetzt von der Wand genommen, um sie zu messen: 29 × 40 × 3 cm. Sie wiegt nur drei Kilo.

Bis vor Kurzem wusste ich nicht einmal, dass Michas Skulptur OHNE TITEL als Skulptur von etwas gedacht ist. Ich war nie auf den Gedanken gekommen, danach zu fragen, da sie mir kein Rätsel aufgab. Ich brauchte es nicht zu wissen, damit die Skulptur ihr Werk verrichten konnte, meine Sinne immer neu zu bündeln, Tag für Tag. Jetzt, da ich ihr Sujet kenne, kann ich Ihnen versichern, dass ihr Inhalt, ihrer Form entsprechend, ein belebender ist.

20 “He almost never thought of riveting topics when out for a walk.” Siegfried Kracauer, *Ginster.* UNTITLED MIRROR, 2016, mirror with Portland cement, Robin Hood Second Hand Shop Rotterdam, photo: Sabrina Chou

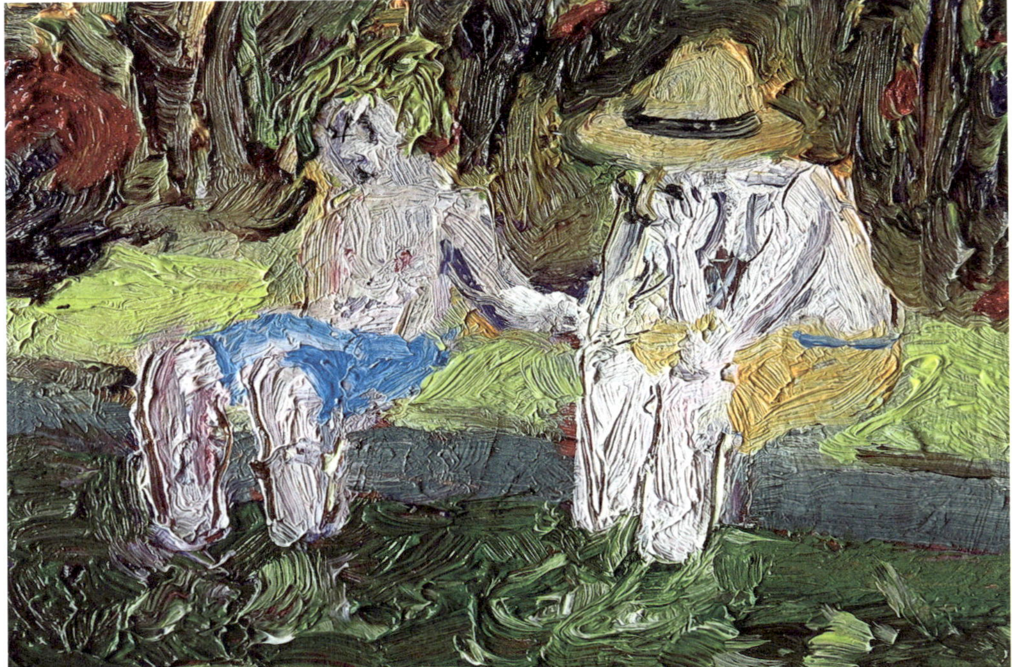

21 "'Are there ants in Heaven?' Sophia asked. 'No', said Grandmother, and laid down carefully on her back. She propped her hat on her nose and tried to sneak a little sleep. Some kind of farm machinery was running steadily and peacefully in the distance." Tove Jansson, *The Summer Book*. UNTITLED (OXFORD MYSTERY SERIES), 2019, oil on wood board

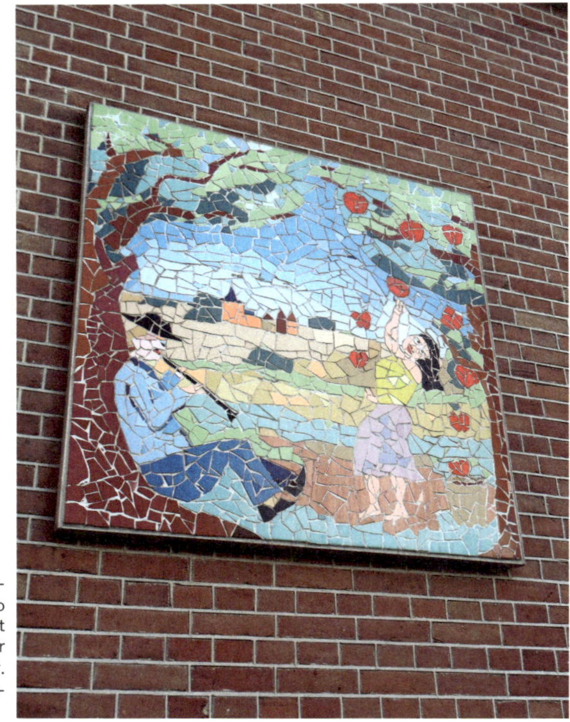

22 "Method of this project: literary montage. I needn't say anything. Merely show. I shall purloin no valuables, appropriate no ingenious formulations. But the rags, the refuse—these I will not inventory but allow, in the only way possible, to come into their own: by making use of them." Walter Benjamin, *Arcades Project*. Michiel Brink, Mosaic, 2016, Clemensstraat, Charlois, Rotterdam

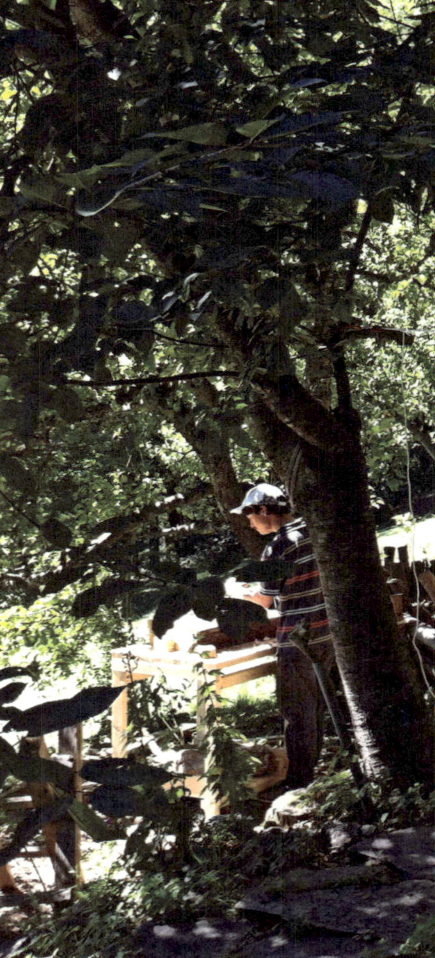

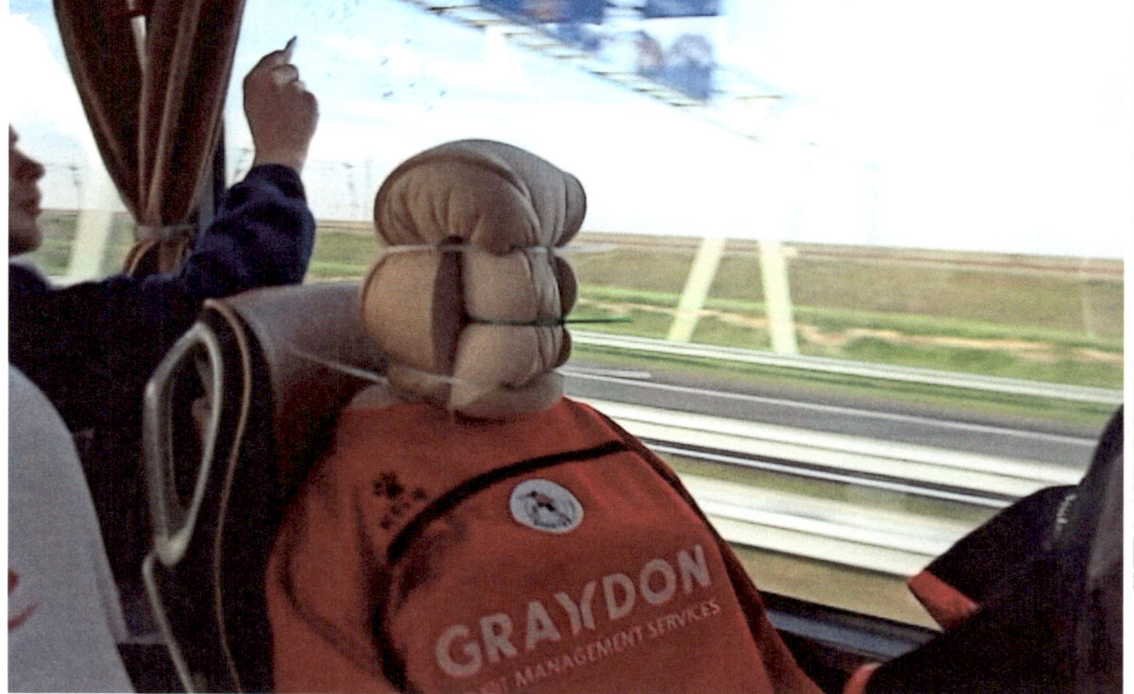

23 "The young people growing up in the broad strata between the proletariat and the bourgeoisie adapt themselves more or less easily to the firm. Many drift along unwittingly and join without ever suspecting that they really do not belong there." Siegfried Kracauer, *The Salaried Masses*. PASSENGER, 2018, foam, clothes, tie-wraps

24 “Ginster looked out his window, the street was empty, nothing had changed. It occurred to him that he was deficient in ‘presence.’ The Assessor had presence. An acquaintance had told him it was improper to greet an inferior familiarly. When the acquaintance entered a bank or administrative offices, he simply walked past the porter and was instantly received by the general manager. He, Ginster, would never get as far as the general manager. Should he stay in the city?” Siegfried Kracauer, *Ginster*. PASSENGER, 2018, foam, clothes, tie-wraps

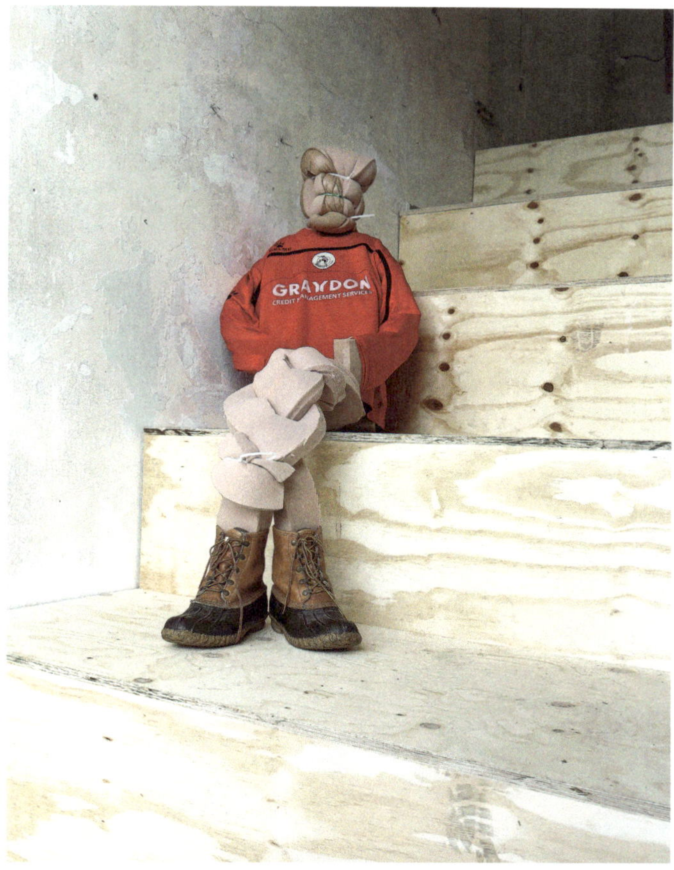

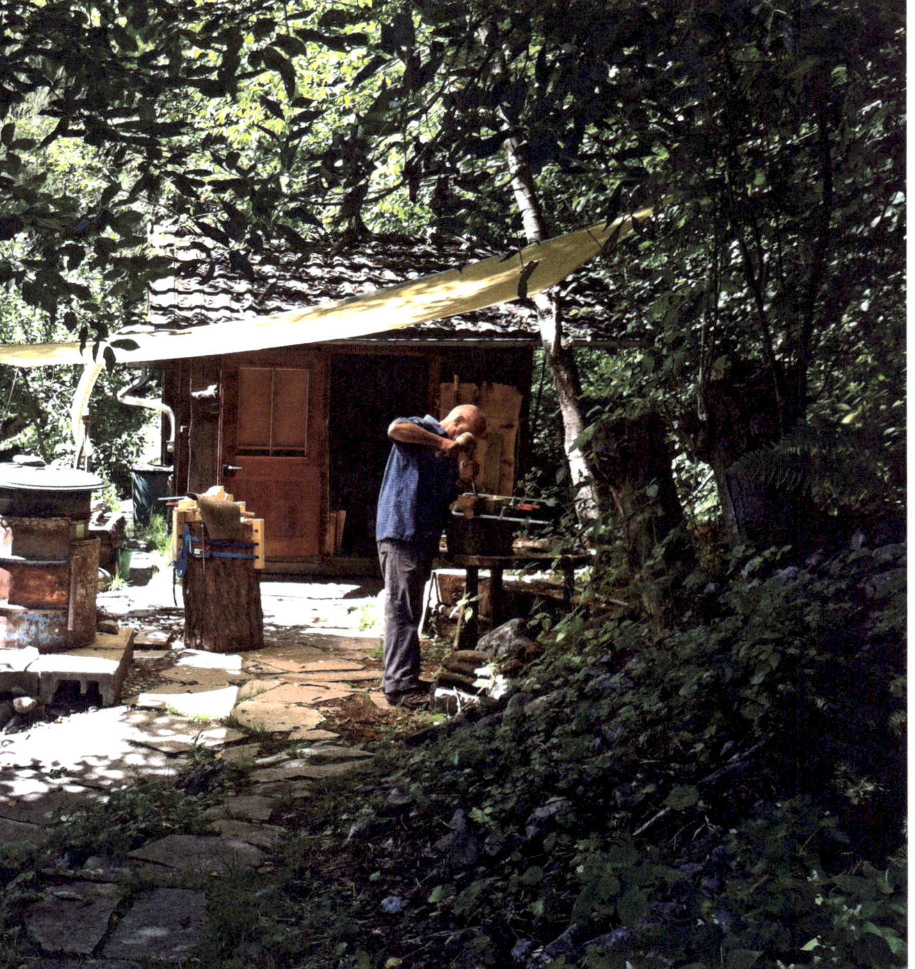

26 “It follows that an art which has fallen into disuse for the period of a generation is altogether lost. There are hundreds of examples of this to which the process of mechanization is continuously adding new ones. These losses are usually irretrievable. It is pathetic to watch the endless efforts—equipped with microscopy and chemistry, with mathematics and electronics—to reproduce a single violin of the kind the half-literate Stradivarius turned out as a matter of routine more than 200 years ago.” Michael Polanyi, *Personal Knowledge*. Tschoma, 2016, photo: Sabrina Chou

25 “The body was, after all, the first human building; the corpse literally became the dwelling-place from where the spirits of evil could be expelled.” Michael Camille, *Image on the Edge*. Wax model for LIFT, 2019

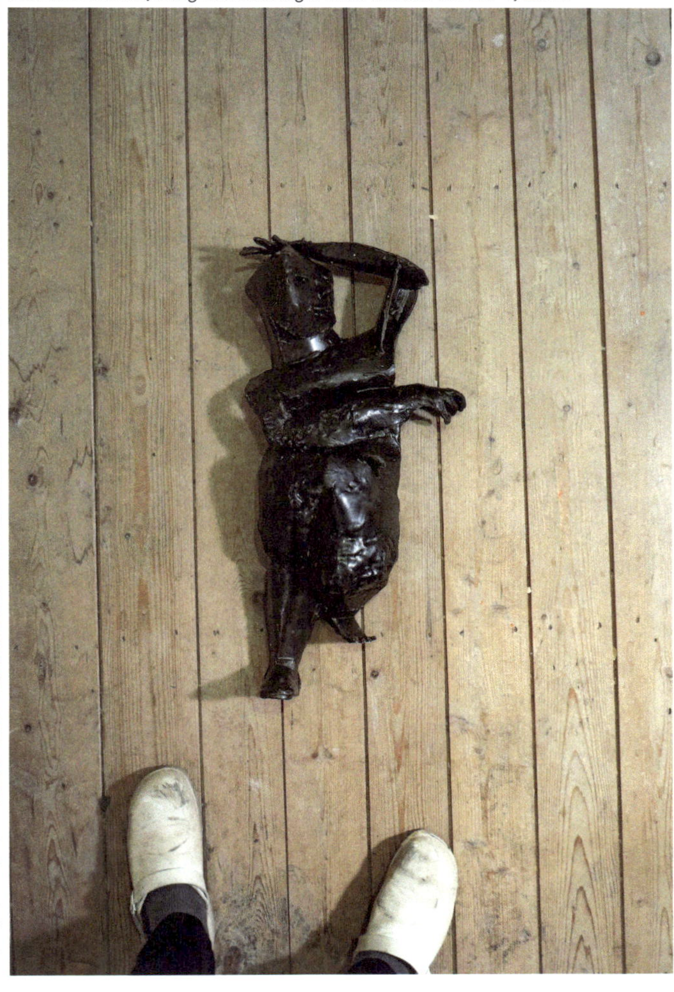

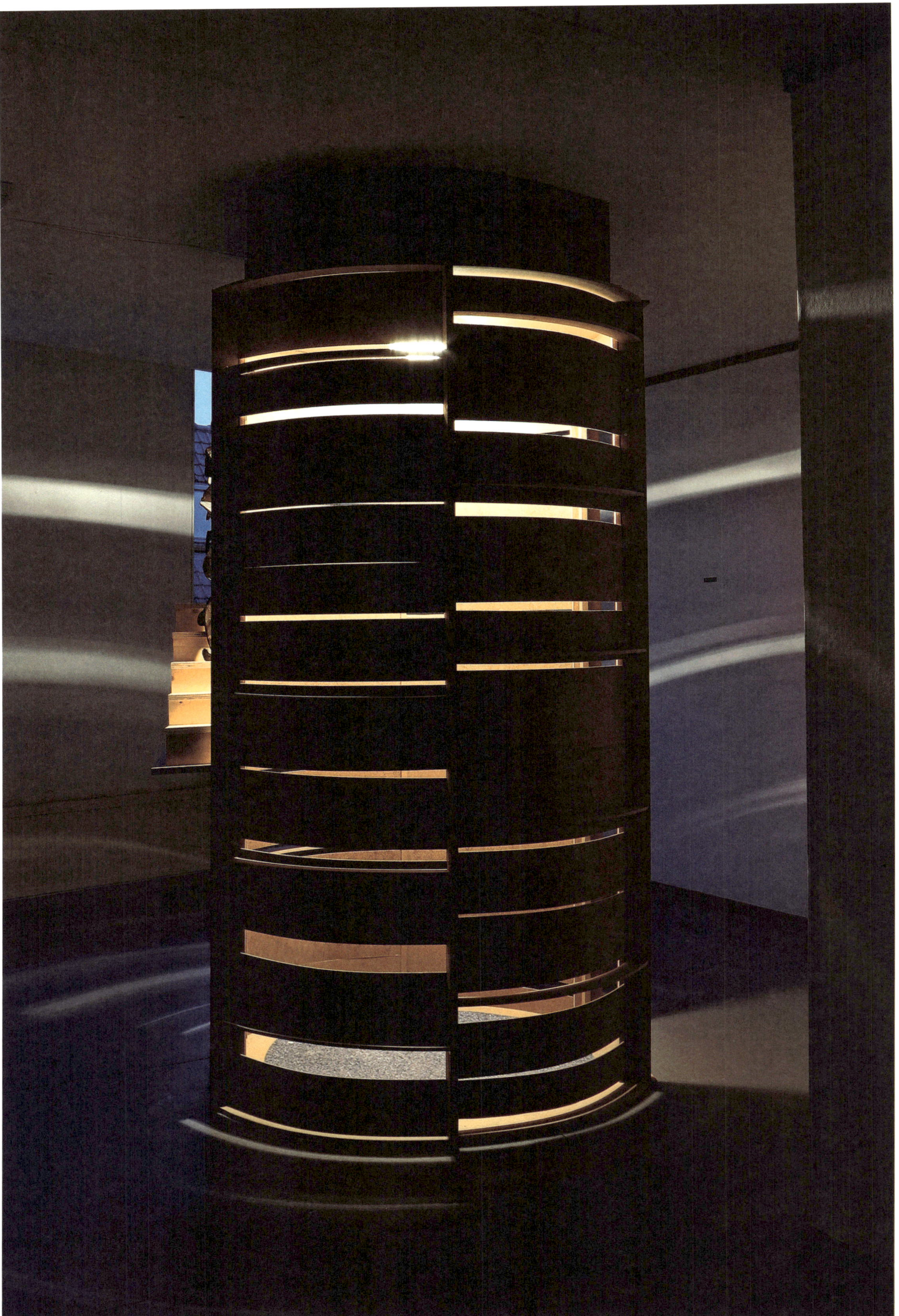

27 “The slow whirr of the cogwheels, the fat sound of the chime that is always striking noon, the hush and stasis that lets the inflated body feel the world rotating underneath it—I feel these things viscerally, as I am sure many viewers do, and want to think about why they touch us so deeply.” T.J. Clark, *Painting at Ground Level*. LIFT, 2019, MDF, plywood, bronze, vinyl flooring, lamp, ONONO Rotterdam

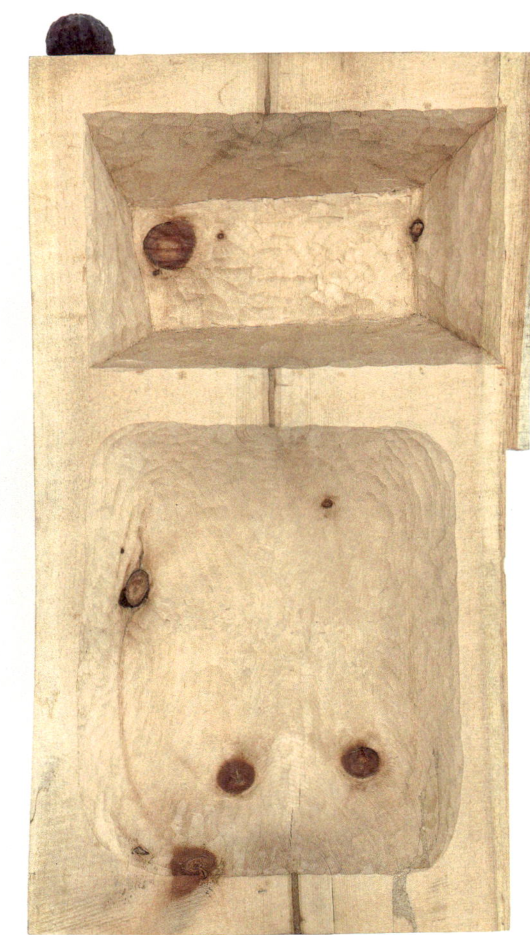

28 “Take for example the identification of a thing as a tool. It implies that a useful purpose can be achieved by handling the thing as an instrument for that purpose. I cannot identify the thing as a tool if I do not know what it is for—or if knowing its supposed purpose, I believe it to be useless for that purpose.” Michael Polanyi, *Personal Knowledge*. PAPADADA, 2016, stone pine, fig, Pracownia Portretu, Łódź, photo: Maciek Łuczak

29 “When she woke up, she lay for a long time and wondered if she should go out or not. It felt as if the night had come right up to the walls and was waiting outside, and her legs ached. The stairs were badly constructed. The steps were too high and too narrow, and then came the rock, which was slippery down toward the woodyard, and then you had to come all the way back again. No sense in lighting a light; it only makes you lose your sense of direction and distance, and the darkness comes closer. Swing your legs over the edge of the bed and wait for your balance to come right.” Tove Jansson, *The Summer Book*. LIFT, 2019, bronze, Kunstmuseum Luzern, photo: Marc Latzel

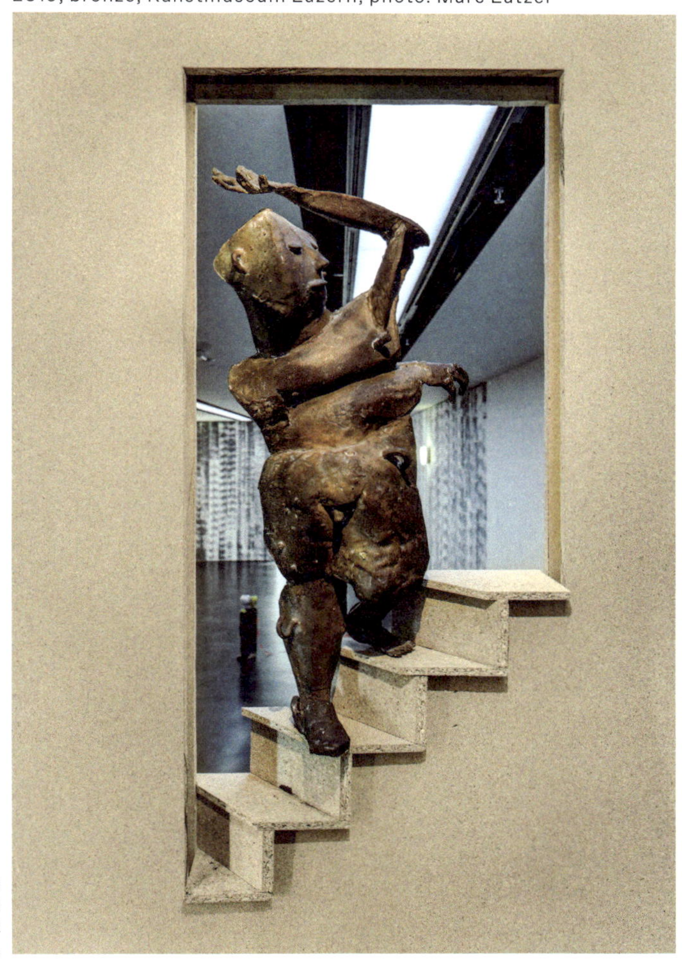

30 “After a while Sophia asked, ‘Are you sure the door is closed?’ ‘It’s open,’ her grandmother said. ‘It’s always open; you can sleep quite easy.’ Sophia rolled up in the quilt. She let the whole island float out on the ice and on to the horizon. Just before she fell asleep, her father got up and put more wood in the stove.” Tove Jansson, *The Summer Book*. LIFT, 2019, MDF, plywood, bronze, vinyl flooring, lamp, ONONO Rotterdam

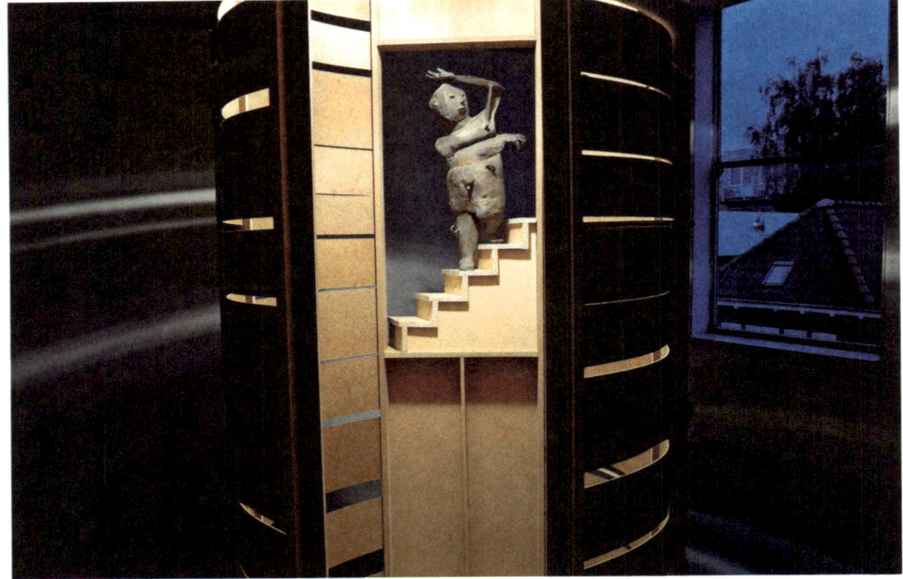

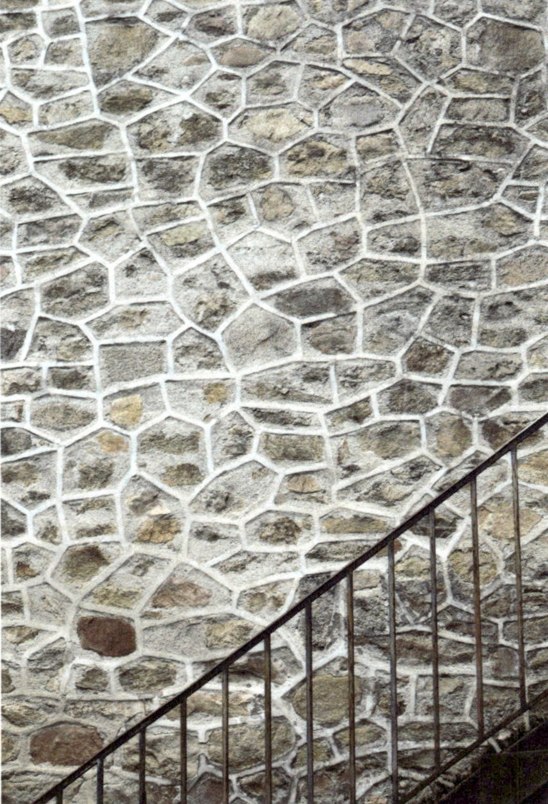

31 “A problem that I have once solved can no longer puzzle me; I cannot guess what I already know. Having made a discovery, I shall never see the world again as before. My eyes have become different; I have made myself into a person seeing and thinking differently. I have crossed a gap, the heuristic gap which lies between problem and discovery.” Michael Polanyi, *Personal Knowledge*. Wall, Treignac Projet, 2018

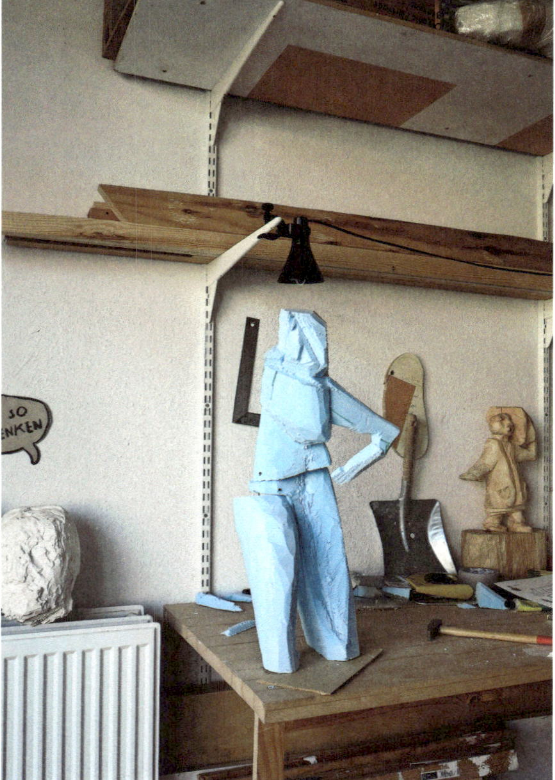

32 “On the other side of the harbor stretch the warehouses, indifferent yellow storage facilities which no one pays attention to. Stevedores haul goods back and forth between them and the docks. I’m attracted to the warehouses, they lie so hidden in broad daylight, and nothing stays in them. And then, all the laborers wear blue blouses. At an early hour, dense clusters of them cling to the trams traveling to the harbor. Blue spritzes itself over everything.” Siegfried Kracauer, *Ginster*. Studio, Charlois, Rotterdam

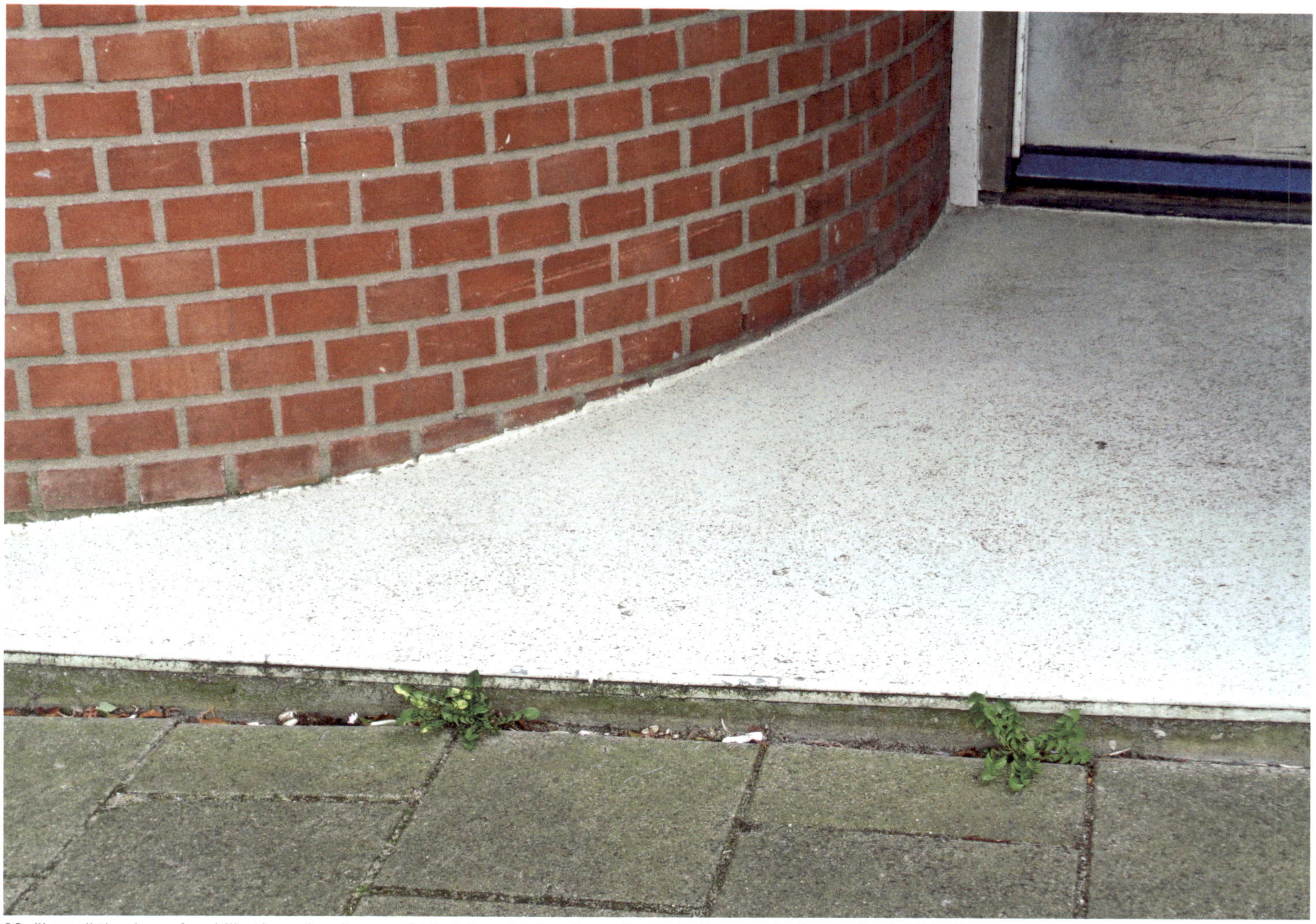

33 "I recall the days of mobilization, when it was said that the minister of war, thanks to the organizational miracle of deployment plans prepared in advance, sat in his peaceful office with nothing to do while outside his troops were on the march. Admittedly, the war itself was then lost." Siegfried Kracauer, *The Salaried Masses*. Entrance, Rotterdam, 2016

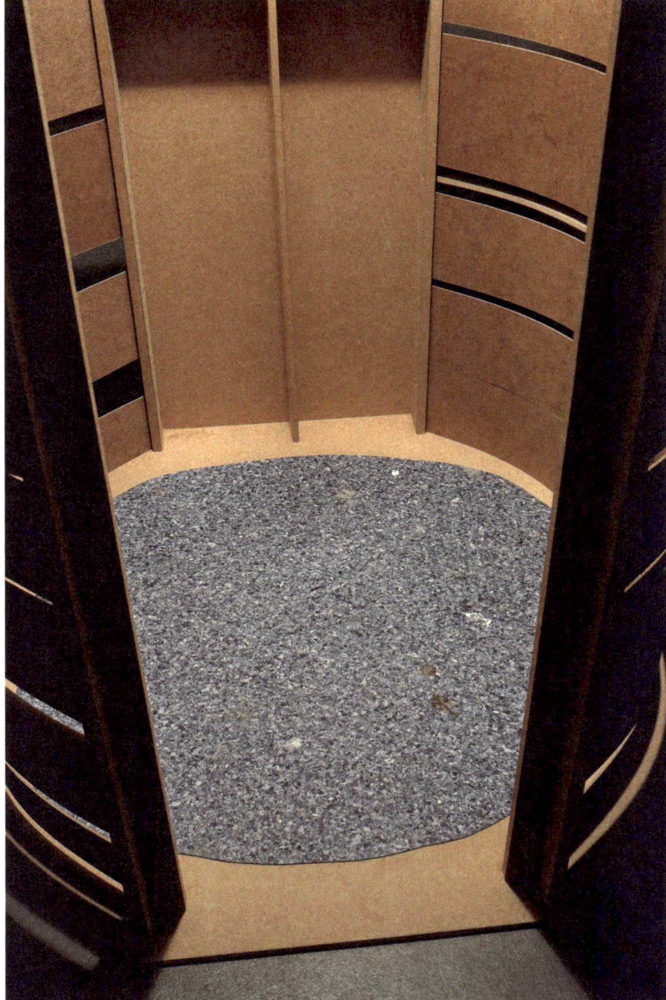

34 "We are aware of fear as soon as we are alone. Some of us are so faint-hearted that we never allow ourselves to be alone for this reason. But artists must of necessity be alone and therefore they must recognize and overcome fear. This is a very long process." Agnes Martin, *Writings*. LIFT, 2019, MDF, plywood, bronze, vinyl flooring, lamp, ONONO Rotterdam

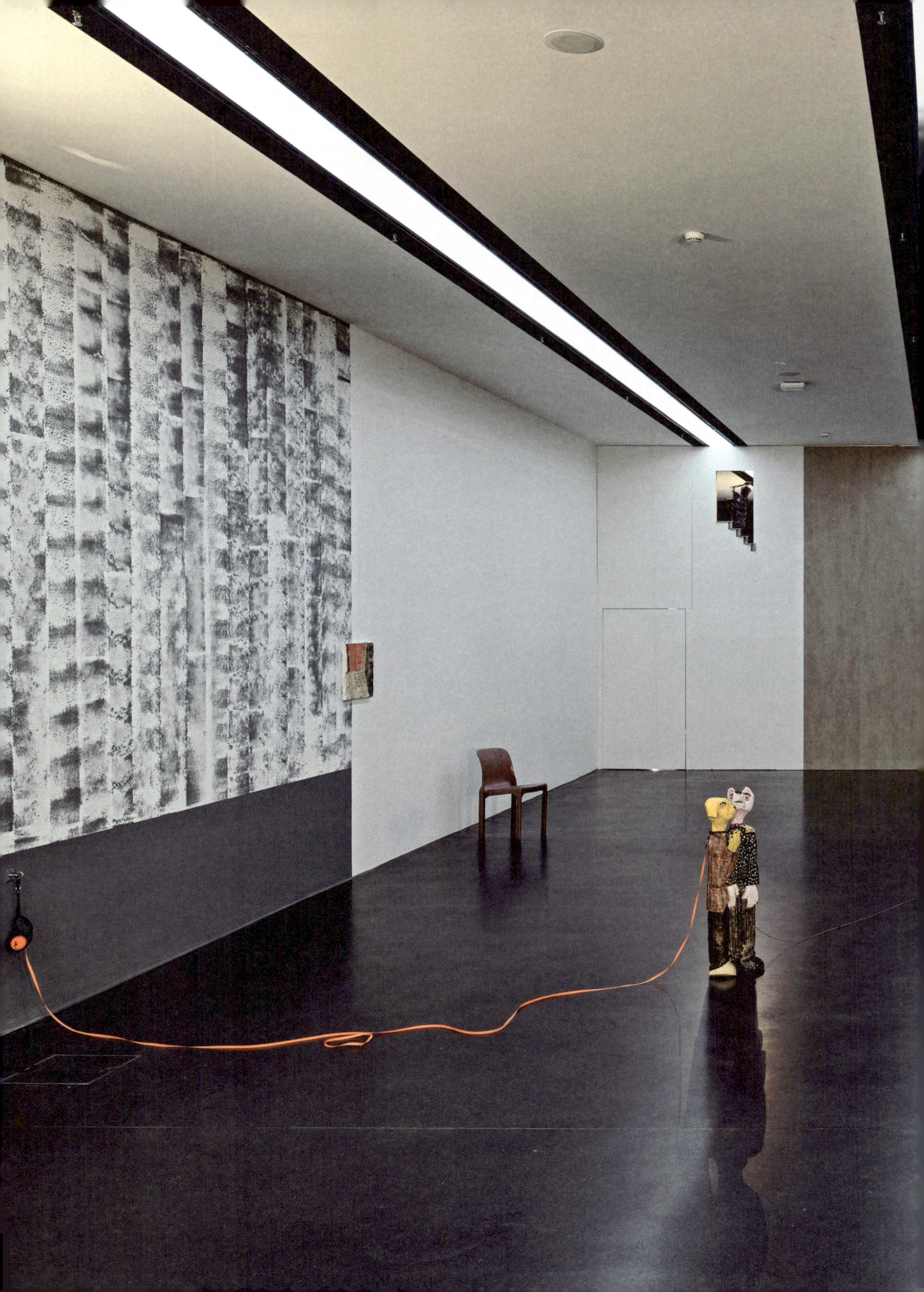

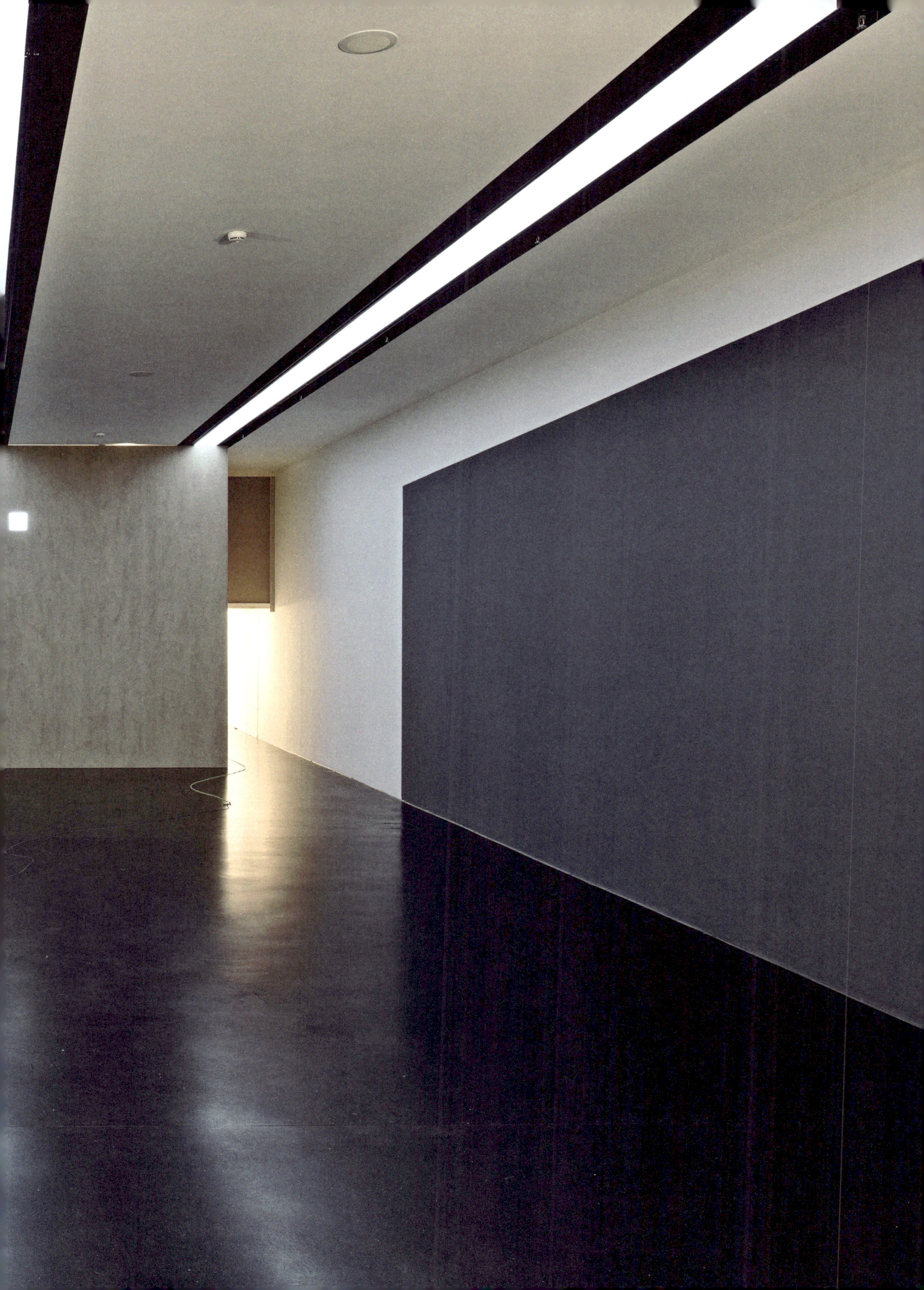

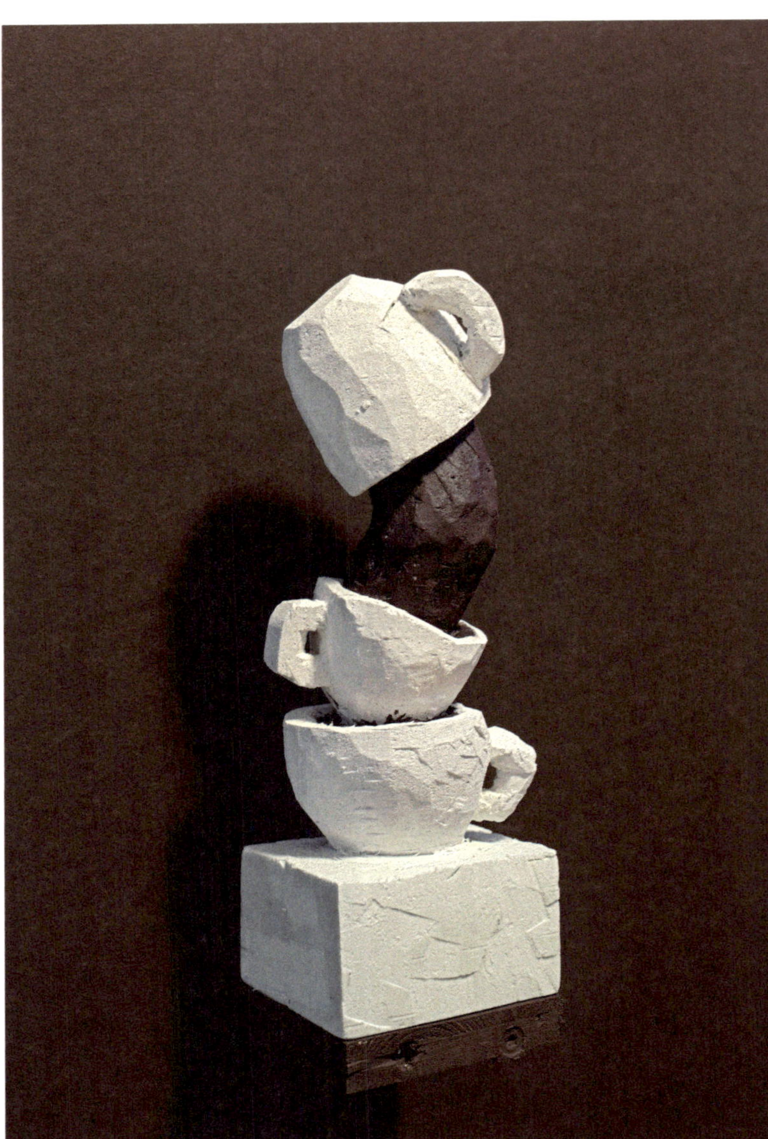

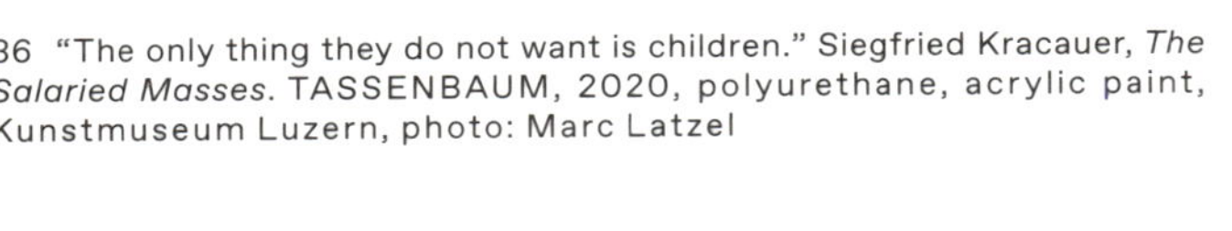

36 “The only thing they do not want is children.” Siegfried Kracauer, *The Salaried Masses*. TASSENBAUM, 2020, polyurethane, acrylic paint, Kunstmuseum Luzern, photo: Marc Latzel

37 “Animals can make mistakes; rabbits fall into traps, fish rise to the angler’s fly, and such errors may be fatal. But animals are exempt from the errors due to elaborate systems of false interpretation, which can be established only in verbal terms.” Michael Polanyi, *Personal Knowledge*. UNTITLED, 2020, brass, photo: Katalin Deér

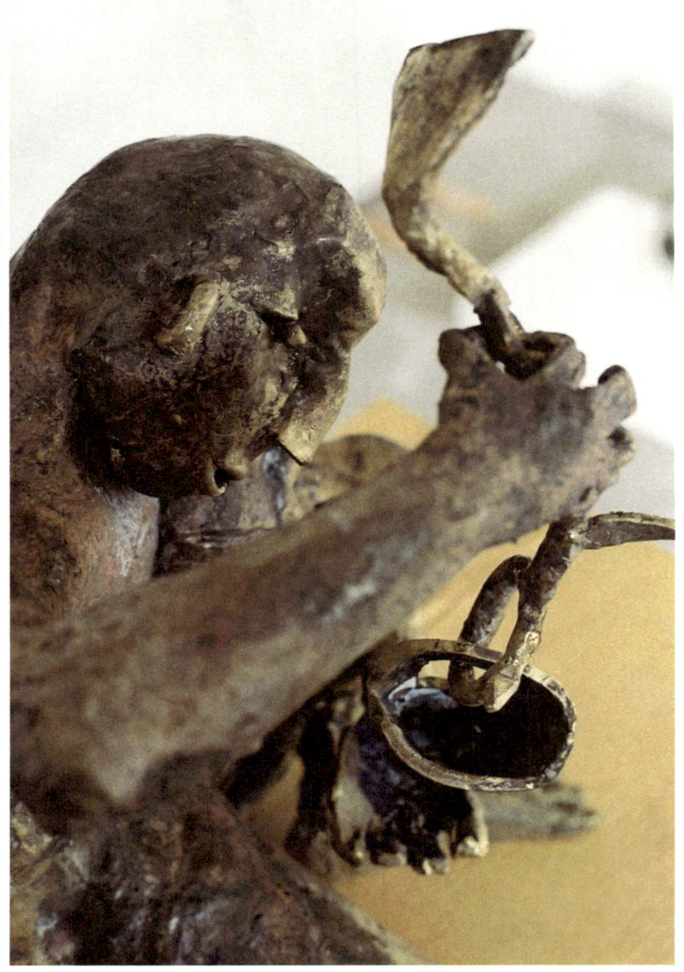

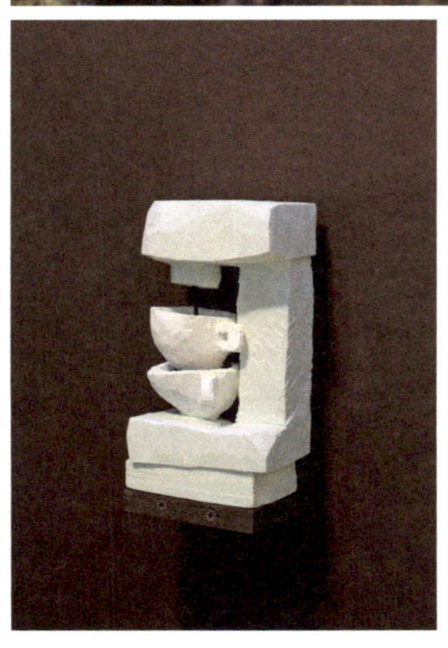

38 “She’s sitting at a lunch counter—greasy churros which she dips into her coffee. Oil dancing on the surface of her coffee in the morning light. Opens her notebook but she’s got nothing to say. It’s just a gleaming hole in the day.” Eileen Myles, *Afterglow (a dog memoir)*. DOPPIO, 2020, polyurethane, acrylic, Kunstmuseum Luzern, photo: Marc Latzel

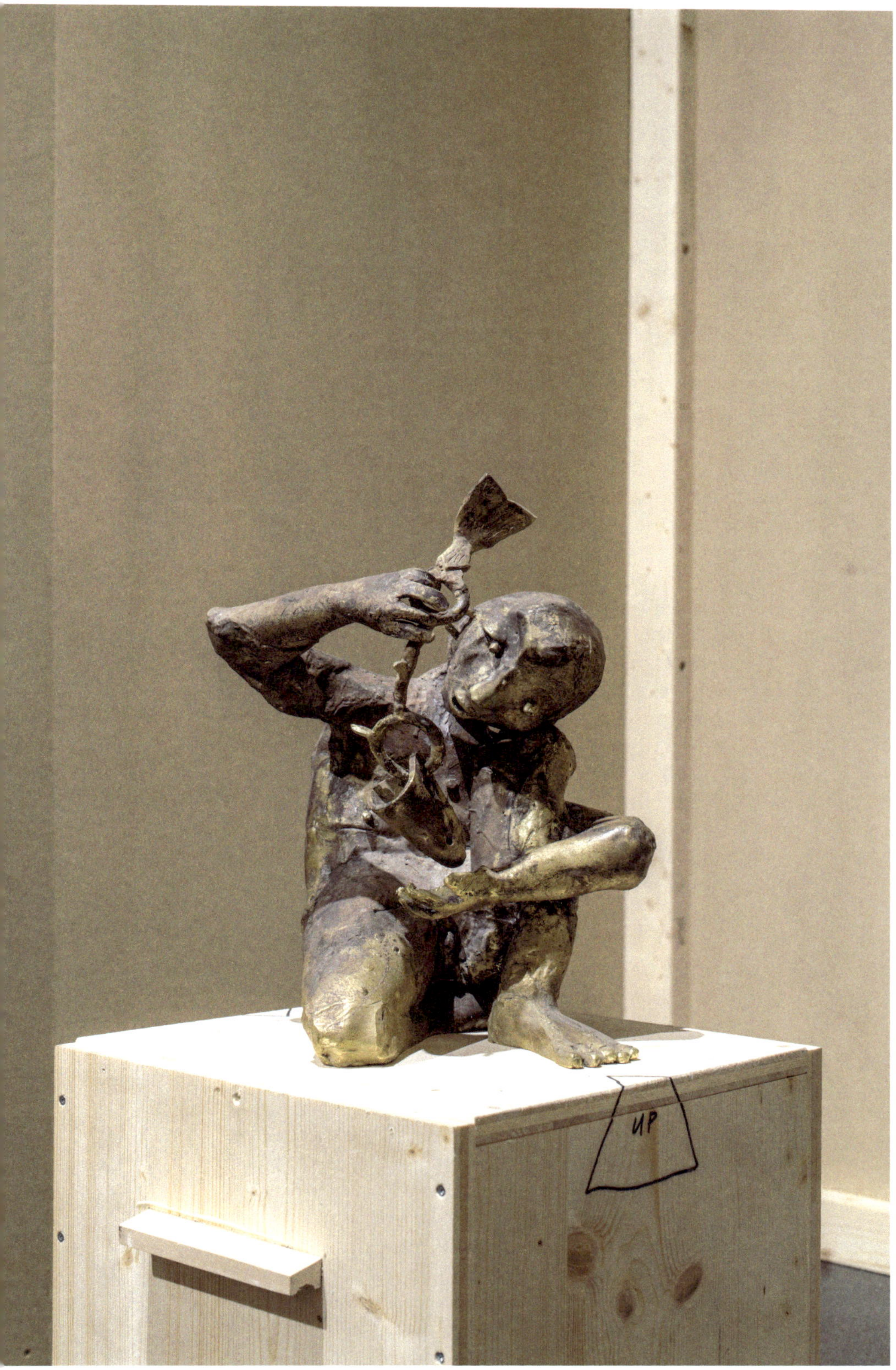

39 “One young salesgirl told me about her friendship with a skilled metalworker, who changed his job under pressure from her father. The father is a court usher, no less, and will consequently tolerate no worker in the family. Her beloved now has to content himself with the lowly position of bank messenger—but in return he has progressed to fiancé.” Siegfried Kracauer, *The Salaried Masses*. UNTITLED, 2020, brass, Kunstmuseum Luzern, photo: Marc Latzel

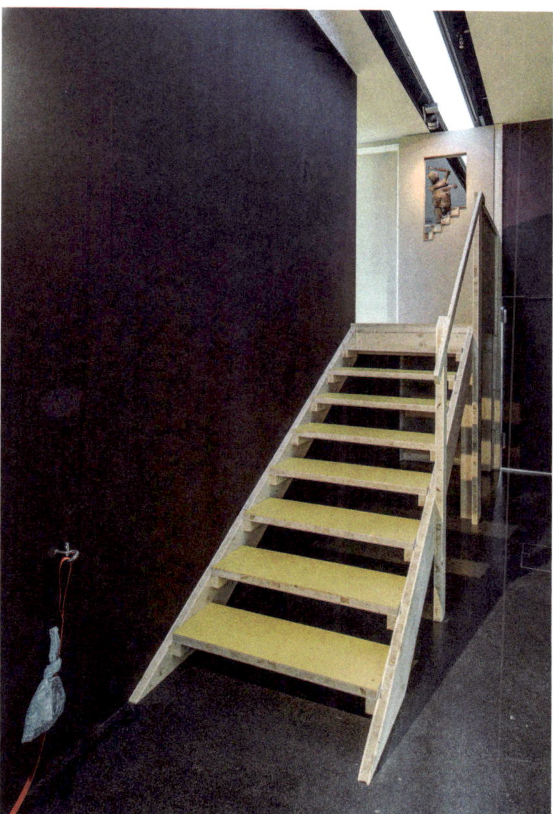

40 “Technology teaches action. This is made plain when it speaks in imperatives, as it often does in cookery books or directions for the use of machinery.” Michael Polanyi, *Personal Knowledge*. ZUR SACKGASSE 4. STOCK, exhibition view Kunstmuseum Luzern, photo: Marc Latzel

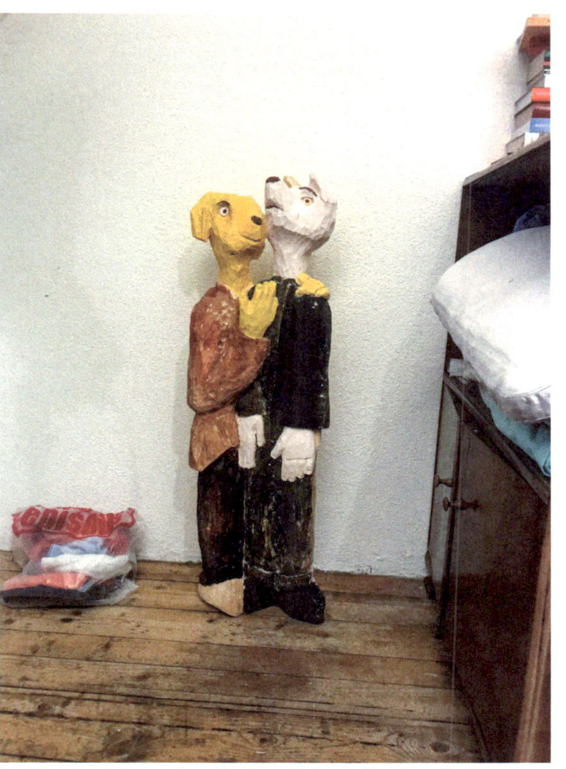

41 “No dog is born alone.” Eileen Myles, *Afterglow (a dog memoir)*. DIE ZWEI FREUNDE, 2020, Swiss stone pine, acrylic paint, nail polish

The Stoppage: An Etiology

Sabrina Chou

As you approach the precipice of doubt, another confrontation smacks you right in the face. But isn't the brink always such a foreshortened plot, where revelation coincides with demise? It appears you have reached the end.

Here is an impasse from which you can only retreat, a halting of progressions that were for so long assumed, a cessation of enlightened expectations which reality steadily reproduced, an obliteration of willing perspectives ahead, until—

But what is it that has stopped you? The speculative plumbers are off duty. So, you must take the plunge yourself, nose-first. This is not an isolated episode (even if vacuums do clog). A stoppage obstructs what it also confirms. What were you expecting to say, "Here lies an unencumbered body, who blocks itself and others?" If you were worried before, let nothing assuage your fears. For, at least there is clarity in vacuity. Instead, you must acquiesce to your other faculties. Detection is only the beginning.

You might ask, what next? Back to the end, of course, and then: reverse this history's circuit. Is it possible to reconstruct the sequence of congestions that agglomerated into this instant? From the tremulous lumps and ridges, to the traceable edges and restless blanks, to coarse planes bristling with apprehension, the boundaries begin to emerge. Against these surfaces you might decipher an institutional imprint, whose poorly repressed conceit scrapes justification off its own walls. This waffling debris, dislodged from the complacency of its cartesian axis, scatters into an anxious frenzy, impossible to grasp. Even as you attempt to clump wads of its linty dregs between your fingers, they disintegrate into paltry protests, collapsing at the slightest demurral. So, you attempt another mode of address.

This stoppage might correspond to interruption, a sputtering stop in the stream. Dams are built against currents, cross-purpose. But your eager inspections do not convey confidence. Rather, you find yourself knee-deep in a mumbling, incoherent morass. The impulse to over-articulate can be thwarted in more than one way; silence is an entitled inhibition. Could this hazy obscurity be strategic? Could it perhaps be a blockade that blurs against the attacks of sympathetic translations and sentimental assimilations? Those who believe in the capacity of language might find themselves immobilized here. Their mouths burst, stuck shut with the rhetorical residues of their narcissistic indulgences. They choke on their own self-seduction. Charm and beauty notwithstanding, motley jams (and their jellies) are stickier than they are virtuous.

Is causation dependent on classification? You wish for a concrete prognosis that can cure itself slowly over time, instead of this viscous restraint. Certainty is a convenience and a comfort. But identifications are brittle. Necessarily they are unwavering, no matter how weighty the load. They bear their own semblance in monoliths. Theirs is an unauthorized archaeology of their own representation. Such excavations expose only the crumbling of their self-sedimented accumulations. All reflections being equal, even the most polished glosses crack under pressure. Subjected to self-reflexive exercises of scrutiny and correlation, similitude loses itself in itself. Anyway, who certifies affinity? Aren't representations built upon belief, with alloys of conviction hammered into the luster of legitimacy?

Still, you confront the face of it, this vertical cul-de-sac. What goes up must come down. Yields refuse to tally up. You return once more to the end, no nearer to conclusion's close. What's more, unscrambled codes only offer diagnostic fields. There you will find hermetic emissaries of symptoms, whose superficial adhesions are impossible to peel off. Disorder, once ordered, lodges itself as complaints into catalogues of purchase and merit, trapped in its aspirations to cohere.

To dredge up provenance, to squeeze proof positive through the pores of authority, to entertain cause as belief—perhaps it's a matter of disposition. What is it that you were doing at the time that the stoppage stopped? Form's alibi is a deferral or a dislocation. And unattempted deformations connotate detours, however plastic they may be. Form is not in presumptive agreement; it is still up for negotiation. You may find your consensuses parched and left shrunken on the vast shores of accord. There, the wreckages of reconciliation shield your cursory affirmations from the aloofness of contact or collision. Preemptive avowals may pour ease into your ears, but confirmation does not promise safe passage, nor does compliance accrue insurance. So, you search for another way, another side. Indeed, inclination and slouching alike can temper even the steepest of bluffs. If this is an appeal to form, then it will reveal itself through its due process.

As you approach the precipice of doubt, another confrontation smacks you right in the face. It appears you have reached the end.

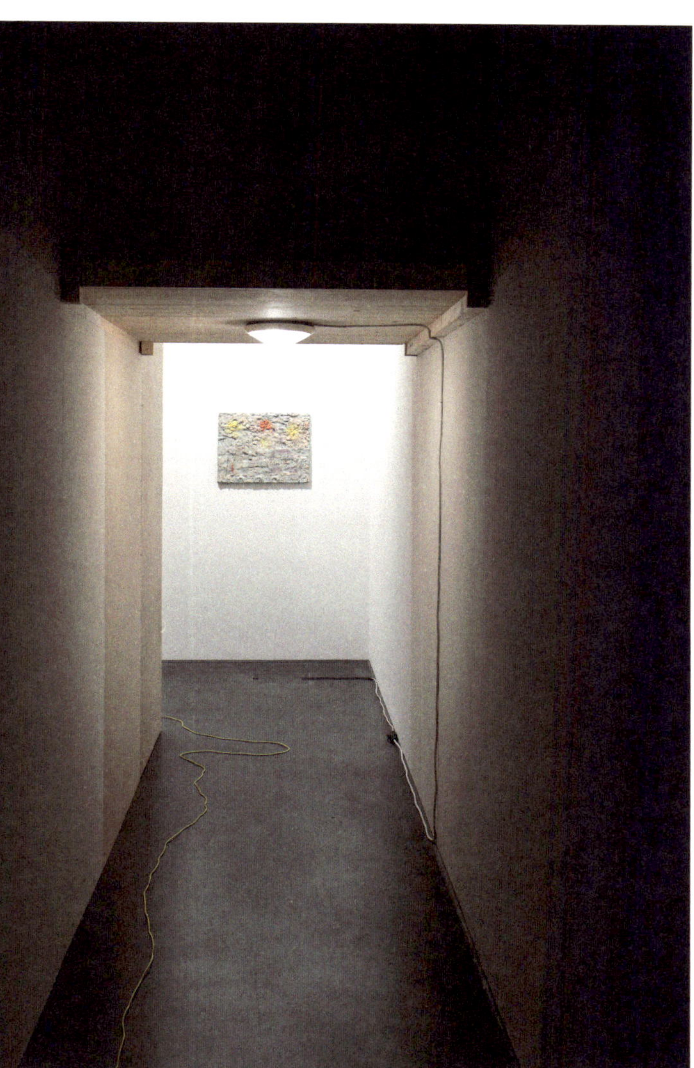

42 “If you want to know the truth you will know it.” Agnes Martin, *Writings*. ZUR SACKGASSE 4. STOCK, exhibition view Kunstmuseum Luzern, photo: Marc Latzel

43 “Light meets everything and it’s where the color goes. It’s what’s left when it’s gone.” Eileen Myles, *Afterglow (a dog memoir)*. ZUR SACKGASSE 4. STOCK, exhibition view Kunstmuseum Luzern, photo: Marc Latzel

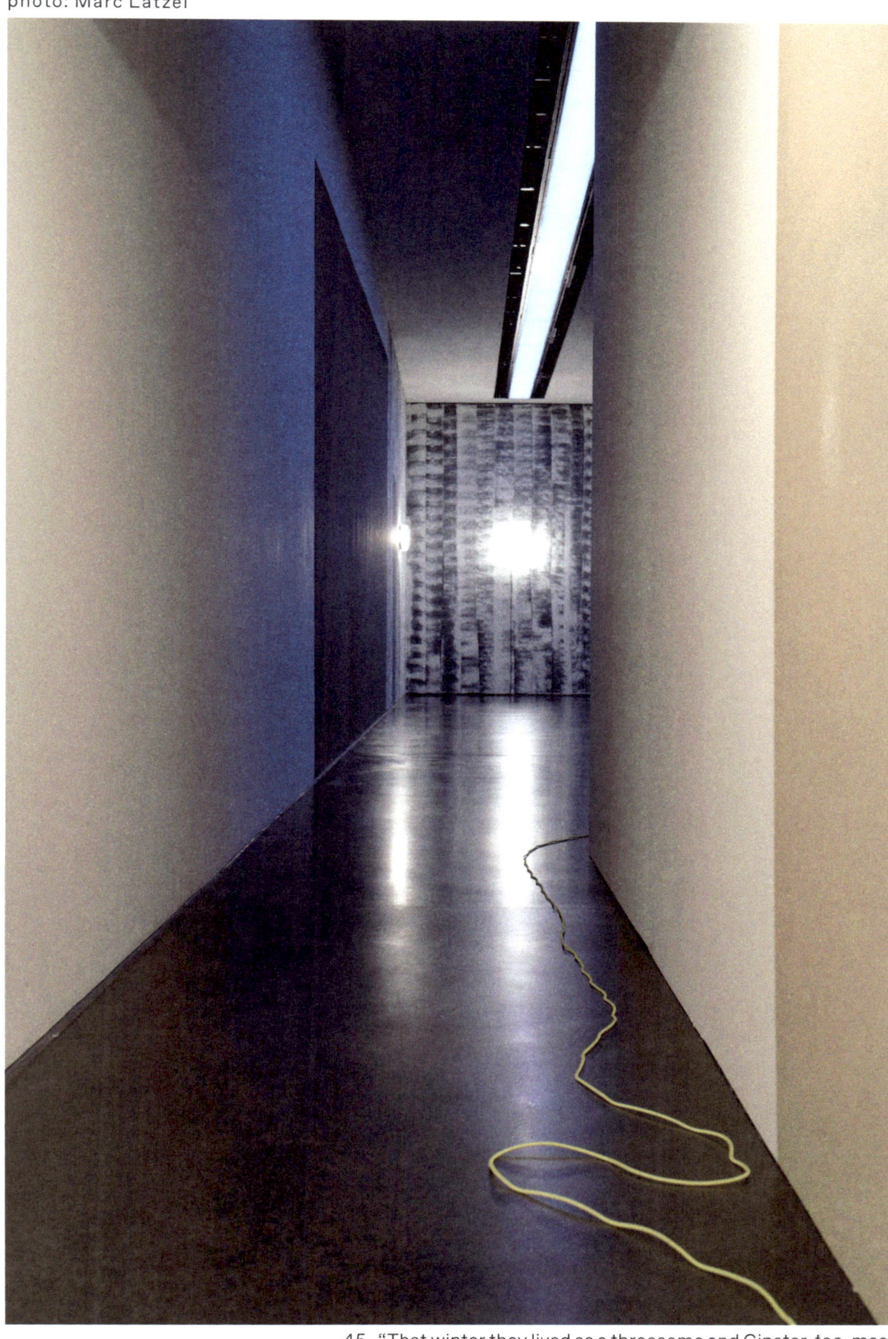

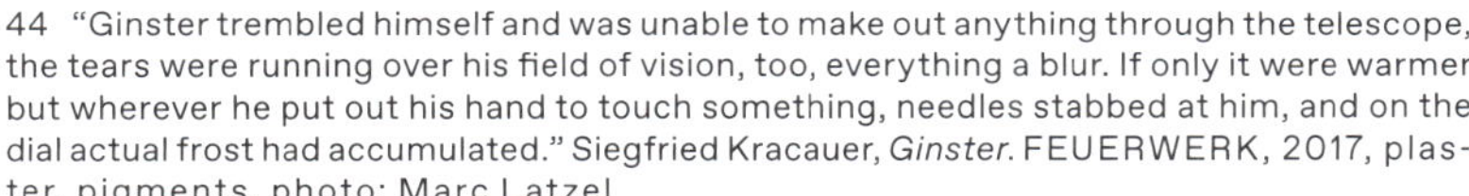

44 “Ginster trembled himself and was unable to make out anything through the telescope, the tears were running over his field of vision, too, everything a blur. If only it were warmer but wherever he put out his hand to touch something, needles stabbed at him, and on the dial actual frost had accumulated.” Siegfried Kracauer, *Ginster*. FEUERWERK, 2017, plaster, pigments, photo: Marc Latzel

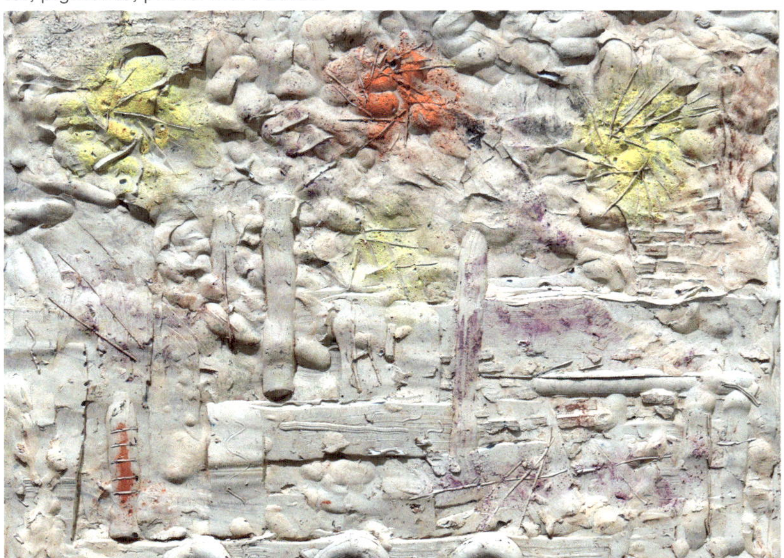

45 “That winter they lived as a threesome and Ginster, too, mastered the private language.” Siegfried Kracauer, *Ginster*. Rheinländerstrasse, Basel, 2020

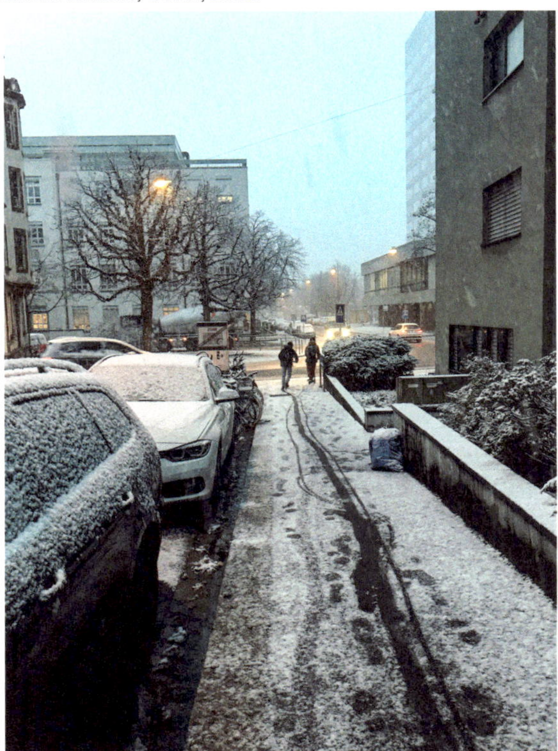

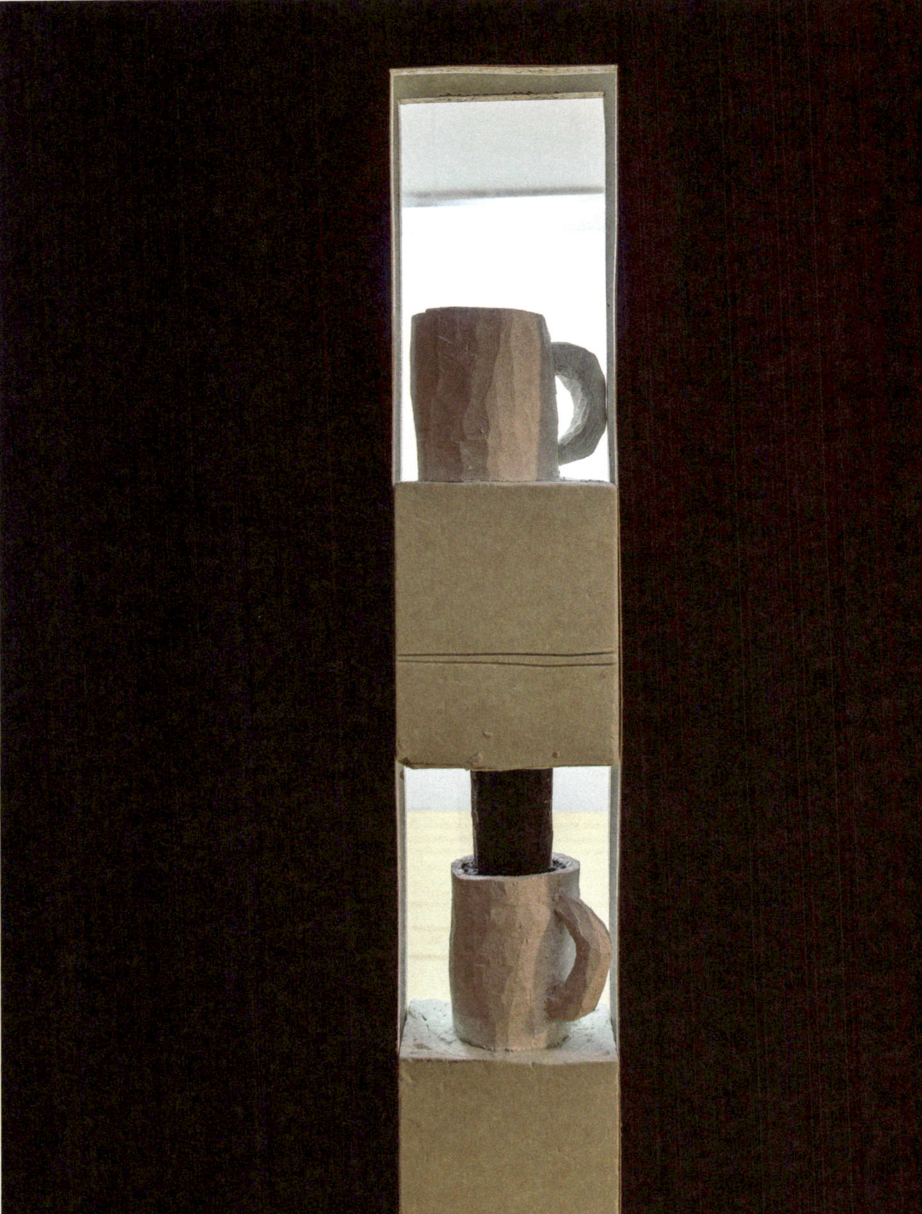

46 "Labour exchanges are reminiscent of marshalling yards, with innumerable tracks along which the jobless are shunted to and fro like wagons." Siegfried Kracauer, *The Salaried Masses*. REFILL, 2020, polyurethane, acrylic paint, Kunstmuseum Luzern, photo: Marc Latzel

47 "By May everyone forgot how fast I was. I jumped up on the table and ate all the food. It was right there on plates. You were in the next room hating each other." Eileen Myles, *Afterglow (a dog memoir)*. Canapés, Luzern, 2020

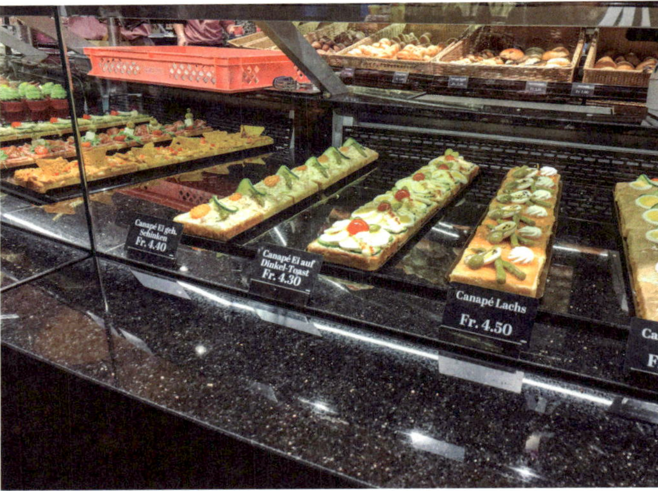

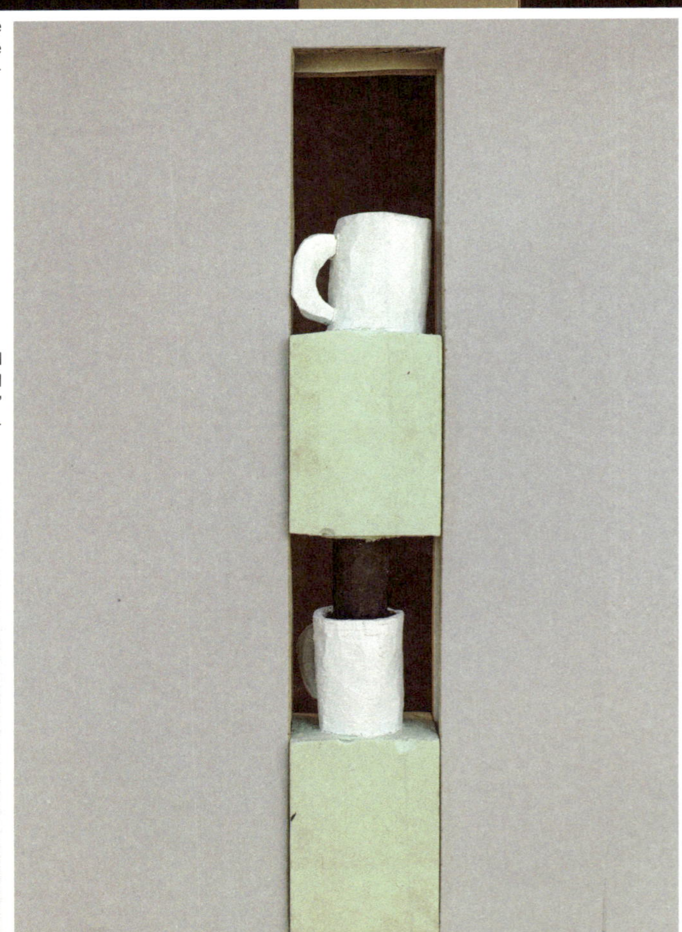

48 "Complaints follow one another in unbroken sequence. They are already sifted before they are brought forward: either by a court official in the registry or, more usually, by the employee organizations." Siegfried Kracauer, *The Salaried Masses*. REFILL, 2020, polyurethane, acrylic paint, Kunstmuseum Luzern, photo: Marc Latzel

49 "To not just blur genres, but to write totally outside of them—it sounds like a wonderful utopia—but is it possible? What kind of marginality is that, free-floating outside the social order like David Bowie's Major Tom? Doesn't genre infect everything we write—or think?" Dodie Bellamy, *Crimes Against Genre* in *Academonia*. DOOR MAT 1, 2017, plaster, pigments, Kunstmuseum Luzern, photo: Marc Latzel

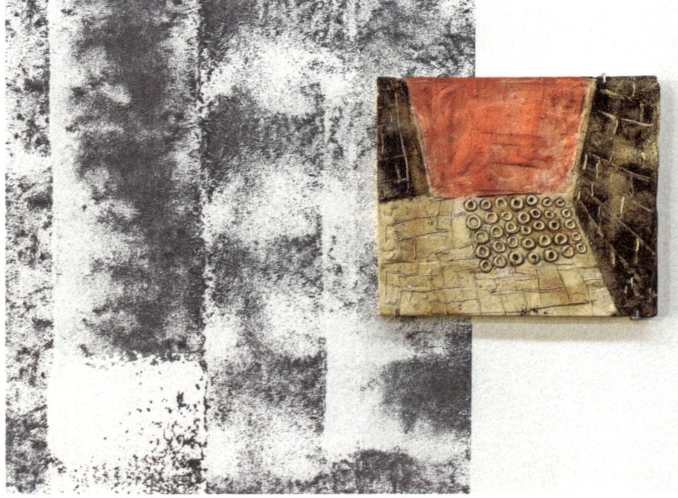

Die Stauung: Eine Ätiologie

Sabrina Chou

Du näherst dich dem Abgrund des Zweifels, da trifft dich ein weiterer Anwurf mitten ins Gesicht. Aber ist der Rand nicht immer ein perspektivisch stark verkürzter Plot, in dem Enthüllung und Niedergang Hand in Hand gehen? Es scheint, als hättest du das Ende erreicht.

Das hier ist eine Sackgasse, du kannst nur noch den Rückzug antreten, ein Stocken von Entwicklungen, die seit Langem als selbstverständlich galten, ein Stillstand aufgeklärter Erwartungen, die die Wirklichkeit stetig reproduziert hatte, ein Schwund guter Aussichten, bis –

Aber was hat dich innehalten lassen? Die spekulativen Klempner haben frei. Du musst selbst tauchen, der Nase nach. Das ist keine isolierte Episode (selbst wenn die Sauger verstopfen können). Eine Stauung blockiert, was sie zugleich bestätigt. Was hast du denn geglaubt, was du sagen würdest? – »Hier liegt ein unbelasteter Körper, der sich selbst und andere blockiert?« Wenn du dich vorher schon gesorgt hast, lass nicht zu, dass deine Ängste beschwichtigt werden. In der Leere gibt es zumindest Klarheit. Du musst deinen übrigen Fähigkeiten nachgeben. Etwas ausfindig zu machen, ist nur ein Anfang.

Was nun, fragst du dich vielleicht. Zurück ans Ende natürlich und dann wird der Kreislauf dieser Geschichte umgekehrt. Lässt sich die Folge von Stauungen rekonstruieren, die in ihrer Summe diesen Augenblick ausmachen? Von den bebenden Klümpchen und Erhebungen über die auszumachenden Kanten und die rastlosen Zwischenräume hin zu den rauen Oberflächen voller böser Ahnungen tun sich die Grenzen auf. In diesen Oberflächen kannst du vielleicht einen institutionellen Abdruck entziffern, dessen nur mühsam unterdrückte Arroganz Rechtfertigung von den eigenen Mauern kratzt. Diese wankenden Trümmer, aus der Gemütlichkeit ihrer kartesianischen Achse gedrängt, zerbersten in einer ängstlichen Raserei, nicht mehr zu fassen. Wenn du versuchst, aus dem faserigen Bodensatz wattige Klumpen zu formen, lösen sie sich sofort auf in armseligem Aufbegehren, zerfallen ob der leisesten Bedenken. Also versuchst du, dich dem auf andere Weise zuzuwenden.

Diese Stauung könnte einer Unterbrechung entsprechen, einem stockenden Einhalt im Strom. Dämme werden gegen die Strömung errichtet, gegenläufig. Doch deine eifrigen Erkundungen fördern keine Zuversicht. Im Gegenteil, du steckst knietief in einem murmelnden, unzusammenhängenden Morast. Der Impuls, dich überdeutlich zu artikulieren, kann auf mehrere Arten erstickt werden; Schweigen ist eine anmaßende Hemmung. Ob diese diffuse Unklarheit eine Strategie ist? Eine Blockade, die mit Unschärfe die Angriffe einfühlsamer Übersetzungen und sentimentaler Anpassungen abwehrt? Diejenigen, die an das Vermögen der Sprache glauben, könnten sich hier gelähmt fühlen. Ihre Münder, versperrt, zum Bersten voll mit den rhetorischen Rückständen ihrer narzisstischen Schwelgereien. Sie ersticken an ihrer Selbstverführung. Ungeachtet ihrer Anmut und Schönheit sind bunte Konfitüren (und Marmeladen) vor allem klebrig, weniger tugendhaft.

Hängt die Kausalität an der Klassifikation? Du sehnst dich nach einer konkreten Prognose, die sich mit der Zeit selbst heilen könnte, statt dieser zähen Hemmung. Gewissheit ist eine Bequemlichkeit und ein Trost. Doch Identifikationen sind spröde und zerbrechlich. Sie müssen unerschütterlich sein, so groß die Last auch sein mag. Sie ertragen ihre eigene Ähnlichkeit in Monolithen. Sie verfügen über eine unautorisierte Archäologie ihrer eigenen Repräsentation. Solche Ausgrabungen legen nichts frei als das Bröckeln ihrer selbstsedimentierten Ablagerungen. Bei im Übrigen gleichen Reflexionen zersplittert auch der bestpolierte Schein unter Druck. Unter der Wirkung selbstreflexiver Übungen der Prüfung und der Entsprechung verliert das Ebenbild sich in sich selbst. Doch wer könnte eine Wesensverwandtschaft denn bezeugen? Beruhen Repräsentationen nicht auf Glauben, mit in den Glanz der Rechtmäßigkeit eingehämmerten Legierungen von Überzeugungen?

Du siehst ihr dennoch ins Gesicht, dieser senkrecht verlaufenden Sackgasse. Was hinaufgeht, kommt auch wieder herunter. Die Gewinne weigern sich, zusammengezählt zu werden. Noch einmal kehrst du ans Ende zurück, einem Abschluss der Schlussfolgerungen kein bisschen näher. Dechiffrierte Codes eröffnen ohnehin nur Felder für die Diagnose. Du triffst dort auf hermetische Sendboten von Symptomen, deren oberflächliche Anhaftungen sich nicht abziehen lassen. Wird die Unordnung geordnet, lagert sie sich in den Verzeichnissen von Erwerb und Verdienst ab, als Beschwerde, gefangen im Bestreben kohärent zu werden.

Eine Herkunft ans Licht bringen, Beweise zu prüfen, sie durch die Poren der Autorität zu quetschen, die Ursache als Glauben zu nehmen – vielleicht ist das eine Charakterfrage. Was hast du getrieben, als die Stauung innehielt? Das Alibi der Form ist ein Aufschub oder eine Verschiebung. Deformationen, die unversucht bleiben, haben etwas von Umwegen, seien sie auch noch so plastisch. Form ist nicht Gegenstand mutmaßlicher Vereinbarungen, sie befindet sich noch in der Aushandlung. Vielleicht findest du deine Einigkeiten verdorrt und eingeschrumpft an der langen Küste der Übereinkünfte. Die Wrackteile der Aussöhnung, die dort sind, schützen deine flüchtigen Bejahungen vor den Distanzen des Kontakts oder der Kollision. Präventive Bekenntnisse mögen dir Behaglichkeit ins Ohr träufeln, doch die Bestätigung gewährt keine sichere Überfahrt und Regeltreue verschafft keine Gewissheit. Also suchst du nach einem neuen Zugang, einer anderen Seite. Neigung wie Schlaffheit können die schroffste Täuschung abmildern. Wenn das ein Aufruf an die Form ist, wird er sich im ordentlichen Verfahren zu erkennen geben.

Du näherst dich dem Abgrund des Zweifels, da trifft dich ein weiterer Anwurf mitten ins Gesicht. Es scheint, als hättest du das Ende erreicht.

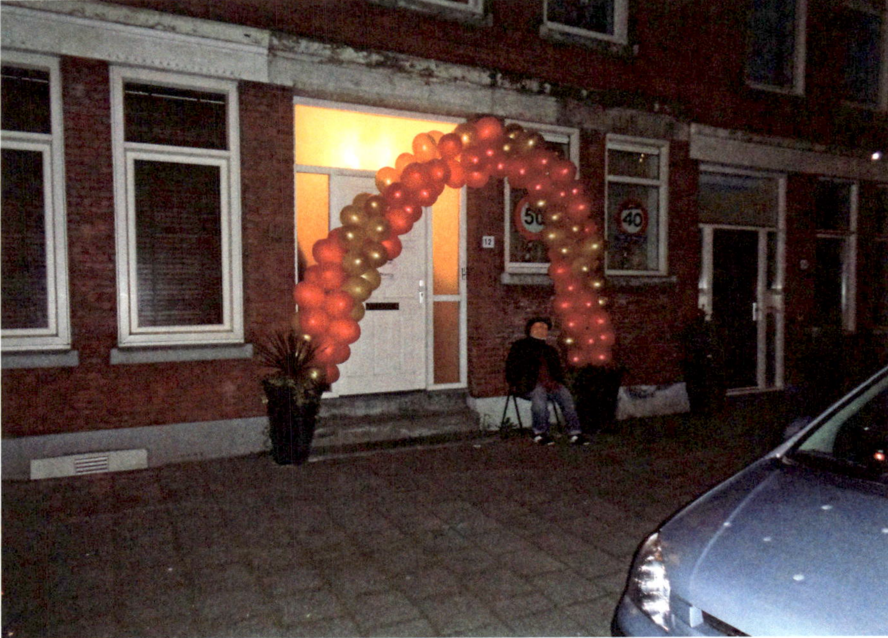

50 "Thousands of young employees dream about canoeing." Siegfried Kracauer, *The Salaried Masses*. Charlois, Rotterdam, 2018

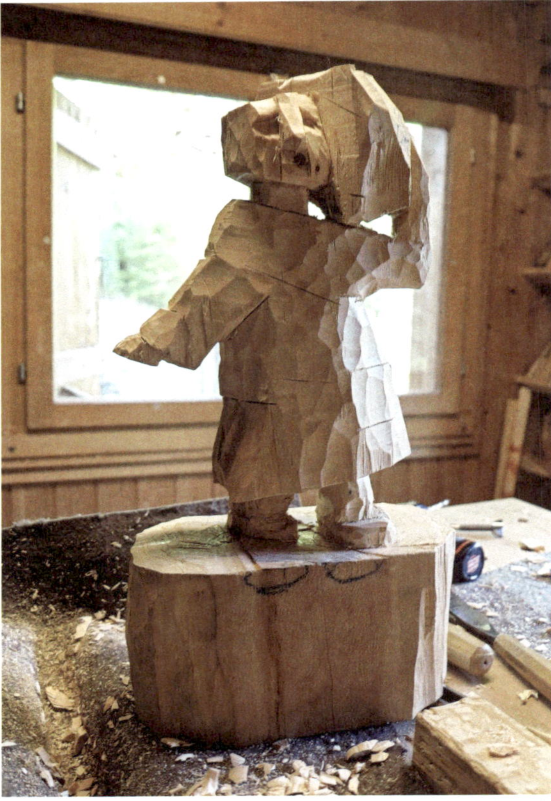

51 "One summer, Sophia's father bought a tent and put it up in the ravine so he could hide there if too many people came. The tent was so small that you had to crawl in on all fours, but inside there was enough room for two if they lay close together." Tove Jansson, *The Summer Book*. Carving STOFFEL, Tschoma, 2018

52 "Many employers have highly subjective notions of a community. The lady supervisors of one well-known department store address their subordinates as 'Child'. Perhaps this family atmosphere does lend wings to the children's enthusiasm, but it is not really very affecting, enforced as it is by checks that express only a limited confidence in its warmth." Siegfried Kracauer, *The Salaried Masses*. UNTITLED, 2018, plywood, paint

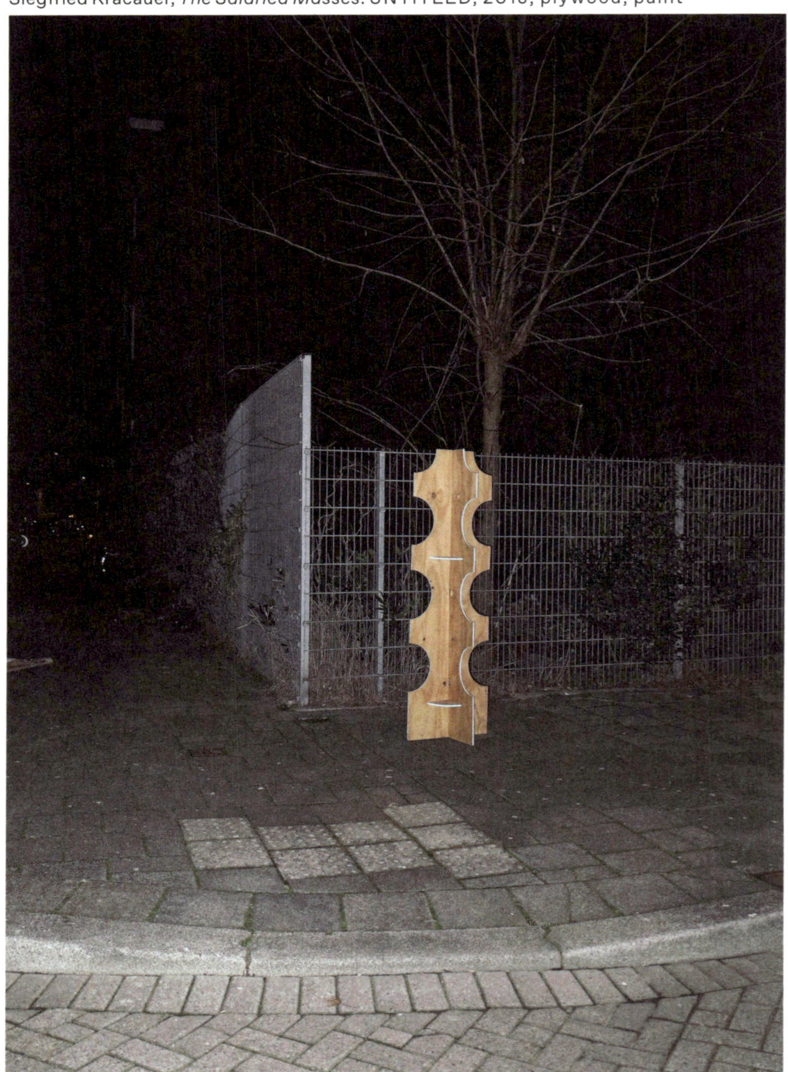

53 "The mouth is an ambivalent part of the body, being the site of both speech and mastication. The monk was meant to feed not on the flesh of animals but on the Word of God in a muscular mastication—*a ruminatio*, so-called, that released the full flavor or meaning of the text. The savor of the text, chewing on its succulent meanings, is a metaphor that can be traced from St Augustine onwards." Michael Camille, *Image on the Edge*. STOFFEL, 2018, carved stone pine, tooth brush, I am not your Guru, Arnhem

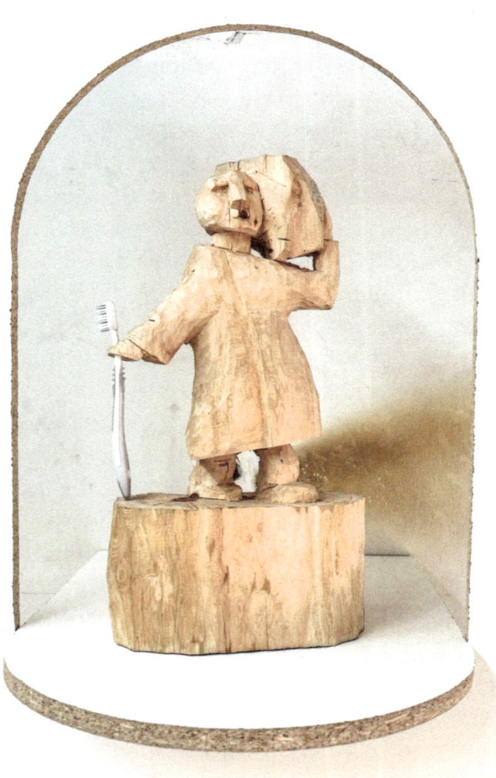

The exhibition title ZUR SACKGASSE 4. STOCK (cul de sac 4th floor) is a signpost that is immediately overlaid metaphorically: by the omnipresent mental state of the year 2020 in which our own four walls became a cul de sac or dead end; by the frenetic standstill of capitalism with supposedly no alternative in which the escalators no longer rise smoothly upwards but instead accelerate downwards, so that we have to run faster and faster to remain on the very same spot. The cul de sac enables a confrontation with our own finitude and limitations.

Alluding to the *Dada Manifesto* (1918), everyday life appears in the work of Micha Zweifel as "a simultaneous whirl of noises, colours and spiritual rhythms" adopted in all its banal reality. In this publication, Eveline Suter describes the details and situations Micha Zweifel records as being "mostly ordinary and sometimes quite ugly". Although this may introduce an irritation, what if the oppositions of complex and banal, beautiful and ugly, high and low are themselves banal? And what if our attention is directed instead at the art practice and the practice of everyday life?

Micha Zweifel cites a passage from *Capital* by Karl Marx as his basic idea behind his artistic work and his conception of himself as human being: "Labour is a process [...] in which both man and nature participate, in which man of his own accord starts, regulates and controls the material re-actions between himself and nature. He opposes himself to nature as one of her own forces, setting in motion arms and legs, head and hand, the natural forces of his body in order to appropriate nature's productions in a form adapted to his own wants. By thus acting on the external world and changing it, he at the same time changes his own nature." Art is labour, because art too is fundamentally nothing more than a kind of metabolism, "material re-actions". This is an insight that leaves the artist and cook Micha Zweifel anchored in everyday life and labour.

The title of Micha Zweifel's work SHORT BREAK FOR VENTILATION (fig. 60, 75–80) cites a chapter heading from *The Salaried Masses* (1930) by the German journalist and sociologist Siegfried Kracauer. Kracauer describes vividly how recuperation merely aims to restore the labour power and the readiness to perform. A machine room wallpapered with pretty pictures and clever calendar sayings providing a temporary escape. We are always working, be it during working hours, when we produce, or in our leisure time, when we consume and optimise ourselves. Zweifel's clothed plaster or foam figures, UNTITLED (STANDING FIGURE) (fig. 110) or MEC (fig. 5) bear witness to rigid and simultaneously flexible humans. Everything that is not swiftly and easily consumable immediately bores them, which is why they fall into a kind of depressive hedonism.

In his correspondence with his father Christoph Zweifel, the artist confesses that, "the idiotic, the not-reaching-beyond-itself" appeals to him. He thus remains faithful to the plane of immanence, capable of being folded like a smooth surface, and prefers to engage with the resistance of the material than with the supposed splendour of the idea. This way, he practices not the glorification but the profanation of the commonplace. There, art is a misappropriation not just of designed everyday life, but also of spectacular art itself. In this he resembles not only Duchamp and Pop Art, but also the Swiss artist duo Fischli / Weiss. Looking at Micha Zweifel's works as rat and bear, perhaps they would also shout out: "Of simple vehemence", "Tender. Strictly decorative".

Micha Zweifel asks his father what it means "to work without a specific intention, without filling the activity with meaning in advance". This "elegant ignorance" resembles the innocence of a child that plays a creative game without asking why. A game in which rules do not exist in advance and the roll of the dice never abolishes chance. And because chance is affirmed every time, once and for all, the child cannot help but win, and is not afraid to fail because the wish is always to fail better.

Play is a paradigm, not only for our actions, but also for our movements. If we walk through a city, a museum or a room, then usually we do so according to a set of rules of a purposeful plan: from A to B, to do C. But why not just wander aimlessly around a city? Go to a museum every day? For a short time one day, for longer the next? This would interrupt the social production of space, misappropriate its rules, which make some things visible, others invisible, and abduct us into another space.

In this vein, Micha Zweifel's new and expansive overall installation at the Kunstmuseum Luzern lets us first drift through another exhibition, then discover hidden sides of the museum. The sculptural gesture is less about imitating a room and more about evoking another bodily awareness of the room in the sense of a pointer. He covers the walls of the room with the relief series CALENDAR (fig. 84, 91). For these he used an identical form that gives him a "formal stability", as he puts it. These forms enable him to be "attentive to other things" during the iterative process of difference and repeating. Organised like a frieze, they have something ornamental about them. His interest in the decorative aspect of art also stems from a distrust of the neutral modern architecture.

The verdict of the Austrian architect Adolf Loos in *Ornament and Crime* (1908) is notorious: "The evolution of culture is synonymous with the removal of ornament from objects of daily use." Siegfried Kracauer by contrast wrote in *The Mass Ornament* (1927): "The position that an epoch occupies in the historical process can be determined more strikingly from an analysis of its inconspicuous surface level expressions than from that epoch's judgments about itself." They, "by virtue of their unconscious nature, provide unmediated access to the fundamental substance of the state of things."

In the end, we again find ourselves in a cul de sac. But it is the very limitation of our freedom of movement that opens the space in such a way that we no longer take the path of least resistance but that of the greatest intensity. So, let us wander aimlessly around and recoil neither at surfaces nor dead ends!

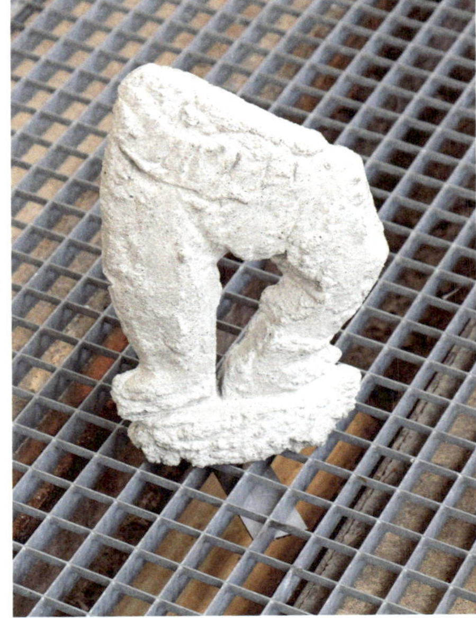

54 "One can go even further and remember that interruption is one of the fundamental devices of all structuring. It goes far beyond the sphere of art. To give only one example, it is the basis of quotation. To quote a text involves the interruption of its context." Walter Benjamin, *What is Epic Theater?* in *Illuminations*. CONTRAPPOSTO, 2014, Portland cement, photo: Sabrina Chou

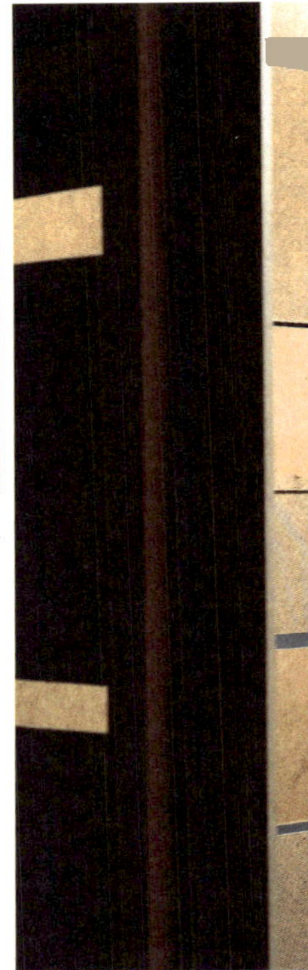

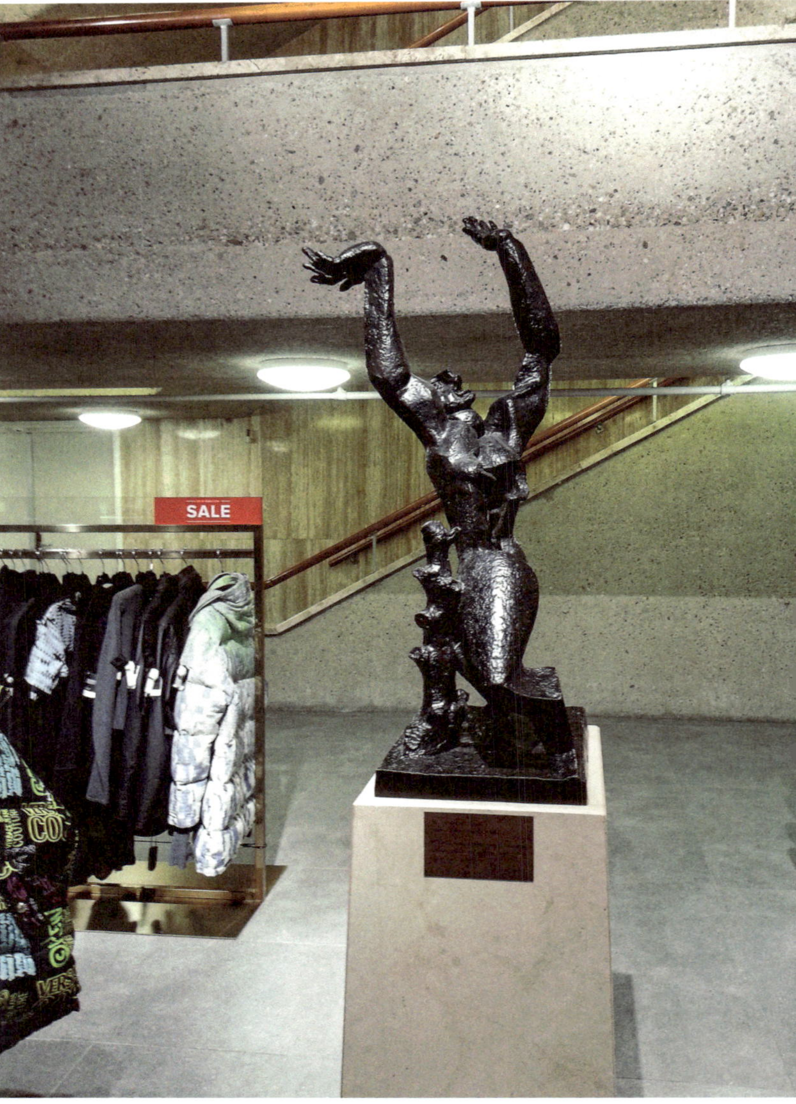

56 "...in other words we who created the expression of the modem composition were to be recognized before we were dead some of us even quite a long time before we were dead. And so war may be said to have advanced a general recognition of the expression of the contemporary composition by almost thirty years." Gertrude Stein, *Composition as Explanation* in *What Are Masterpieces?*. Miniature of *The Destroyed City* by Ossip Zadkine, Bijenkorf department store, Rotterdam, 2019

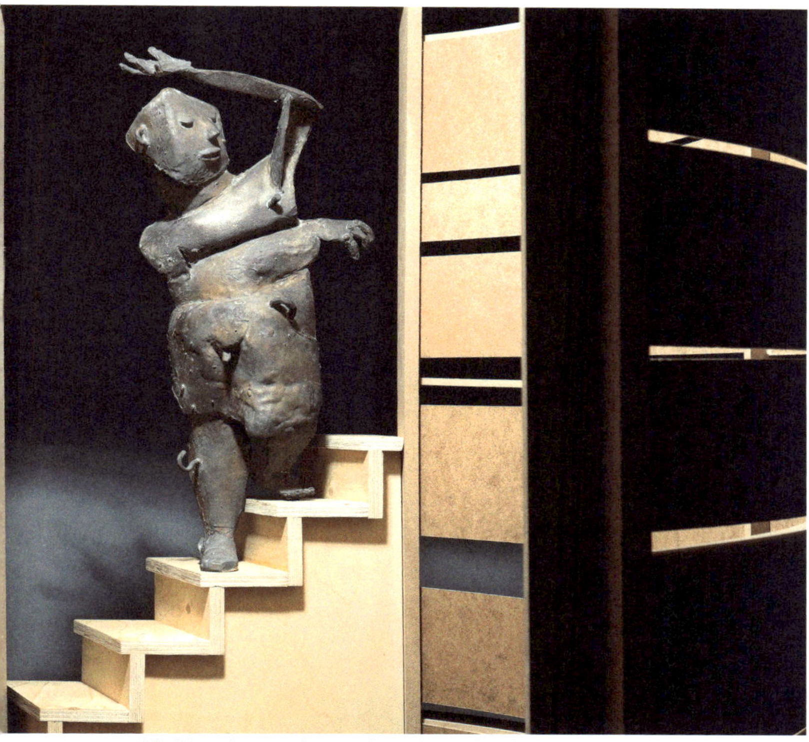

55 "A serious and sometimes incurable form of it is 'stage-fright', which seems to consist in the anxious riveting of one's attention to the next word—or note or gesture—that one has to find or remember. This destroys one's sense of the context which alone can smoothly evoke the proper sequence of words, notes, or gestures." Michael Polanyi, *Personal Knowledge*. LIFT, 2019, MDF, plywood, bronze, vinyl flooring, lamp, ONONO Rotterdam

Der Ausstellungstitel ZUR SACKGASSE 4. STOCK ist ein Wegweiser, der sogleich metaphorisch überlagert wird. Von der allgegenwärtigen Befindlichkeit des Jahres 2020, als unsere eigenen vier Wände zu Sackgassen wurden. Vom rasenden Stillstand des alternativlos scheinenden Kapitalismus, in dem die Rolltreppen nicht mehr gemächlich vorwärts nach oben fahren, sondern beschleunigt rückwärts nach unten, so dass wir immer schneller rennen müssen, um noch am selben Ort zu bleiben. Die Sackgasse ermöglicht die Konfrontation mit der eigenen Endlichkeit und Beschränktheit.

Bei Micha Zweifel erscheint das Alltagsleben, in Anlehnung an das *Dadaistische Manifest* (1918), »als ein simultanes Gewirr von Geräuschen, Farben und geistigen Rhythmen«, das in seiner gesamten banalen Realität übernommen wird. Die von ihm festgehaltenen Details und Situationen beschreibt Eveline Suter in dieser Publikation als »meist von ausgesprochener Gewöhnlichkeit und manchmal eher hässlich«. Dies mag irritieren. Doch was, wenn die Gegensätze von komplex und banal, schön und hässlich, hoch und niedrig selbst banal werden? Und unser Interesse stattdessen auf das Handeln der Kunst und die Kunst des Handelns gelenkt wird?

Als Grundgedanke seiner künstlerischen Arbeit und seines Selbstverständnisses als Mensch zitierte Micha Zweifel eine Stelle aus Karl Marx' *Das Kapital*: »Der Arbeitsprozess ist zunächst ein Prozess zwischen dem Menschen und der Natur, ein Prozess, worin er seinen Stoffwechsel mit der Natur durch seine eigne Tat vermittelt, regelt und kontrolliert. Der Mensch tritt dem Naturstoff selbst als eine Naturmacht gegenüber. Die seiner Leiblichkeit angehörigen Naturkräfte, Arme und Beine, Kopf und Hand, setzt er in Bewegung, um sich den Naturstoff in einer für sein eignes Leben brauchbaren Form zu assimilieren. Indem er durch diese Bewegung auf die Natur ausser ihm wirkt und sie verändert, verändert er zugleich seine eigne Natur.« Kunst ist Arbeit, da sie im Grunde ebenfalls nichts anderes ist als eine Art Stoffwechsel. Eine Erkenntnis, die den Künstler und Koch Micha Zweifel im Alltag und in der Arbeit verankert bleiben lässt.

Micha Zweifels Werk KURZE LÜFTUNGSPAUSE (Abb. 60, 75–80) zitiert im Titel eine Kapitelüberschrift aus *Die Angestellten* (1939) des deutschen Journalisten und Soziologen Siegfried Kracauer. Plastisch beschreibt Kracauer, wie die Erholung einzig der Wiederherstellung der Arbeitskraft und Leistungsbereitschaft diente. Ein Maschinenraum, gepflastert mit schönen Bildern und klugen Kalendersprüchen für den temporären Eskapismus. Wir arbeiten immer, sei es in der Arbeitszeit, wenn wir produzieren, sei es in der Freizeit, wenn wir konsumieren und uns selbst optimieren. Micha Zweifels bekleidete Figuren aus Gips oder Schaumstoff wie UNTITLED (STANDING FIGURE) (Abb. 110) oder MEC (Abb. 5) zeugen vom erstarrten und gleichzeitig flexiblen Menschen. Alles, was nicht schnell und einfach konsumierbar ist, langweilt diesen sofort, weshalb er in eine Art depressiven Hedonismus verfällt.

In der Korrespondenz mit seinem Vater Christoph Zweifel bekennt der Künstler: »Mir gefällt das Idiotische, das Nicht-über-sich-hinausgreifende.« Er bleibt damit der Immanenzebene treu, die wie eine glatte Oberfläche gefaltet werden kann und setzt sich lieber mit der Widerständigkeit des Materials auseinander, als mit der angeblichen Herrlichkeit der Idee. Er betreibt damit keine Verklärung des Gewöhnlichen, sondern

57 “In the night inspiration falls on the world like rain and penetrates our minds when we are asleep. It is because of this that we are so eager, so desperate for sleep.” Agnes Martin, *Writings*. Rotterdam harbor, 2017

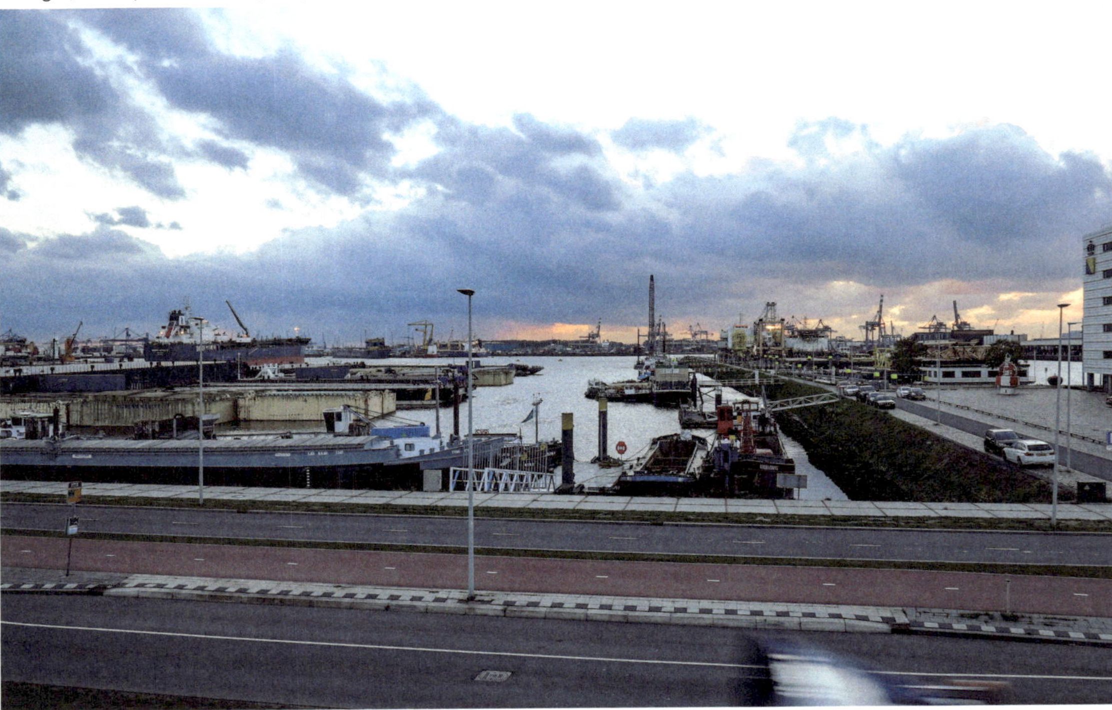

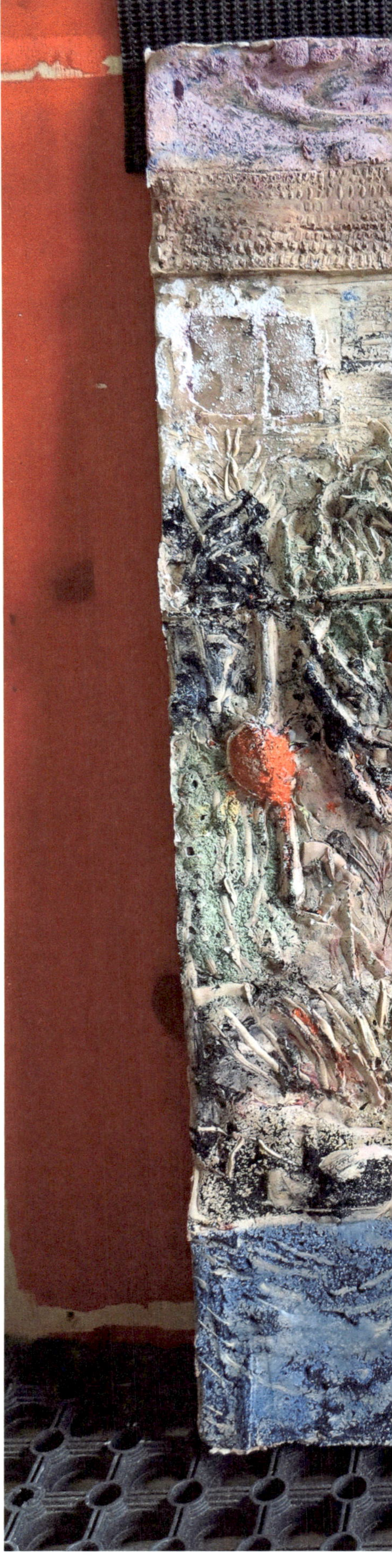

dessen Profanierung. Kunst nicht nur als Zweckentfremdung des designten Alltagslebens, sondern auch der spektakulären Kunst selbst. Darin ähnelt er Duchamp, der Pop-Art, aber auch dem Schweizer Künstlerduo Fischli / Weiss. Vielleicht würden sie als Ratte und Bär auch beim Anblick von Micha Zweifels Arbeiten ausrufen: »Von schlichter Heftigkeit«, »Zart. Streng dekorativ«.

Micha Zweifel fragt seinen Vater, was es bedeute, »ohne bestimmte Absicht zu arbeiten, ohne die Tätigkeit bereits mit Bedeutung zu füllen«. Diese »elegante Ignoranz« ähnelt der Unschuld des Kindes, das ohne Warum sein Spiel des Schaffens spielt. Ein Spiel, in dem die Regel nicht im Voraus existiert und der Würfelwurf nie den Zufall tilgt. Und weil der Zufall jedes Mal und für allemal bejaht wird, kann das Kind nur gewinnen. Denn es hat keine Angst vor dem Scheitern, weil es stets besser scheitern will.

Das Spiel ist ein Paradigma, nicht nur für unsere Handlungen, sondern auch für unsere Bewegungen. Gehen wir durch eine Stadt, ein Museum oder einen Raum, dann meist nach festgelegten Regeln eines zweckmässigen Plans: Von A nach B, um C zu machen. Doch warum nicht ziellos durch die Stadt schweifen? Jeden Tag ins Museum gehen? An einem Tag nur kurz, an einem anderen für eine längere Dauer? Dies würde die soziale Produktion des Raumes unterbrechen, deren Regeln, die manches sichtbar, anderes unsichtbar machen, zweckentfremden und uns in einen anderen Raum entführen.

So lässt uns Zweifels neue raumgreifende Gesamtinstallation im Kunstmuseum Luzern zuerst durch eine andere Ausstellung schweifen und dann ausgeblendete Seiten des Museums sehen. Die skulpturale Geste imitiert weniger einen Raum, als dass sie im Sinne eines Fingerzeigs eine andere körperliche Raumerfassung evoziert. Die Wände des Raumes kleidet er mit der Relief-Serie KALENDER (Abb. 84, 91) aus. Für diese verwendete er eine identische Form, die ihm eine »formale Stabilität« geben, wie der Künstler sagt. Dies ermöglicht ihm eine »Aufmerksamkeit für anderes« beim iterativen Prozess von Differenz und Wiederholung. Organisiert wie ein Fries, erhalten sie etwas Ornamentales.

Sein Interesse am dekorativen Aspekt der Kunst rührt auch aus einem Misstrauen gegenüber der neutralen modernen Architektur.

Berüchtigt ist das Verdikt des österreichischen Architekten Adolf Loos in *Ornament und Verbrechen* (1908): »Evolution der Kultur ist gleichbedeutend mit dem Entfernen des Ornamentes aus dem Gebrauchsgegenstande«. Siegfried Kracauer dagegen schrieb in *Ornament der Masse* (1927): »Der Ort, den eine Epoche im Geschichtsprozess einnimmt, ist aus der Analyse ihrer unscheinbaren Oberflächenerscheinungen schlagender zu bestimmen als aus den Urteilen der Epoche über sich selbst.« Denn sie geben »ihrer Unbewusstheit wegen einen unmittelbaren Zugang zu dem Bestehenden«.

Am Ende finden wir uns in einer Sackgasse wieder. Doch gerade die Beschränkung der Bewegungsfreiheit öffnet den Raum, so dass wir nicht mehr den Weg des geringsten Widerstands gehen, sondern den intensivsten. Also, schweifen wir ziellos umher und scheuen wir weder Oberflächen noch Sackgassen!

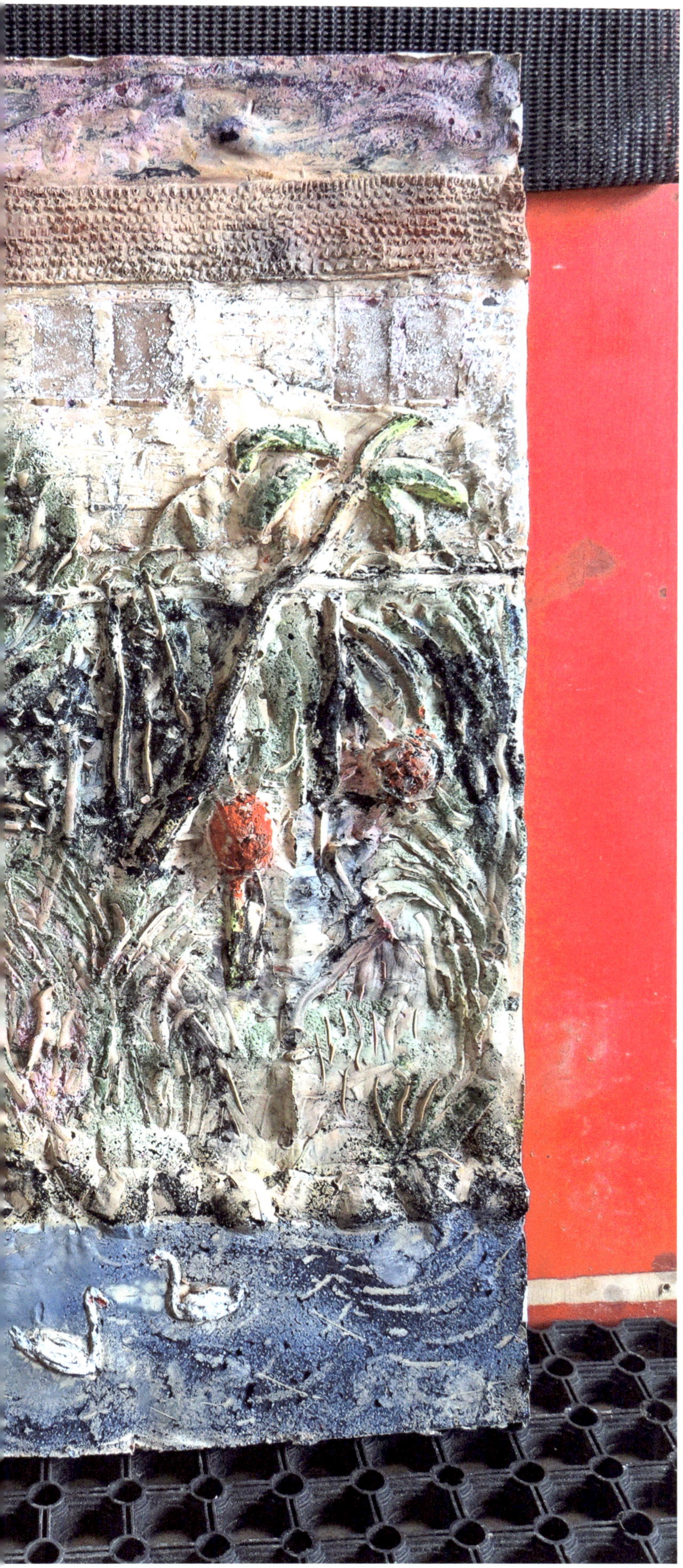

58 “Herr Allinger had entrusted Ginster with drafting the design for a swimming pool that he wished to realize together with him on behalf of a ceramics firm with whom he had business ties. He was an Arts and Crafts man and attracted to the leisurely production of landscapes. He himself belonged in his painted meadows. Usually a sun would be setting.” Siegfried Kracauer, *Ginster*.
UNTITLED (RENÉ DANIËL'S SWANS), 2017, plaster, pigments

59 “It was nice and cool under the pine trees and they weren't in any hurry, so they slept for a while. When they woke up they crawled on to the cave, but Grandmother was too big to get in. 'You'll have to tell me what it's like,' she said.” Tove Jansson, *The Summer Book*.
UNTITLED, 2017, plaster, pigments

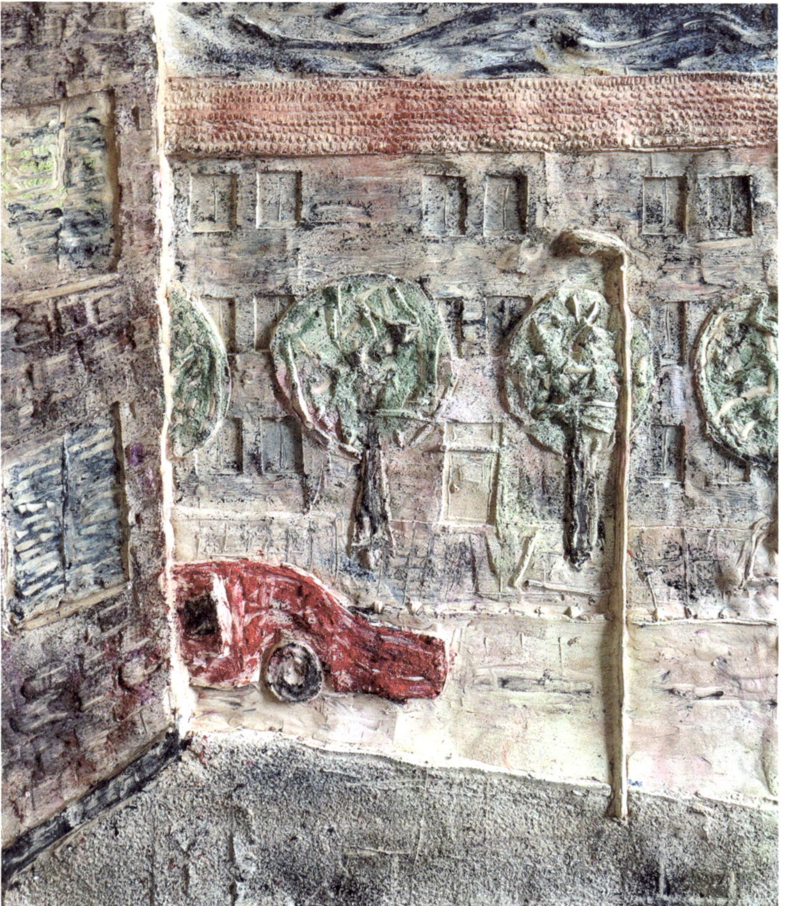

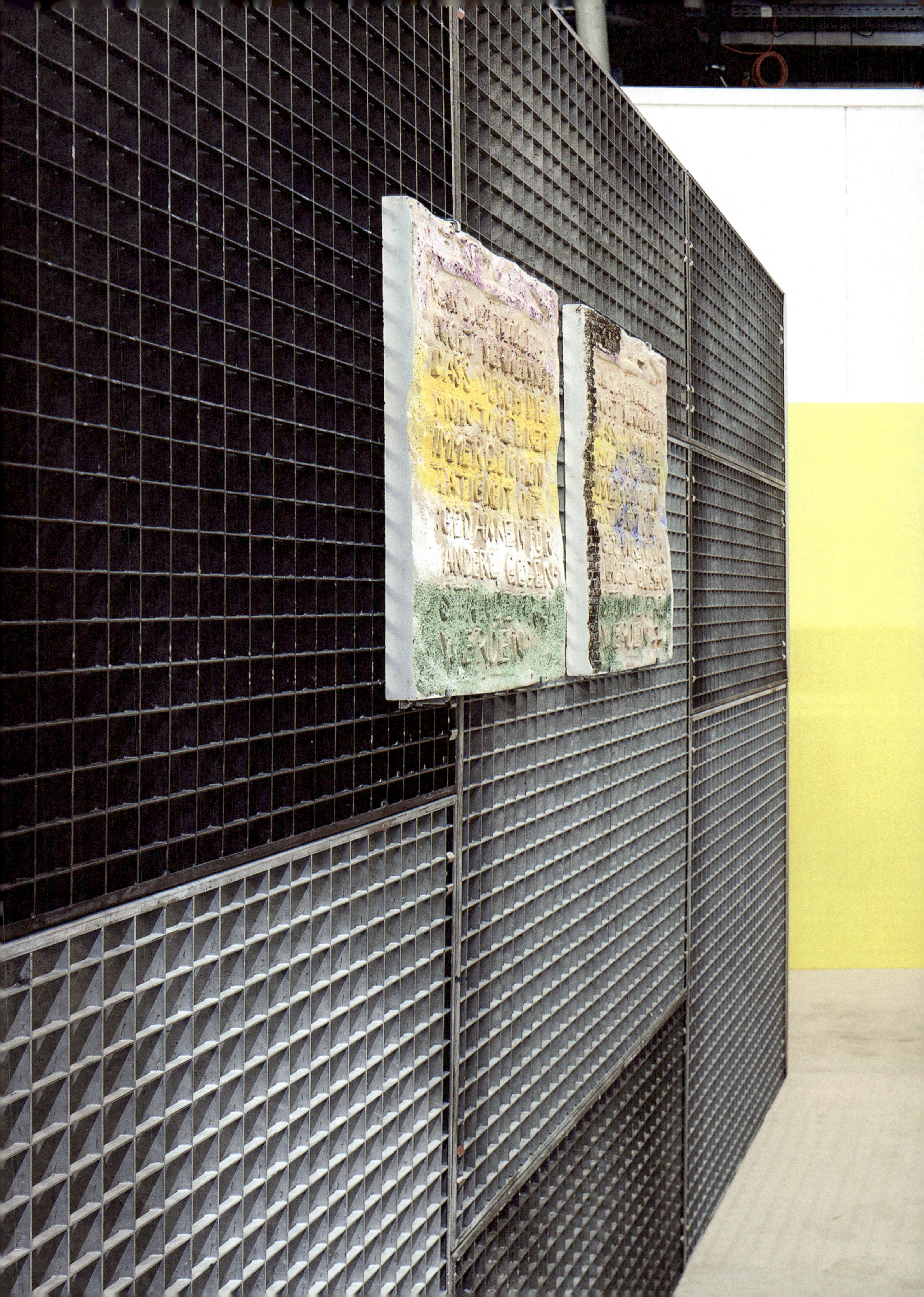
GEDANKEN FÜR
ANDERE GEGEN-

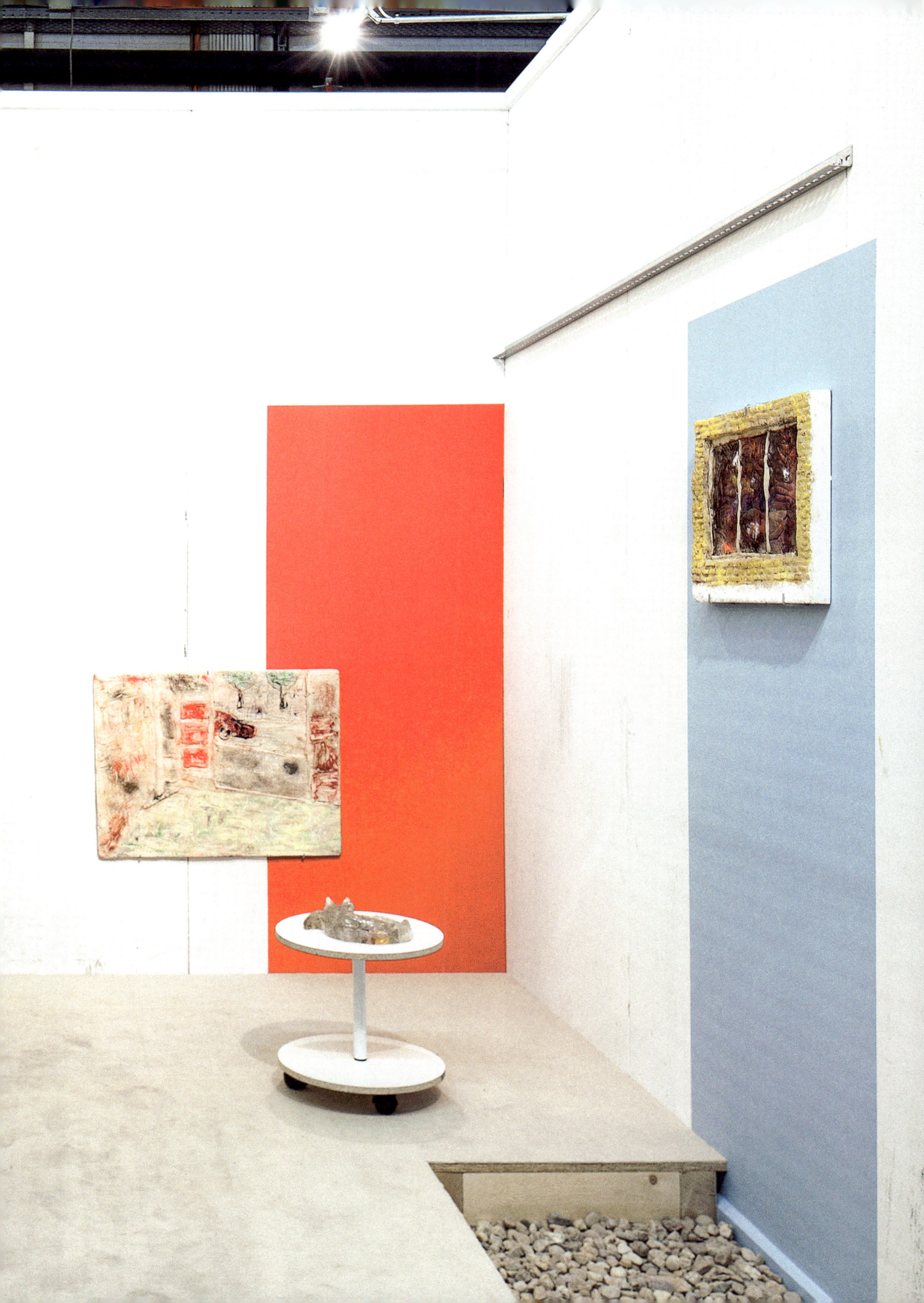

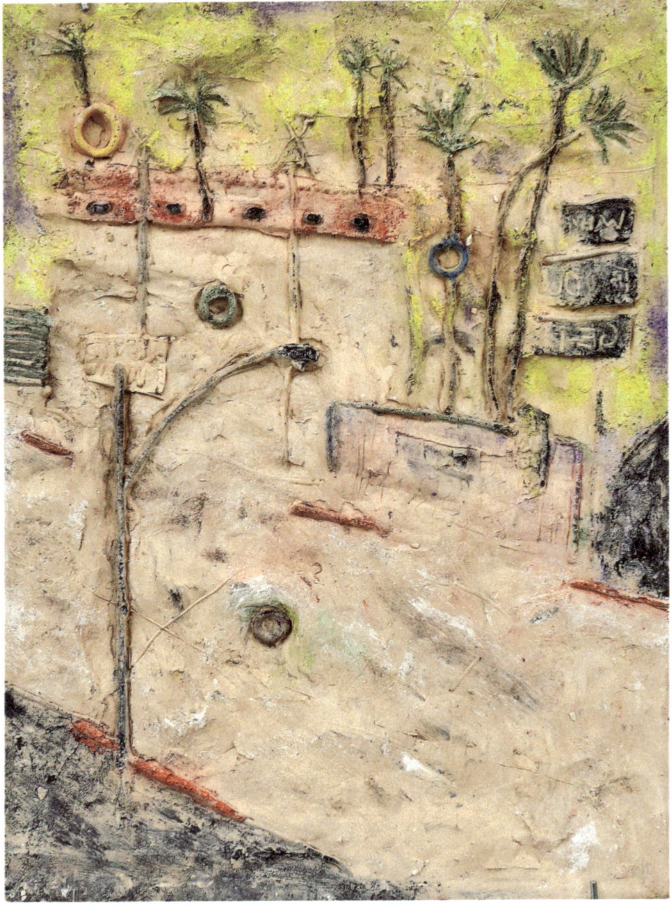

61 “We intuitively know that everyday life doesn’t conform to the simple outlines of well-made genres. In fact any event (and I include the acts of writing-reading, performing on or off the page in this category) is surprising largely to the degree that it transgresses its own generic expectations. When it really does this, going beyond the calculated surprise of an artful plot, or screamingly censurable subject matter, it’s instantly recognized as a crime by those who police aesthetic expectations.” Joan Retallack quoted by Dodie Bellamy, *Crimes Against Genre* in *Academonia*. STREET VIEW, 2017, plaster, pigments

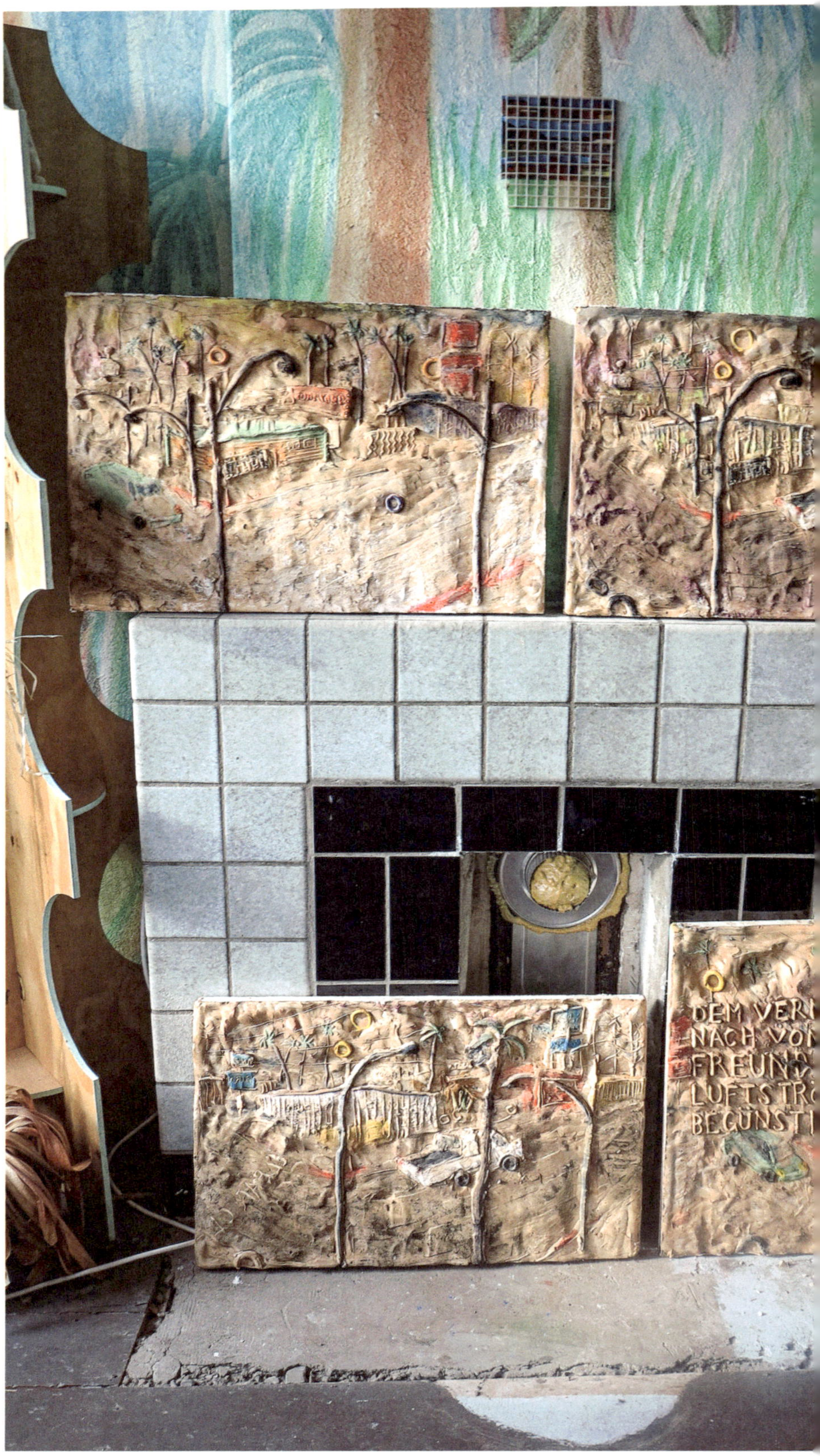

62 “No dog, only its repetition.” Eileen Myles, *Afterglow (a dog memoir)*. STREET VIEW, 2017, plaster, pigments, studio view

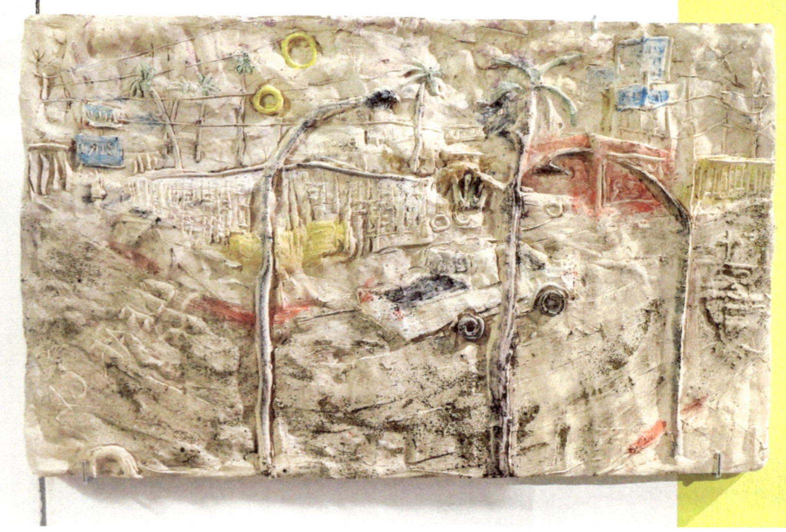

63 “Stage fright is eliminated and fluency recovered if we succeed in casting our mind forward and let it operate with a clear view to the comprehensive activity in which we are primarily interested.” Michael Polanyi, *Personal Knowledge*. STREET VIEW, 2017, plaster, pigments, Swiss Art Awards, photo: Sabrina Chou

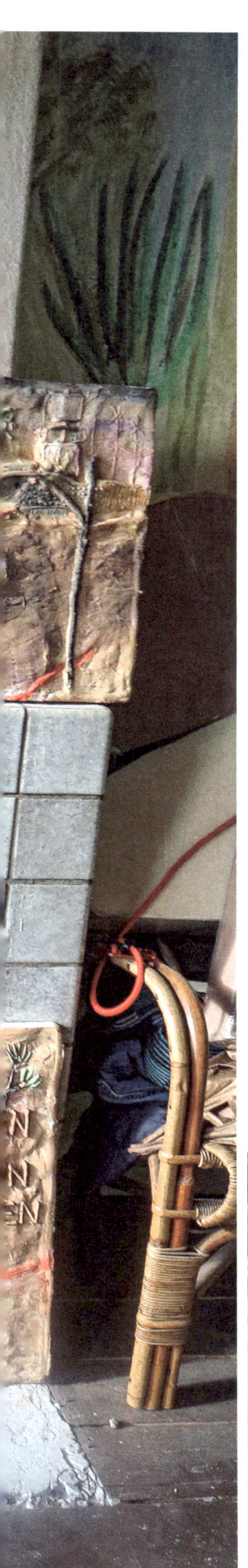

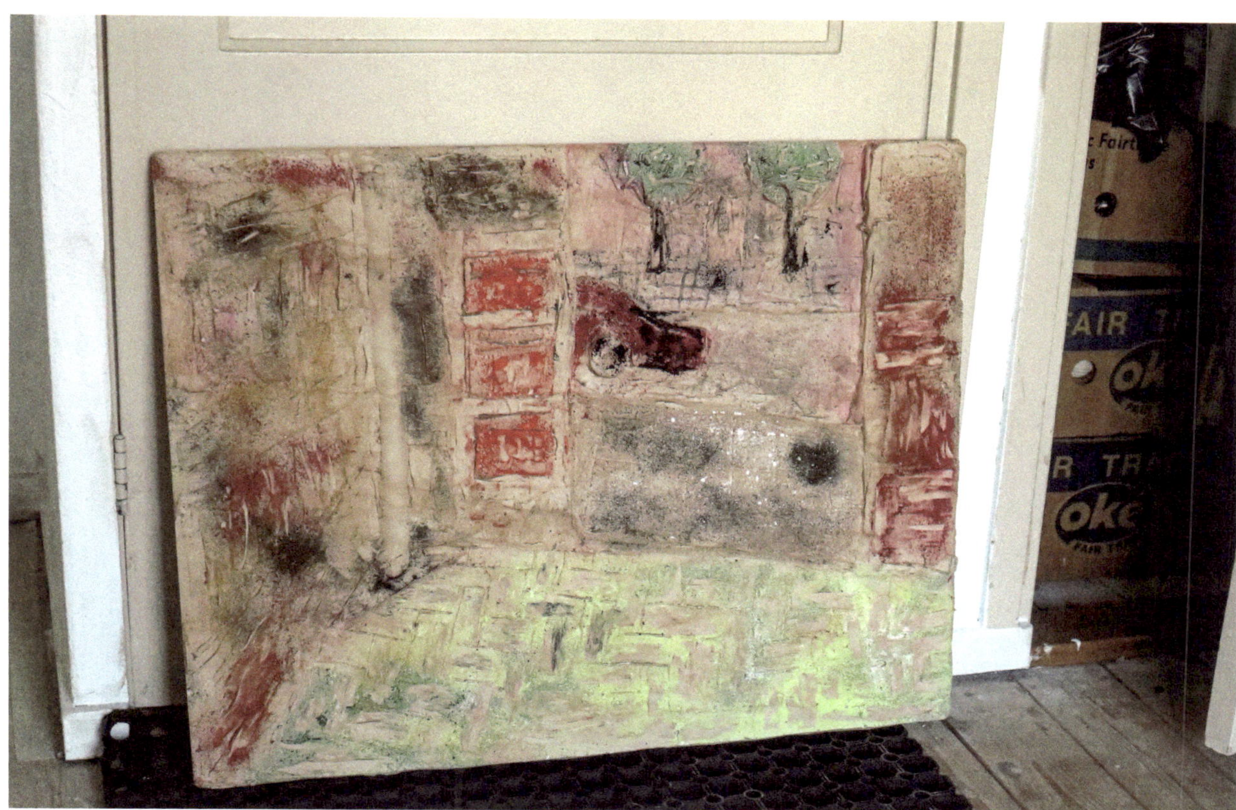

64 “He was often unlucky and was plagued by bad weather and engine trouble. His herring nets would rip or get caught in his propeller, and fish and fowl would fail to turn up where he had expected them. And if he did have a good catch, the price would go down, so it was always six of one or half a dozen of the other.” Tove Jansson, *The Summer Book.* VERBOOMSTRAAT 182-184 ROTTERDAM, 2017, plaster, pigments

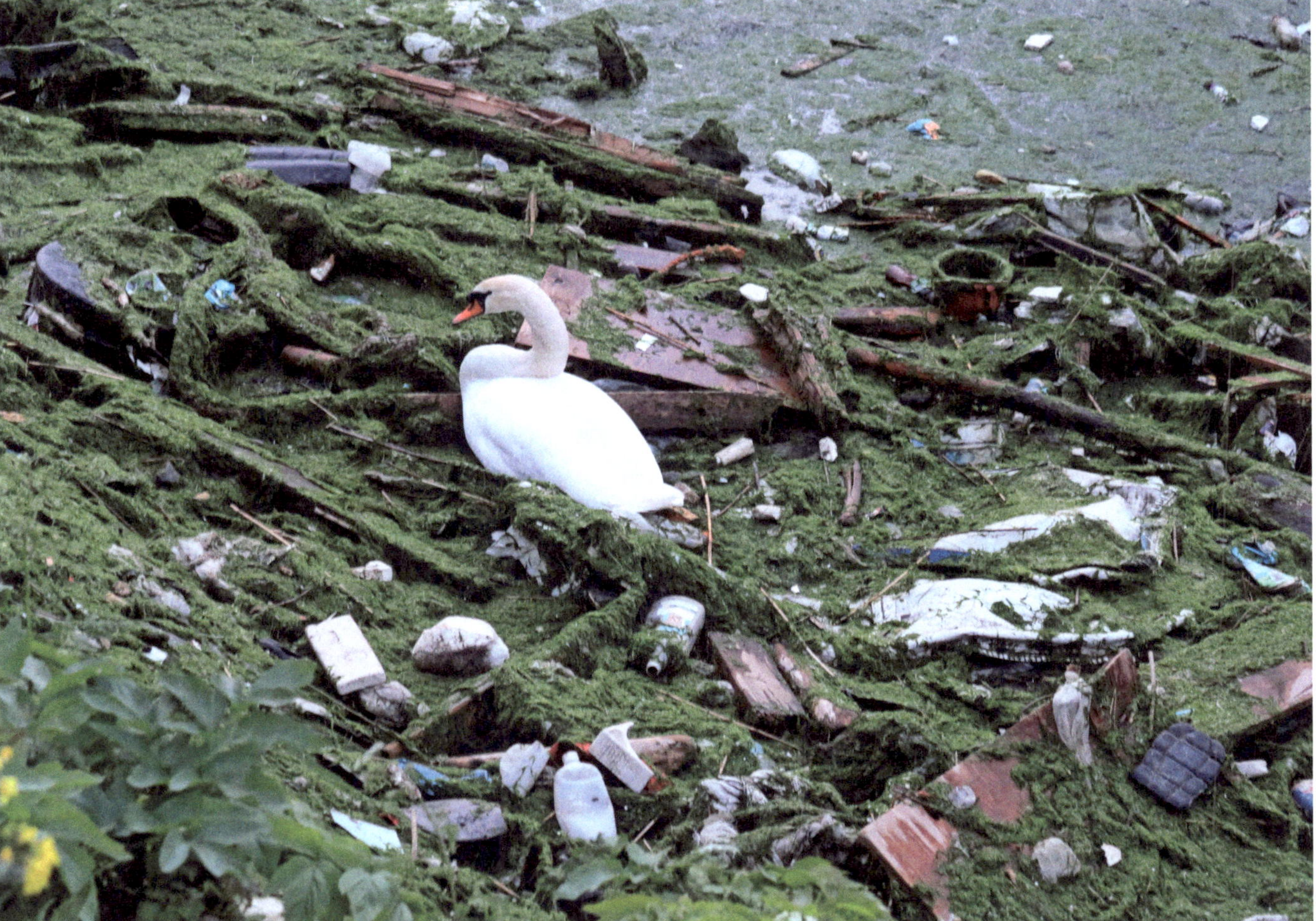

65 “The edge of the water was where wisdom revealed itself; spirits were banished to the spaceless places ‘between the froth and the water’ or ‘betwixt the bark and the tree’. Similarly, temporal junctures between winter and summer, or between night and day, were dangerous moments of intersection with the Otherworld. In charms and riddles, things that were neither this nor that bore, in their defiance of classification, strong magic.” Michael Camille, *Image on the Edge.* Swan at the harbor, Rotterdam, 2017

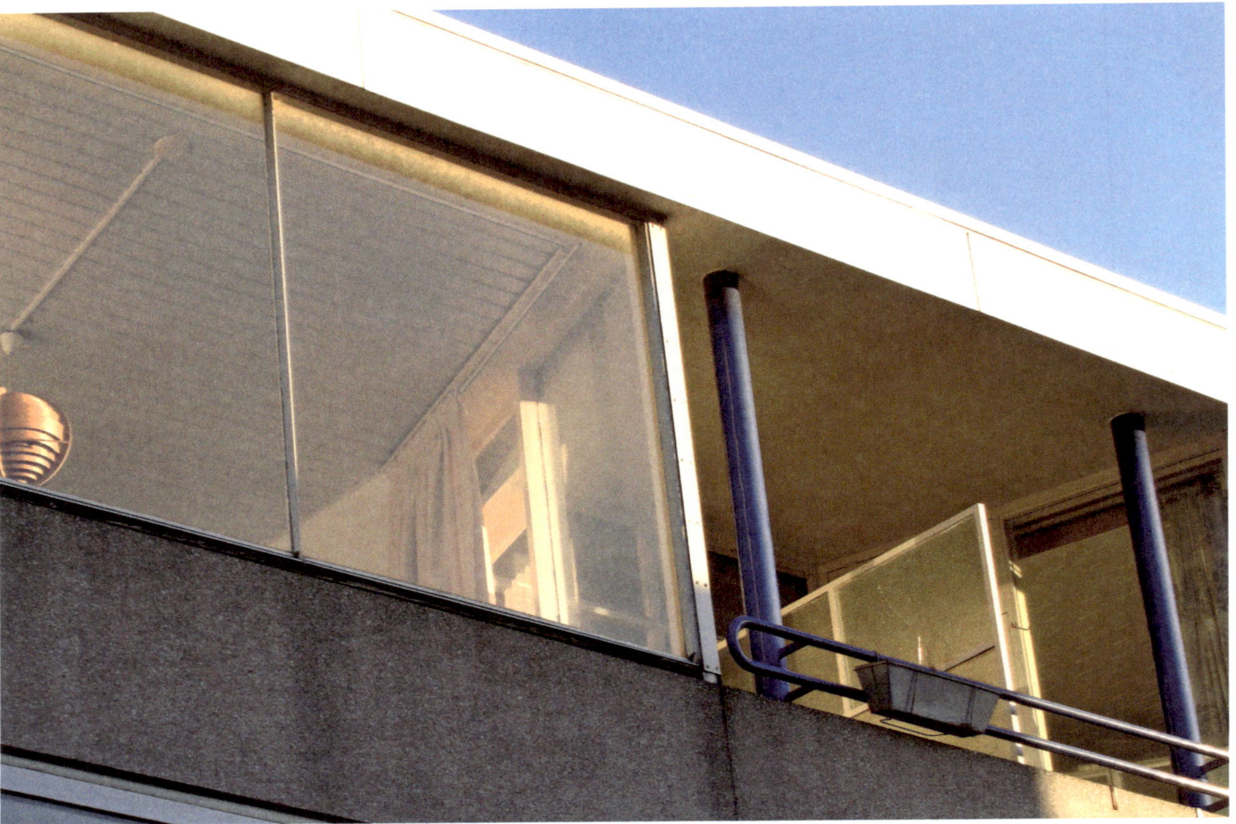

66 “We go out every evening. Sometimes he takes me to the café with him in the afternoon too, and then we don’t go back again. Do you see my shoes? I wear my shoes out every few months, dancing.” Siegfried Kracauer, *The Salaried Masses*. Residential apartment block, Charlois, Rotterdam, 2016

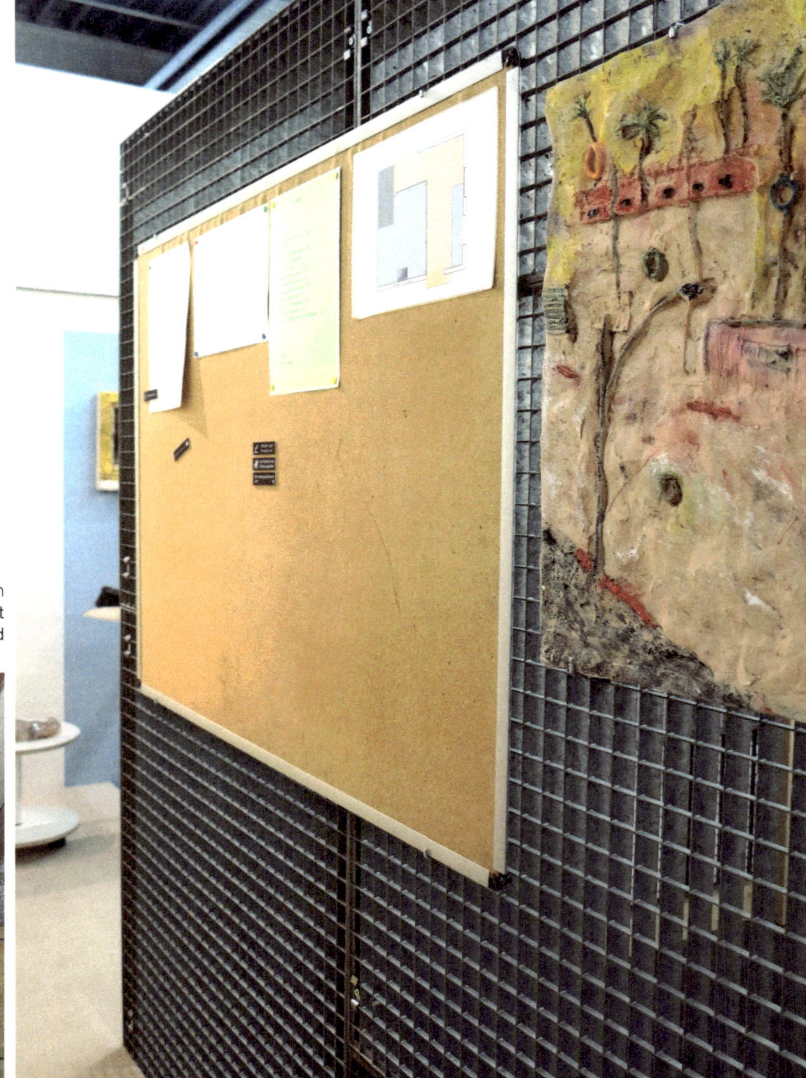

68 “For private clients, he dreamed up porcelain plates and coffee pots that bulged out after careful deliberation. They were like English ladies alone on tour in Italy who seat themselves on a bench in a secluded cypress grove and read novels.” Siegfried Kracauer, *Ginster*. SHORT BREAK FOR VENTILATION, 2017, exhibition view, Swiss Art Awards, photo: Sabrina Chou

67 “On the pink surface of the ham slices Ginster created a star-shaped composition from units of cucumber. Cookies and berries lent themselves to similar creations. The fact that the two dined together as host and guest called for a brief period of adjustment.” Siegfried Kracauer, *Ginster*. Rubber door mat, 2017

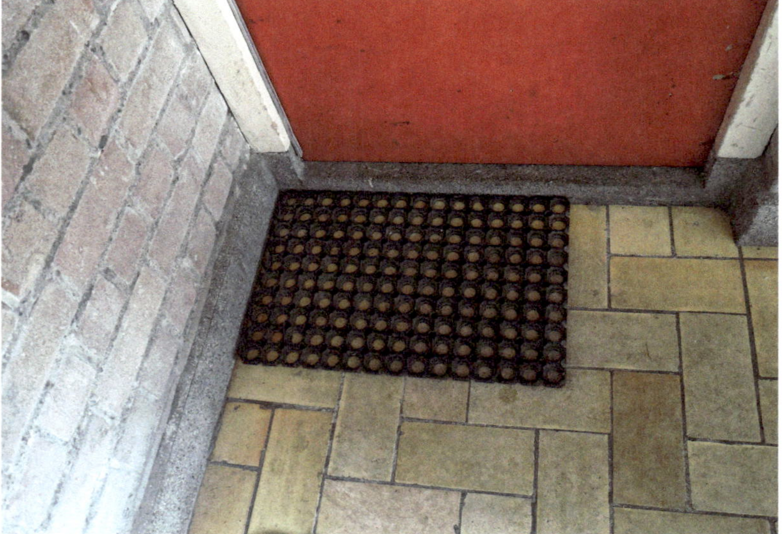

69 "There is no such thing as 'contemporary' art. Any material may be used but the theme is the same and the response is the same for all art work." Agnes Martin, *Writings*. Entrance Verboomstraat 182–184, Rotterdam, 2017

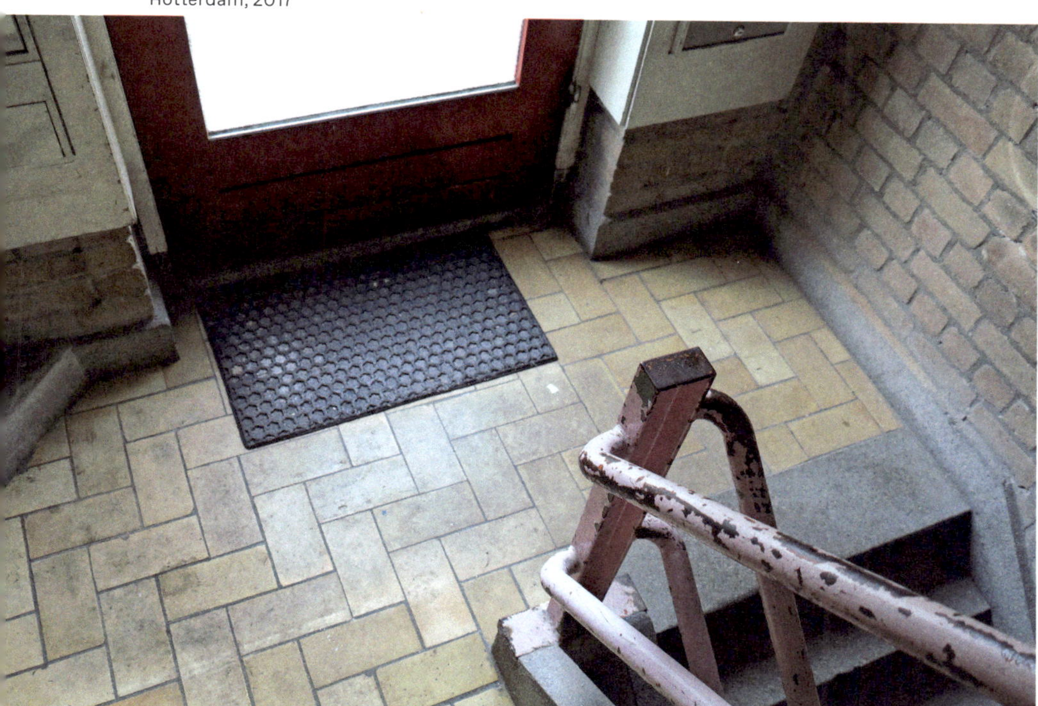

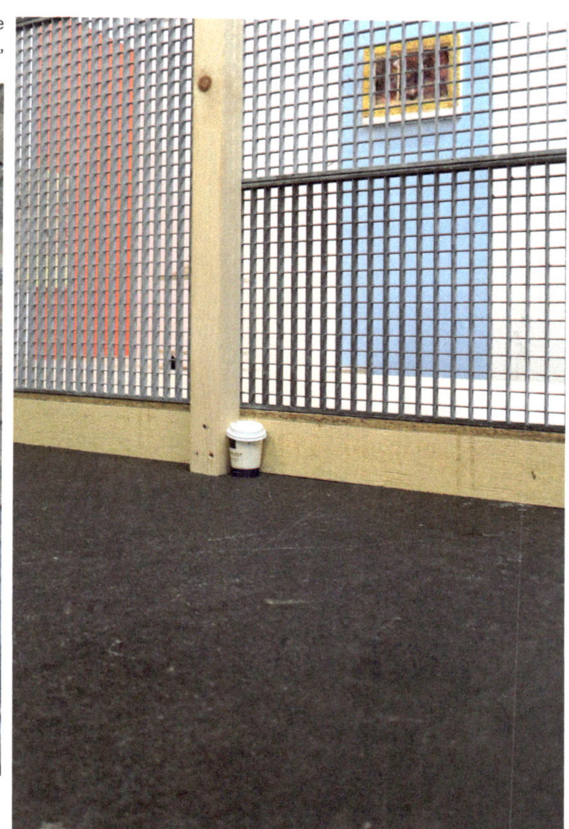

70 "Scientists—that is, creative scientists—spend their lives in trying to guess right. They are sustained and guided therein by their heuristic passion. We call their work creative because it changes the world as we see it, by deepening our understanding of it. The change is irrevocable." Michael Polanyi, *Personal Knowledge*. SHORT BREAK FOR VENTILATION, 2017, exhibition view, Swiss Art Awards, photo: Sabrina Chou

71 "On the outside of the island, beyond the bare rock, there was a stand of dead forest. It lay right in the path of the wind and for many hundreds of years had tried to grow directly into the teeth of every storm, and had thus acquired an appearance all its own. From a passing rowboat it was obvious that each tree was stretching away from the wind; they crouched and twisted, and many of them crept. Eventually the trunks broke or rotted and then sank, the dead trees supporting or crushing those still green at the top. All together they formed a tangled mass of stubborn resignation." Tove Jansson, *The Summer Book*. Wall painting, Charlois, Rotterdam, 2017

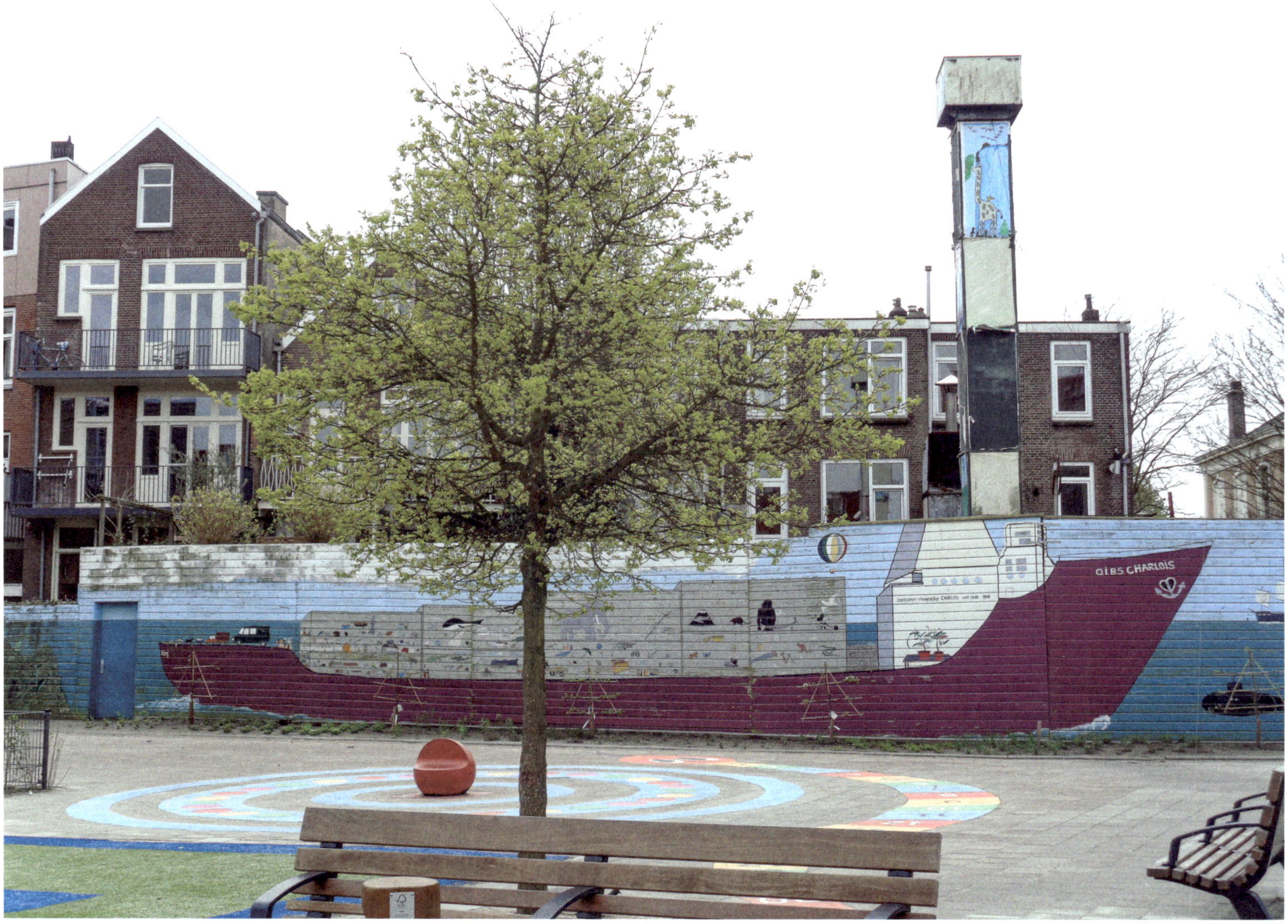

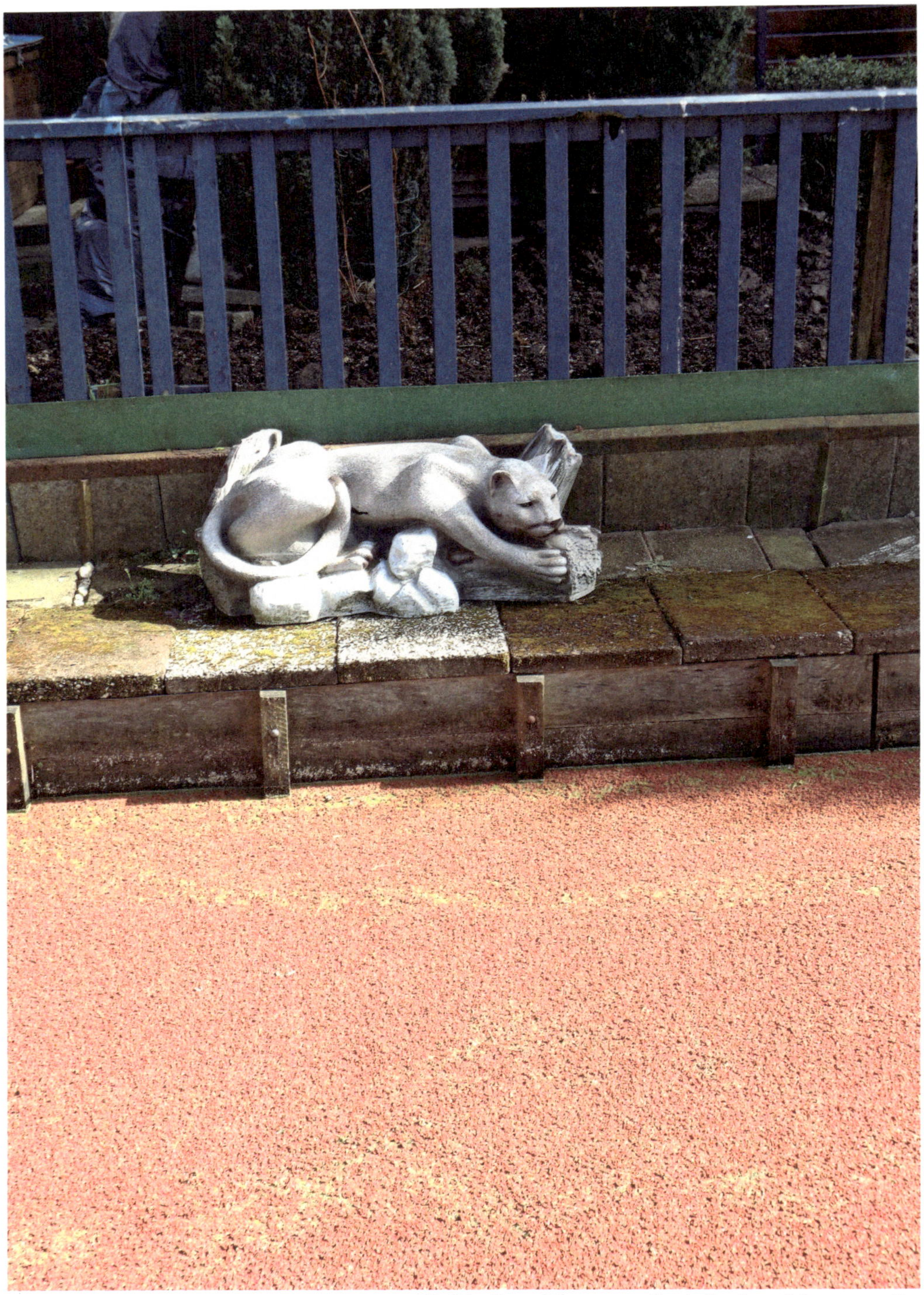

72 "Because we have so cleanly separated feces from everything else in our lives, its medieval status, interwoven with the sacred text, makes us uneasy. Instead of turds being just what they are—matter—they become mysterious signs that we are unable to read, savor and enjoy with the gusto of our ancestors." Michael Camille, *Image on the Edge*. Allotment, Rotterdam, 2017

73 "The time of the composition is the time of the composition. It has been at times a present thing it has been at times a past thing it has been at times a future thing it has been at times an endeavor at parts or all of these things. In my beginning it was a continuous present a beginning again and again and again and again, it was a series it was a list it was a similarity and everything different it was a distribution and an equilibration. That is all of the time some of the time of the composition." Gertrude Stein, *Composition as Explanation* in *What Are Masterpieces?*. Horse and donkey, Treignac, 2018

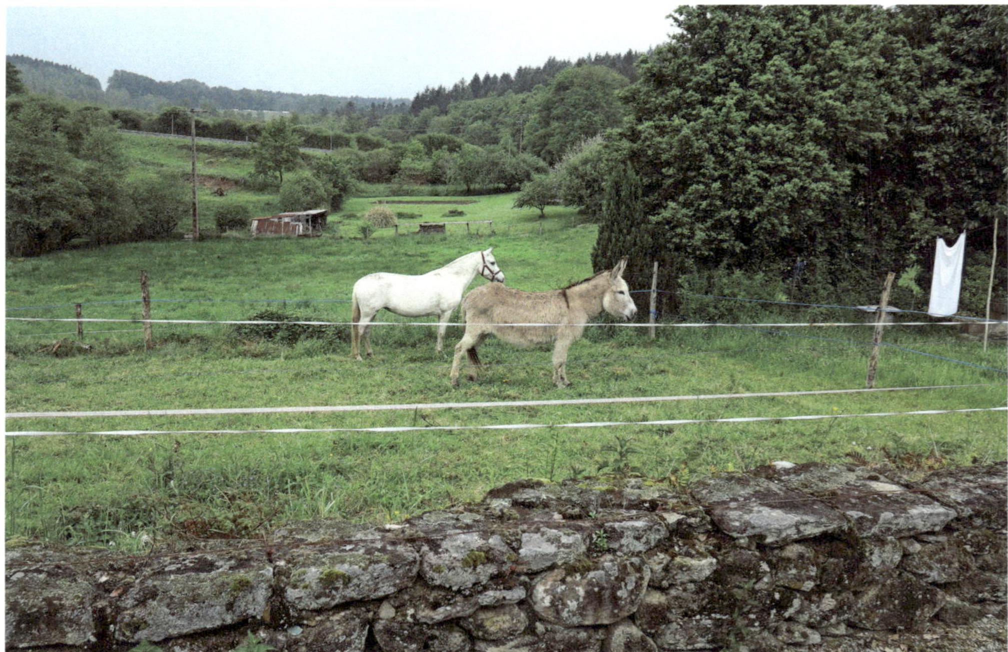

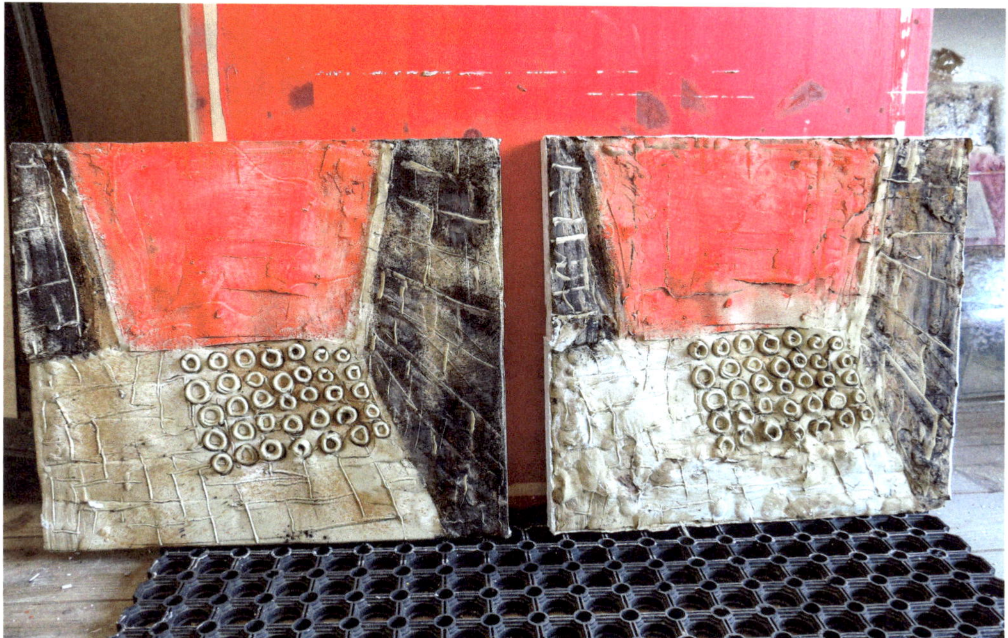

74 "Doubling was too extravagant for Herr Valer tin. Better when the figures were smaller and not so frivolously rounded off. It annoyed Valentin that the soldiers fell a little at a time instead of being all set for the cemetery the day before yesterday." Siegfried Kracauer, *Ginster.* DOOR MAT 1 & 2, 2017, plaster, pigments

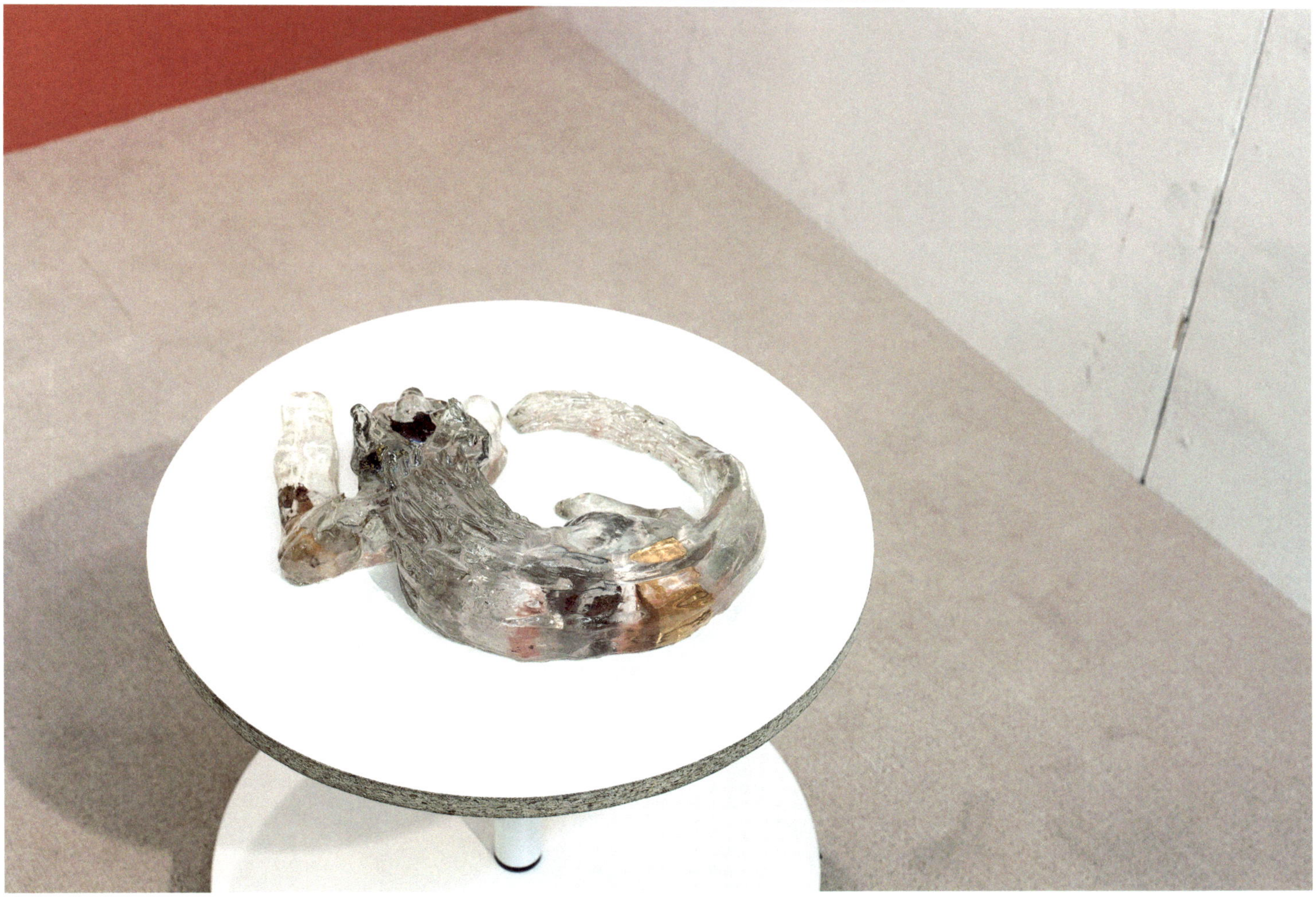

75 "The following used to happen to me regularly in bed before I would fall asleep: First I would lie on one side, that is, the side on which I normally slept. Then I would shift about, to the other side, whereupon I noticed that I remained in the less comfortable position for approximately as long a time as I had in the first one. Only after completing this daily bed-assignment did I consider myself permitted to fall asleep. When my mother, who nearly always paid me an evening visit, inquired as to the reason for such inexplicable behavior, I answered laconically: 'to take the crooked path.'" Siegfried Kracauer, *Ginster.* BÜSI, 2013, resin, bouillon cube, cigarette butts, Swiss Art Awards, photo: Sabrina Chou

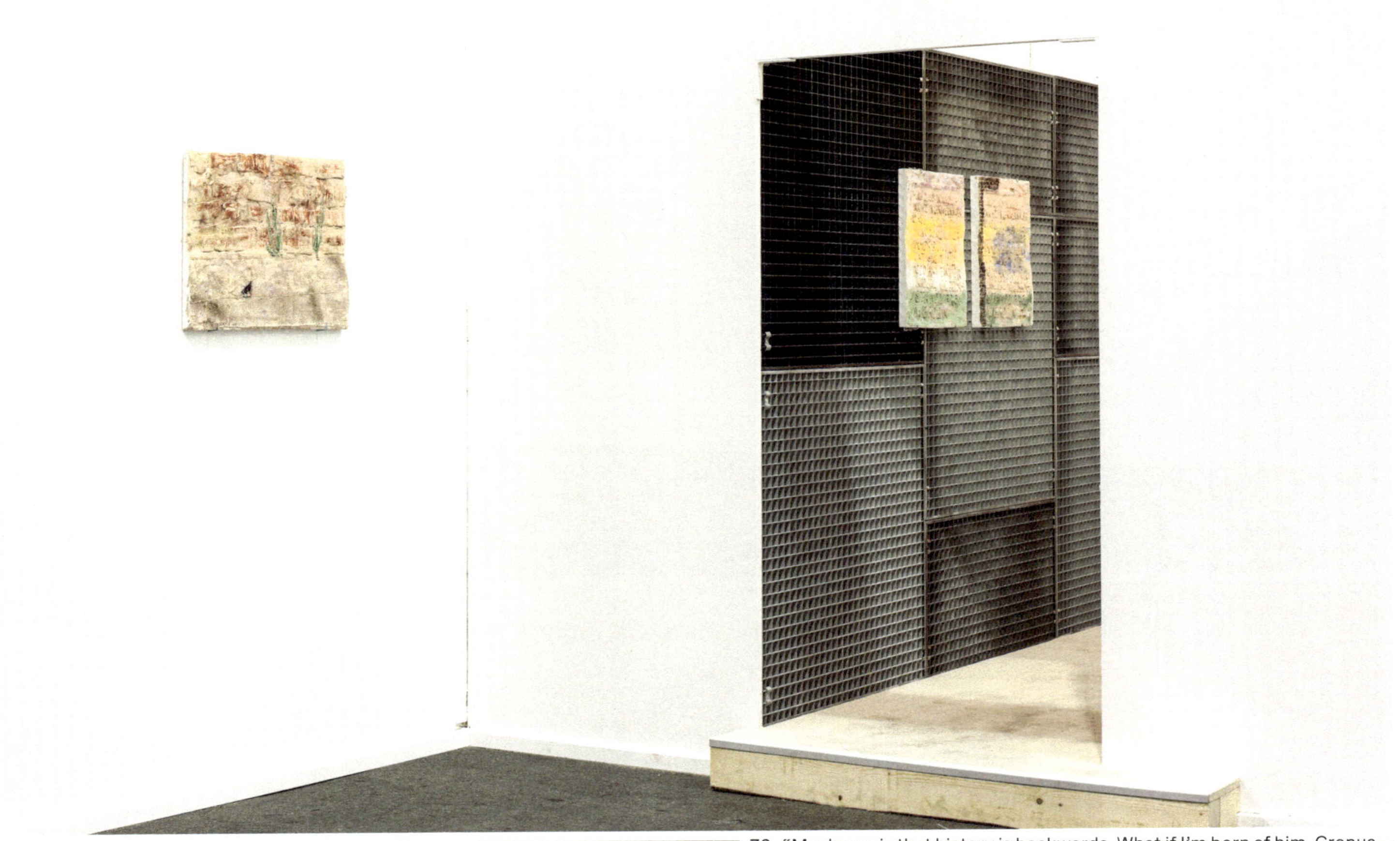

76 “My dream is that history is backwards. What if I’m born of him, Cronus—of his anger and his drunkenness and the ripe destruction of his father’s weapons. I’m for it. And I know these men.” Eileen Myles, *Afterglow (a dog memoir).* SHORT BREAK FOR VENTILATION, 2017, Swiss Art Awards, photo: Guadalupe Ruiz

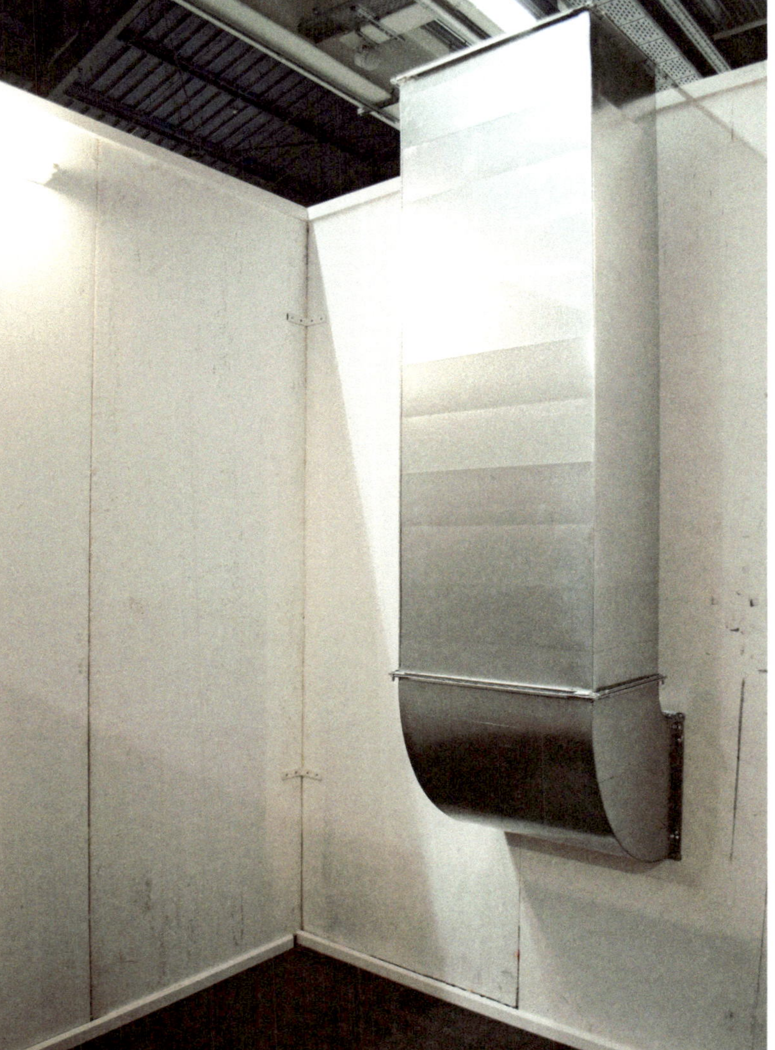

77 “Gentlemen tend the heavy monsters, whose racket vastly surpasses the monotonous clatter of the punching girls. I ask the office manager about the machine-girls’ work routine. ‘The girls’, he replies, ‘punch for only six hours and during the remaining two hours are employed as office clerks. In this way we avoid overtaxing them. All this takes place in a predetermined cycle, so that each employee encounters all tasks. For hygienic reasons, moreover, from time to time we slip in short breaks for ventilation.’” Siegfried Kracauer, *The Salaried Masses.* SHORT BREAK FOR VENTILATION, 2017, vent with hidden speaker, Swiss Art Awards, photo: Sabrina Chou

78 “Perhaps this is why the things on the ground are so affecting. It is not so much that they stand for what has to be discarded in order for ecstasy to happen, it is that ultimately we feel them as standing for the state toward which ecstasy is directed.” T.J. Clark, *Painting at Ground Level.* ON/OFF, 2017, plaster, pigments, Swiss Art Awards, photo: Guadalupe Ruiz

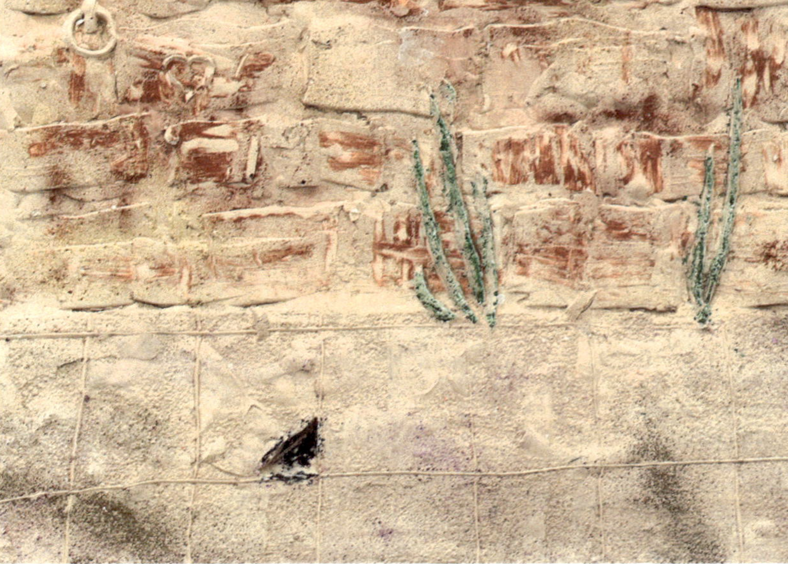

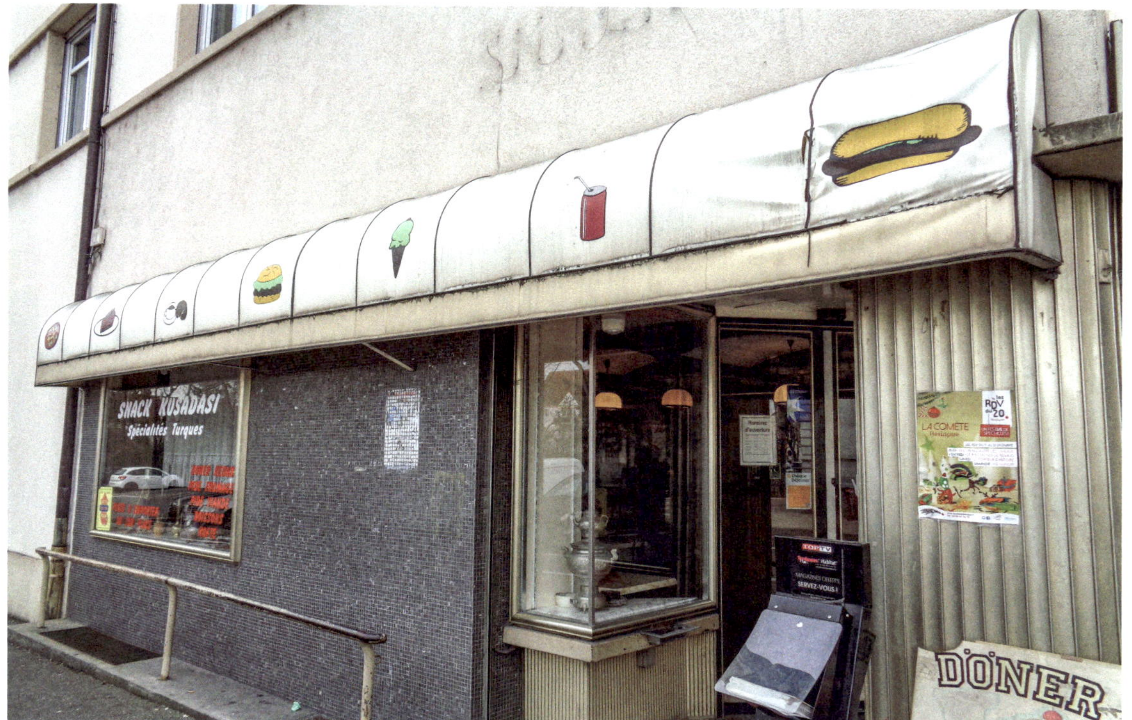

79 “The exterior at Aulnay is a noxious cartiledge—infested, crawling with legions of slimy and furry vermin on its corbels, window splays and corners, and sprouting from shadowy corbels. This idea of placing grinning demons and other forms, mostly heads, along the upper walls as supports for other members, is deep-rooted in ancient history; in the North it is related to the Celtic custom of worshipping decapitated heads.” Michael Camille, *Image on the Edge*. Snack bar in St. Louis, 2017

80 “With an odd kind of tenderness, she examined the nameplates of boats long since broken up, some storm indications that had been written on the wall, penciled data on dead seals they had found and a mink they had shot, and she dwelled particularly on the pretty picture of the hermit in his open tent against a sea of desert sand, with his guardian lion in the background. How can I ever leave this room? She thought.” Tove Jansson, *The Summer Book*. SHORT BREAK FOR VENTILATION, 2017, exhibition view, Swiss Art Awards, photo: Guadalupe Ruiz

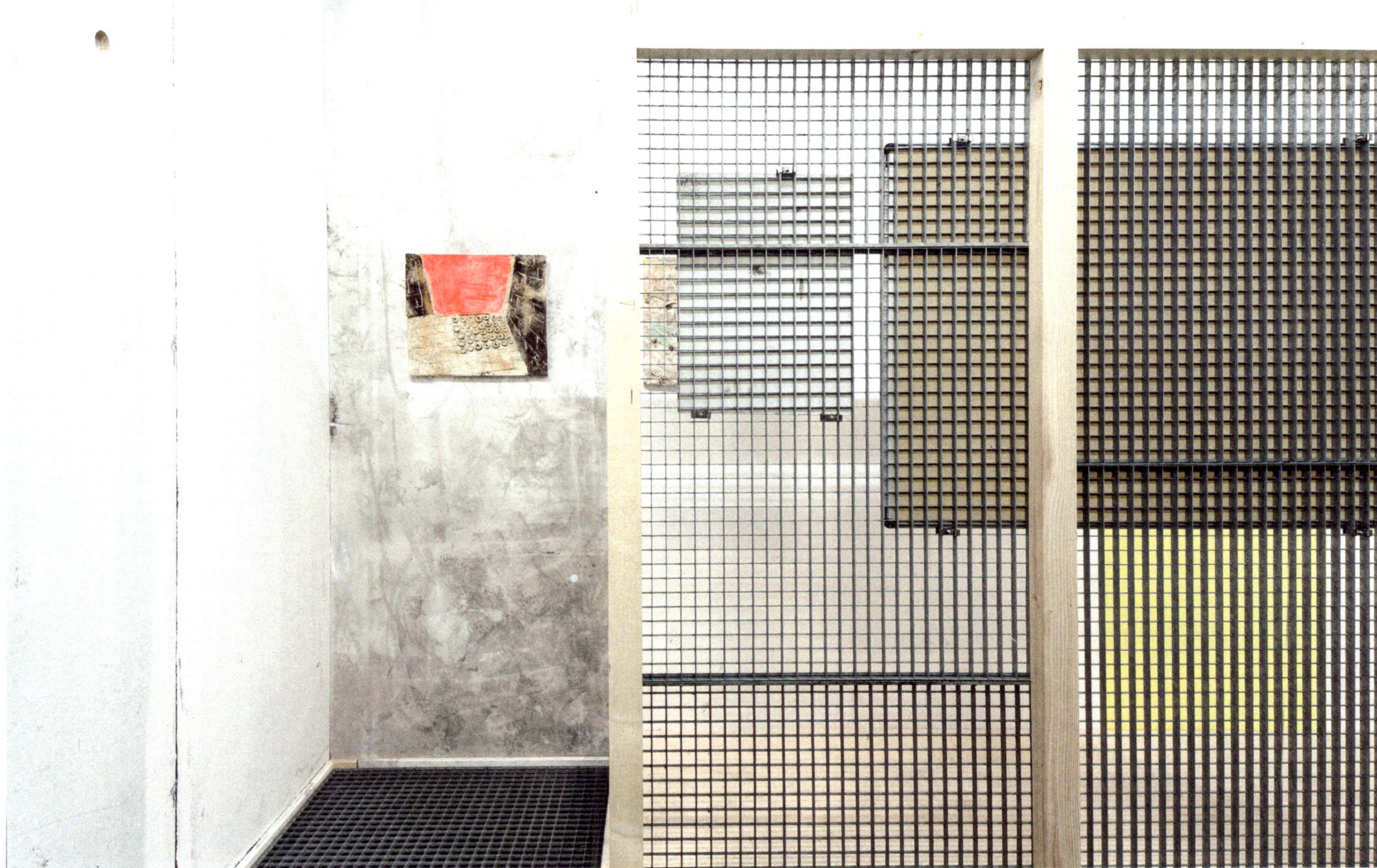

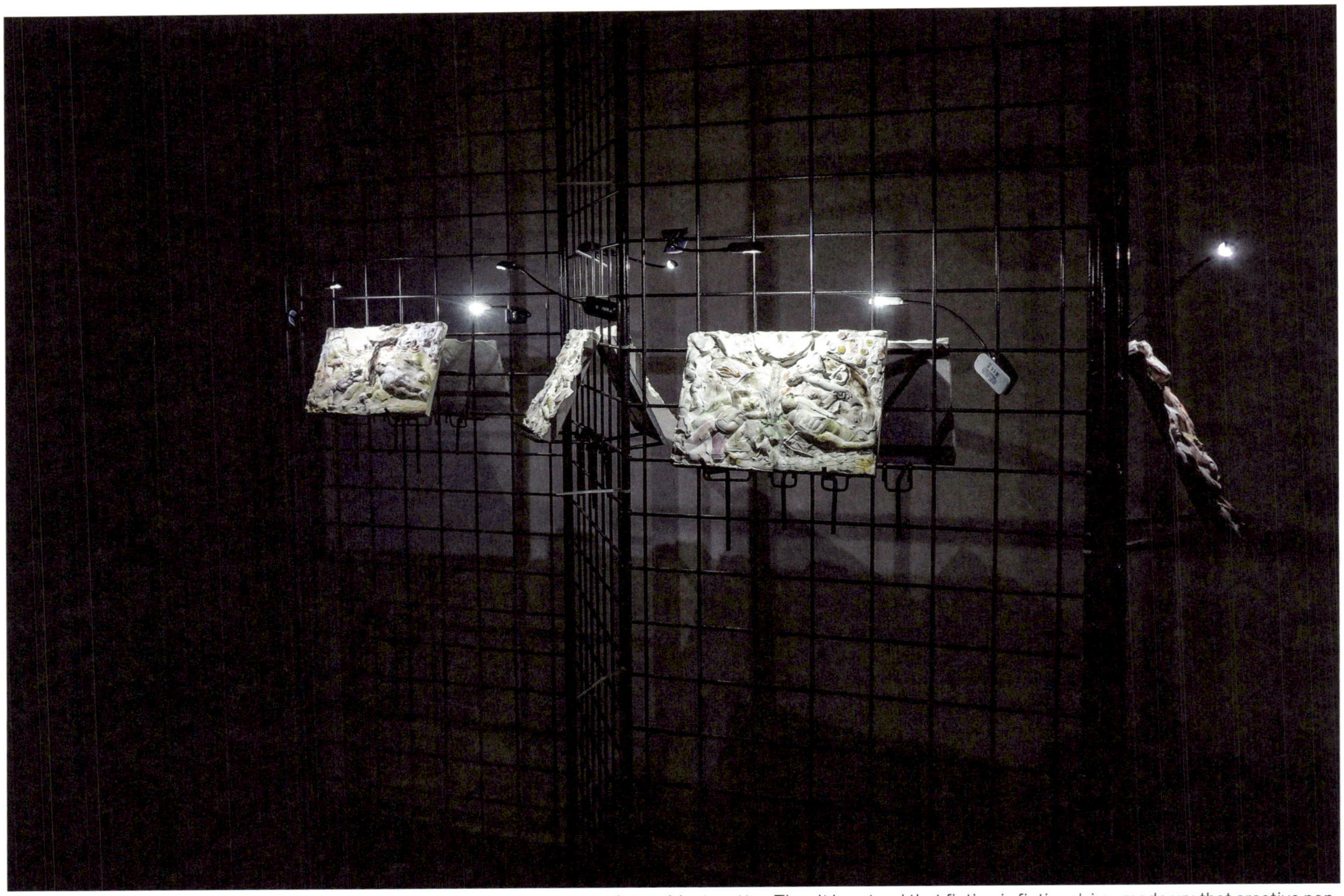

81 "Genres are inherently distinct and each shapes itself around the appropriate subject matter. Thus it is natural that fiction is fictional, i.e., made up; that creative non-fiction is factual (although it is allowed a little bit of leeway, the way Hollywood starlets are expected to lie about their age); that poetry builds to an epiphany. And all these forms have a sort of generic Teflon that protects them from overt sexual content. Sex—if it belongs anywhere—is outcast to the degraded arenas of trash novels and porn." Dodie Bellamy, *Crimes Against Genre* in *Academonia*. LUILEKKERLAND 1–8 (AFTER PIETER BRUEGEL THE ELDER), 2018, exhibition view, I am not your Guru, Arnhem

83 "We are most concerned because having experienced joy we know that it prevails and we think that with violence, destructiveness, possessiveness and frustration we are off the track. The transcendent response that is free from and unrelated to the concrete environment is so blissful and seems so much more innocent that we wish to seek to maintain it at the expense of a concrete response. But it is not possible and it is not desirable." Agnes Martin, *Writings*. Studio, Treignac Projet, 2018

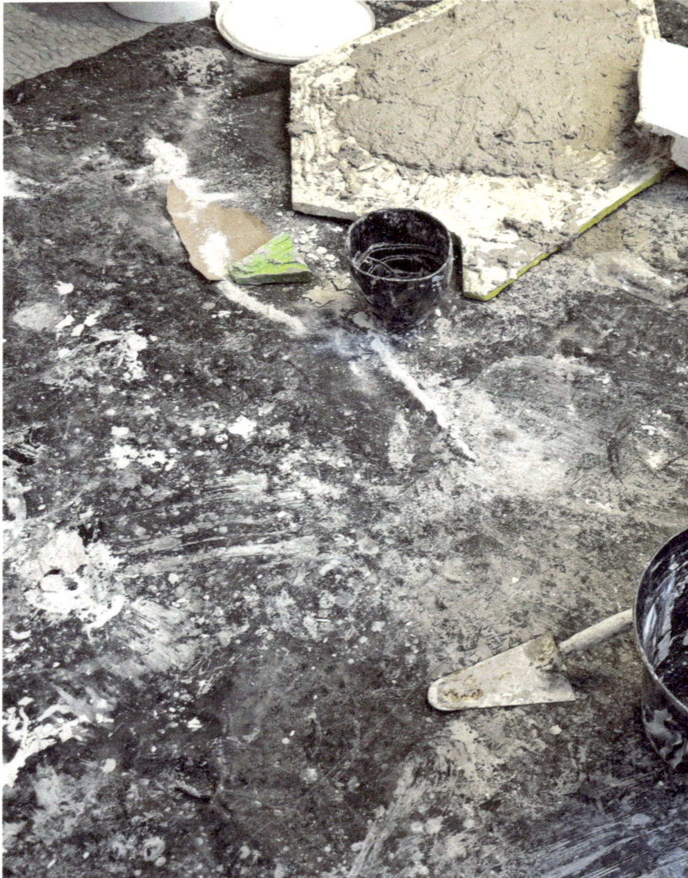

82 "This noble family wallows in excrement, however, and the son, Audiger, takes on as one of his opponents an incontinent old woman, who forces him to eat three-and-a-half of her turds for breakfast, telling him 'and then you will kiss my cunt and the crack of my ass.' She eats, digests and recycles him repeatedly, analogous to the omniphagic orgies pictured in Gothic marginal art." Michael Camille, *Image on the Edge*. Chickens at Bouwmaat, Rotterdam, 2018

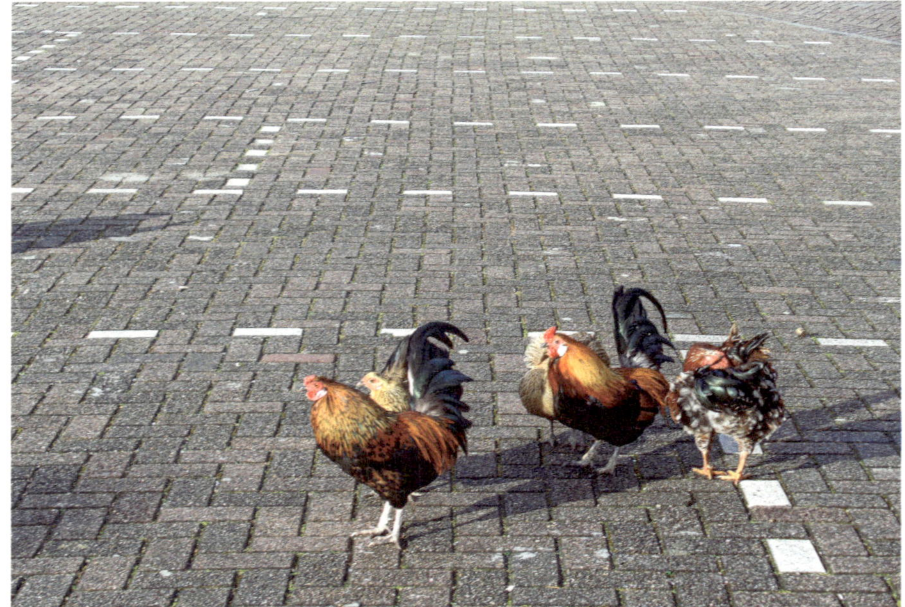

Next Spontaneous Horizontal Restaurant:
Micha Zweifel Makes New Time
Lisa Robertson

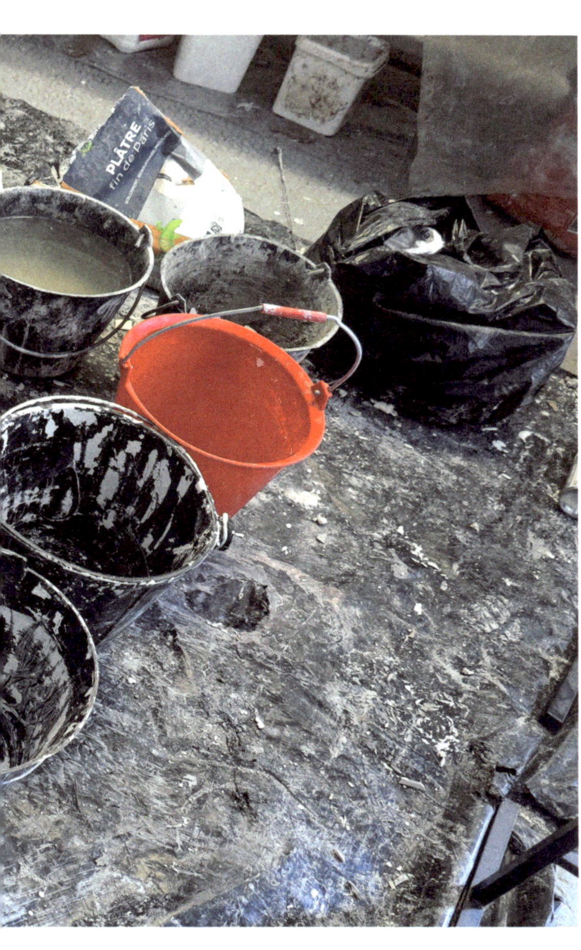

Dwelling for a while—so deliciously, so tentatively—within the social agreement called art, which here we will consider as an unlimited making, a seriously playful making which is liberated, through always renewing collective co-habitation, from the brutality of force (or is it rather the economics of force?)—even temporarily, but ideally for ever (where "for ever" would nonetheless upset every stability, every hegemony to come, would rekindle each appetite)—, we are free to rethink value in its relationship to time.

Why not live together in this convivial proposition for as long as we can? Something unanticipated may alight.

Who is this collective? What does this agreement concern? Have we solicited this contract, or has it slipped into our consciousness unnoticed, as might an atmospheric scent, the texture of a well-worn garment, or a habit of feeling? In our life of making things, we prefer passionate attachments, happened-upon communities, as difficult as such living-together can sometimes become. Is there a passionate collectivity with room for both delight and disagreement? We believe that there is, but usually we do not choose the company our play will keep. The many little clinamens that have thrown in our way the possibility of a meeting, a being together, are as unintentional as atoms. The collective swerves. The things we make swerve also, in their interpretability, their welcome, their stamina. Always something crucial escapes intention. In this way the works themselves are like subjects: quite unpredictable, even slippery. So they have a role in inflecting whatever community is. It's not that they cause or determine their community, but that the way people come together is altered by art. This will be our premise. Quarrelsome, often foundering and imploding, we are the willing misinterpretors of the arrhythmic signatures carrying such ruckus to our perception, our badly scaled desire, and our trained sequences of exchange: some relationships are not received but muddled through, and their apparent lack of institutional frame does not ease or neutralize their complexity. Sometimes this is love. What difficult grace! We refer also to the dulled aching sensation of a space of absence where quite simply somebody or something unnamed is missing. There are collectives that have not yet declared themselves as such; they will recognize themselves only retrospectively, and so will be compelled to aestheticize their transmission. And some collectives do not share a time; some will be the contemporaries of their ancestors or of future communities only. Friction, as with unplaned wood, which leaves little inflammatory splinters beneath our skin, bringing our entire apprehension of the concept of surface into an involved questioning: such is our preference. Here is the incentive to think together with the materials.

The season has changed. We have called it a season, but it is an extremely long received speech tradition. It is buoyed with a learned emotion. There exist longterm hivernal moods. Time isn't quartered and neither are elements. In some places there is no springtime, or no autumn. There may be three different summers of various humidities. Nevertheless here we are, in our elaborately nonchalant layers of garments, with our autumnal sentiments and detailed appetites. The sky has changed. We're in it, beneath it, beside it, eating its overripe fruits, letting them blacken our teeth and the palms of our hands, spitting out the rot, metabolizing the slanted light, cleaving and roasting decorative

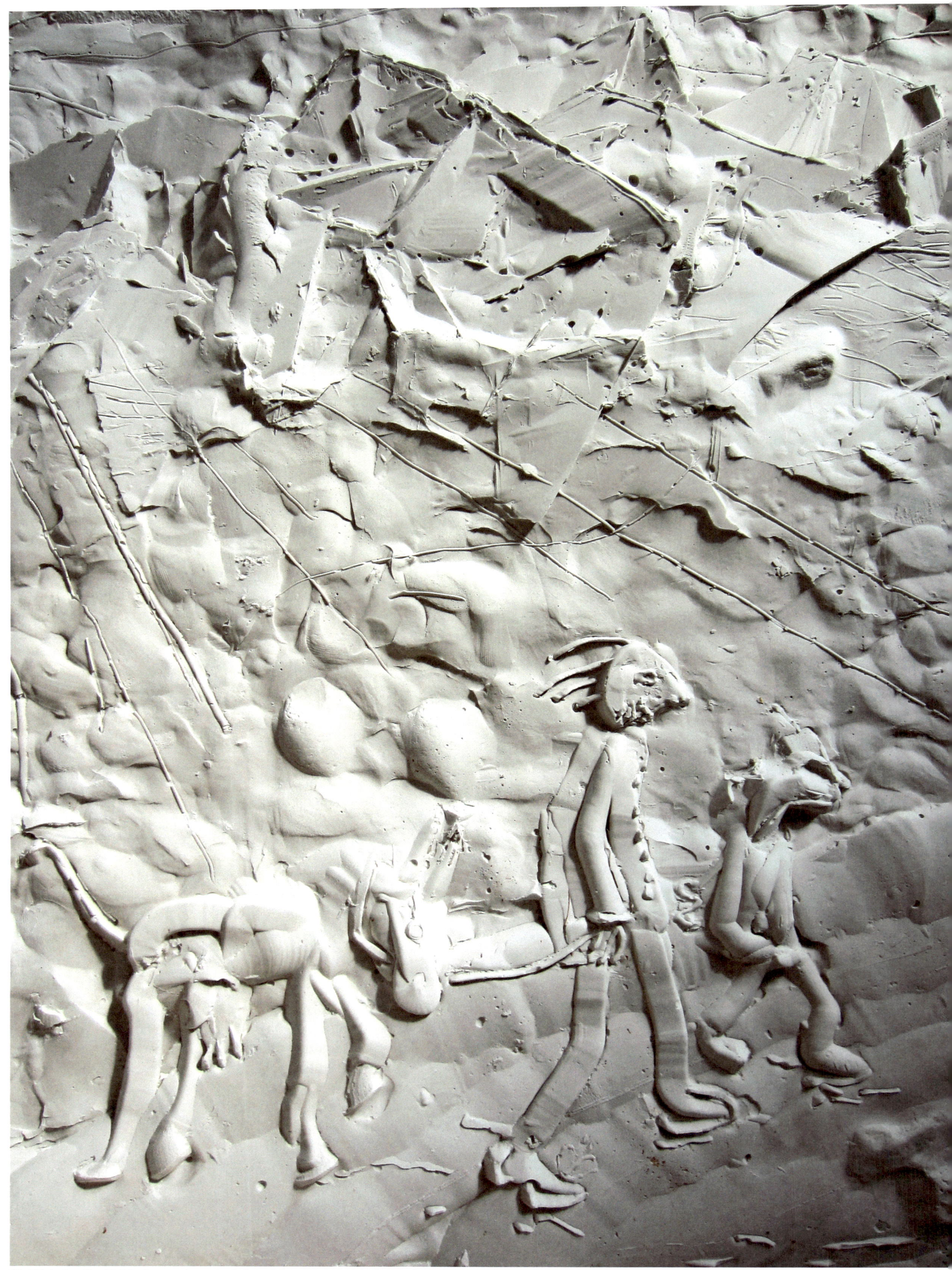

84 “If during the Middle Ages patrons had shared the margins with the monkeys, jongleurs and peasants they in reality lorded over, in later centuries the forms of representation split to demarcate distinct class positions. The ‘grotesque’ became a category in which to place everything barbaric and ‘medieval’ until such things came to titillate the Romantic sensibility in the nineteenth century.” Michael Camille, *Image on the Edge*, CALENDAR, 2020 (Detail), plaster

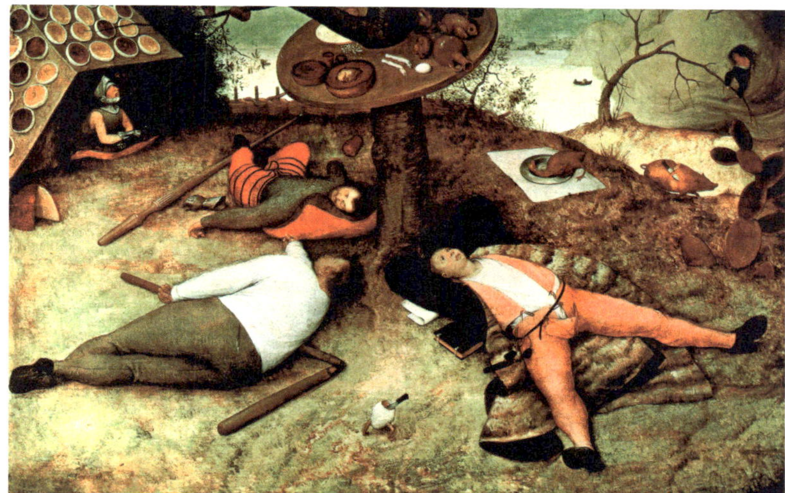

85 "This is Schlaraffenland, or Luilekkerland, as the Netherlanders had it ('Lazy-greedy-land' is, I gather, the proper translation), or what the French and English called The Land of Cockaigne. It is the kingdom where cooked food is everywhere, falling fresh-roasted from the air into the idler's mouth, laid out on tables attached to every other tree, or roaming the landscape in search of consumers—pigs with carving knives sheathed in holsters of their own crackling. No one here will ever again eat his bread in the sweat of his brow." T.J. Clark, *Painting at Ground Level*. Pieter Bruegel the Elder, *The Land of Cockaigne*, 1567, Alte Pinakothek, Munich

87 "What Cockaigne said back to religion—and surely its voice in this was that of peasant culture itself, in one of its ineradicable modes—was that all visions of escape and perfectibility are haunted by the worldly realities they pretend to transfigure. Every Eden is the earth intensified; immortality is mortality continuing; every vision of bliss is bodily and appetitive through and through." T.J. Clark, *Painting at Ground Level*. LUILEKKERLAND 6 (AFTER PIETER BRUEGEL THE ELDER), 2018, plaster, pigments

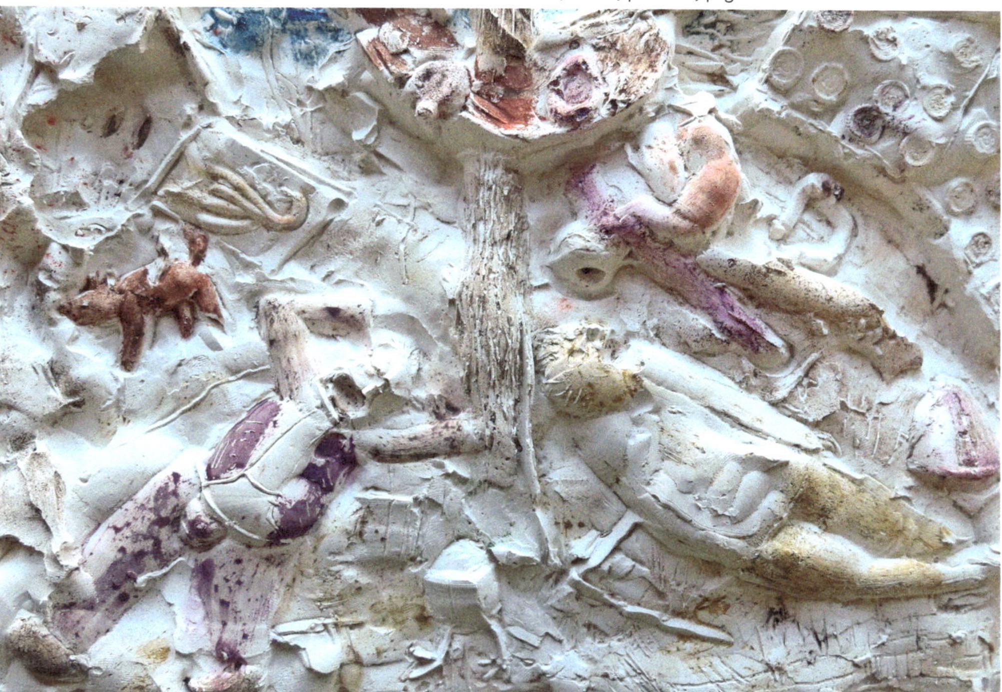

86 "She thought about migratory birds, and the thrush on a summer evening, and the cuckoo—yes, the cuckoo—and the great, cold birds that sail and watch, and the very small birds that sweep in for hasty visits in large late-summer parties, chubby, dumb, and unafraid, and about the swallows that only honor houses where the people are happy. It seemed remarkable that the impersonal birds should have become such powerful symbols." Tove Jansson, *The Summer Book*. Geese, Waal, Rotterdam, 2018

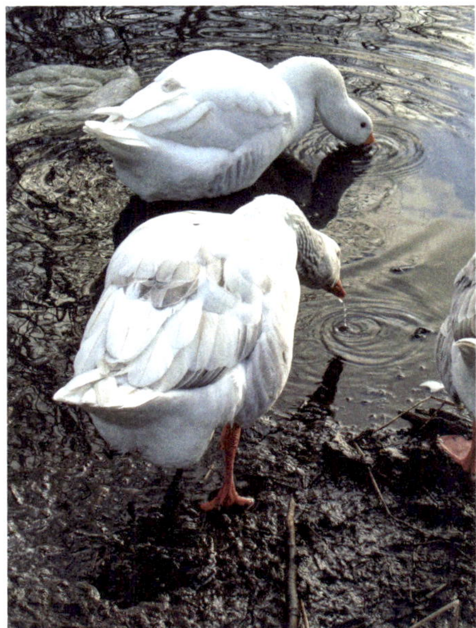

88 "A problem... is a conception of something we are striving for. It is an intellectual desire for crossing a logical gap on the other side of which lies the unknown, fully marked out by our conception of it, though as yet never seen in itself. The search for a solution consists in casting about with this purpose in mind." Michael Polanyi, *Personal Knowledge*. LUILEKKERLAND 5 (AFTER PIETER BRUEGEL THE ELDER), 2018, plaster, pigments

gourds. Perhaps we regret the previous season or we long for some season to follow. We witness this nostalgia without judging it. Later we will undertake its analysis. Now we want a completely new season, an uncharted experience of time. We ache for a temporality that has not yet been recorded, that has never before been experienced. We'll be the ones to supplement cosmology, to synthesize a fresh element. What are calendars to us? Our skin is dry and we want to eat roots. We climb slipshod steps to a metaphysical mezzanine, glimpsing the received season, with its mythologized nomenclature, downwards through the gaps between the planks. It makes us slightly dizzy, a dizziness not so much symptomatic of some hackneyed pathology as redolent with an anticipation of an ideal saturation. And we look up again, continue upwards, curious, careful not to trip on the slightly irregular surfaces. We arrive at the next spontaneous horizontal restaurant.

This is the fucking elegant future. Here is a replete pause in appetitive becoming. Here philosophy is a superfood that accentuates our synapses. Our hunger is a clock. What are we hungry for? We are hungry for time; time is the convivial medium. We want to taste it, savor it, devour it, rub it, bathe in it, both together and apart. This hunger links us with each other and with the things that anyone makes. Stepping onto the temporary mezzanine, we arrive at this robust yet contemplative synthesis. Unsuspected views open onto a previously familiar landscape. A frieze representing a mixture of archaic and invented customs invites us to linger. It is a restaurant because it proposes something newly shared and valued regarding the sensory manifold, in order to entertain us. (To entertain, says Samuel Johnson's dictionary, means to treat at table, and to foster in the mind.) An altered duration is offered to the known, by grace of a work-a-day mysticism, for the sake of a newly opened critical pleasure. It is non-sequential and highly figured. What shall the restaurant restore? Most agile and beautiful, in its anarchic abundance, its swerving grace, its unmeasurable bliss, its scarcity and its relentlessness: the very time that we crave. A time completely outside regulation and measure, which pours from our bodies and opens our thoughts. Kant called time a synthetic a priori. Which is to say that time is a medium of all experience and cognition, both constructed and given, yet necessarily unsolicited. What connects concepts when experience doesn't? A synthetic and active always-ness on which cognition depends. Time is intrinsic to our perception, and we have made it ourselves, as we have transmitted it, by continuing to speak and to eat together, by speculating on our observations and by making mistakes. But our part in time's synthesis is not volitional. This is deeply frustrating and stimulating. Because we are stubborn and insatiable, we want to find a way to glimpse the very matrix of the a priori. By what means shall the restaurant restore time? How do we exit the metrics and savor the sensorium? Here the approach to the concept of temporal extremity is both architectural and gustative. Architecturally the restaurant is a speculum. It gently opens the intuition of sensing to patient broths, liaisons, amuse-bouches, stimulants and calmants and other clandestine potions, little poems, kitsch commemorations, light snacks, midnight suppers, collective breakfasts, O'Hara-esque lunches, anarchic collations, controlled decay, saltings and picklings, pungent reductions, and very temperately, exclusively in early research stages, synthesized foams:

89 "Every so often, far, far in the distance, there would appear the mirage of a mountain range, thin as the edge of a knife, a sort of woods. And then we'd know that on the other side of this woods, whose margins we would reach after many hours, more endless plains stretched. From time to time, shots were fired." Robert Walser, *Jakob von Gunten*. Karl Walser, *View from the Weissenstein*, 1899

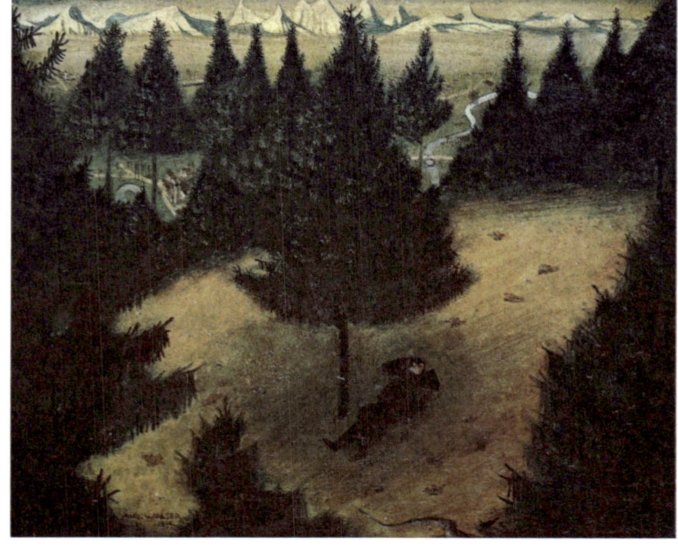

all of these on a raised carpentry platform, of elegantly utilitarian installation, already scheduled for dismounting. The restorative cuisine plays out its techniques, both received and invented, in idiosyncratic rhythms, in the synthesized medium of time, by posing questions, and permitting appetitive ornament. Taste is part memory and part synapse, enjoying as it gently but briefly expands a space of experimental conviviality.

It will be a season of the duration of an exhalation or a lucid dream and it will not be fixed in any recognizable sequence. The season will arrive when necessary perhaps. It will ornament necessity.

"It is high time to replace the Kantian question 'how are synthetic judgements possible' by another question: why is belief in such judgements necessary" Nietzsche claimed, at the beginning of *Beyond Good and Evil.* To honor this moral proposition, we purposely yet accidentally yet dreamily synthesize a new season not just because we can, but because we too believe it is necessary. Our season advances the restoration of a convivial temporality that completely rejects force. We'll raise a quivering platform to the continuance of shared accident and ornament. We'll call this season a restaurant. It is a kind of grace; it models the experiment of consent. It may or may not be perceptible. You may enter this artifice at your pleasure. Falsity is not objectionable—to deny falsity, Nietzsche says, "would amount to a renunciation of life, a denial of life". The fictive, which is to say the *made* nature of the spontaneous restaurant, the utopian season, the proposal of consent, requires us to act *as if* our fictions were necessary to flourishing. Because now is a good time to flourish together despite the totalizing frame of the general economy, not only in order to evade it or negate it, but to learn afresh how to value the difficult tenderness we discover in the temporary gift, the ludic contract.

Stay! We call
To the season
Which unfurls
Like a comic-strip

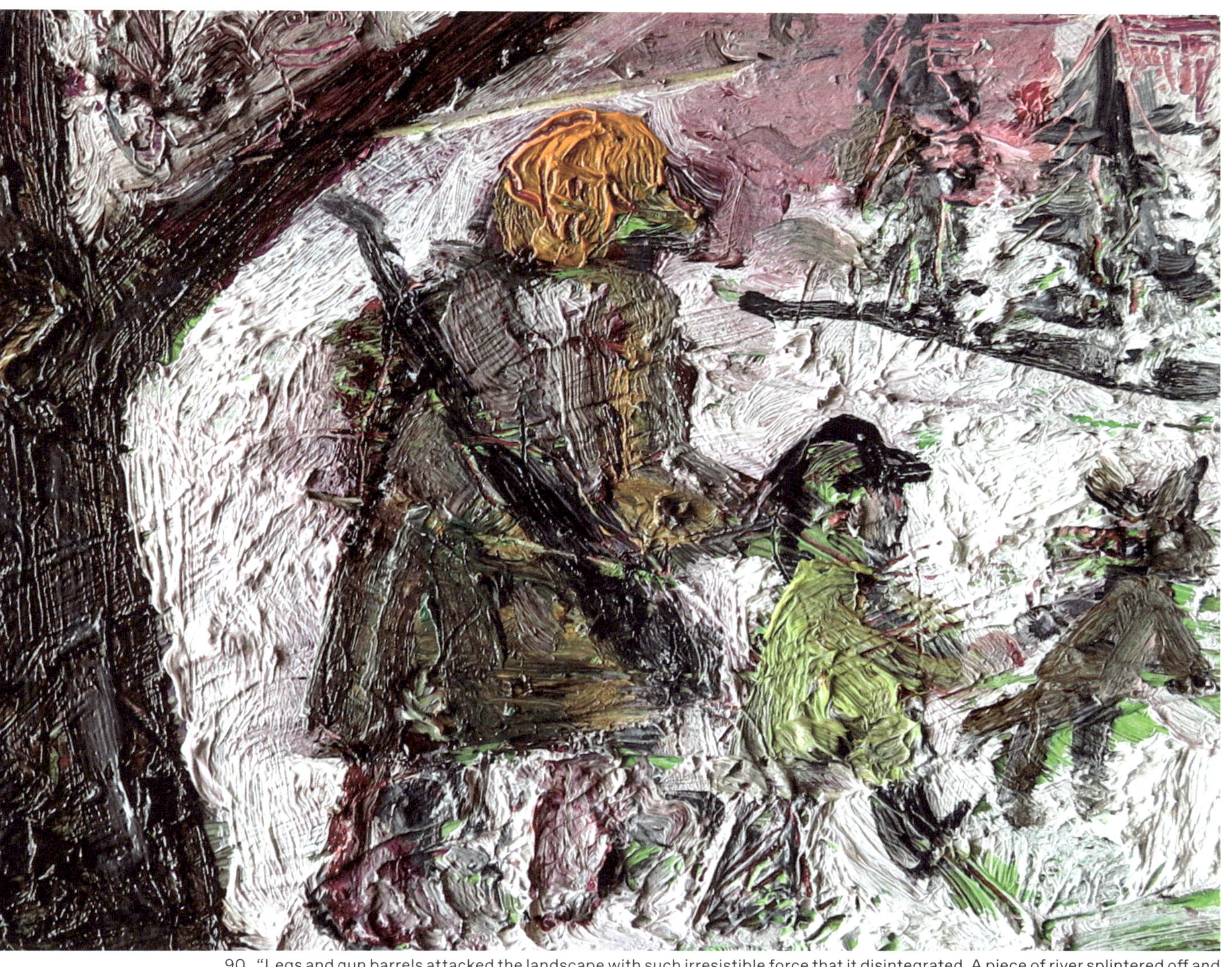

90 "Legs and gun barrels attacked the landscape with such irresistible force that it disintegrated. A piece of river splintered off and fell into the sky, fields were sliced through, the water flew up out of puddles. In front of them a regiment of hop-poles emerged, bent on preventing their advance. The poles with the hops grew rapidly larger, long, lean things about which dangerous spirals wound, but the legs strode into their midst and hurled them into the river." Siegfried Kracauer, *Ginster.* UNTITLED (OXFORD MYSTERY SERIES), 2019, oil on wood board

Das nächste spontane horizontale Restaurant:
Micha Zweifel bereitet neue Zeit
Lisa Robertson

Bewohnen wir für eine Weile – so köstlich, so vorläufig – die gesellschaftliche Vereinbarung namens Kunst, die wir hier als endloses Entstehen begreifen wollen, ein ernsthaft spielerisches Entstehen, das, indem es das kollektive Mitbewohnen unablässig erneuert, von der Brutalität eines Zwangs (oder ist es die Ökonomie eines Zwangs?) befreit – vielleicht nur zeitweise, im besten Fall aber für immer (wobei »für immer« dennoch an jeder künftigen Stabilität, jeder Hegemonie rütteln, jedes Begehren wieder entfachen würde) –, sind wir frei, Wert in seinem Verhältnis zu Zeit neu zu denken.

Warum nicht zusammen leben, in diesem gastlichen Vorschlag, so lange wir können? Vielleicht stellt Ungeahntes sich ein.

Wer ist dieses Kollektiv? Was umfasst diese Vereinbarung? Haben wir diesen Vertrag eingefordert oder ist er unbemerkt in unser Bewusstsein gehuscht wie ein Umgebungsgeruch, die Beschaffenheit eines oft getragenen Kleidungsstücks oder die Gewöhnung eines Gefühls? In unseren Leben, in dem wir Dinge herstellen, wünschen wir uns leidenschaftliche Zugewandtheit, durch Zufall geformte Gemeinschaft, wie schwierig ein solches Zusammenleben manchmal auch sein mag. Gibt es eine leidenschaftliche Kollektivität, in der Entzücken und Uneinigkeit einander nicht ausschließen? Wir glauben daran, aber normalerweise suchen wir uns die Gesellschaft für unser Spiel nicht aus. Die vielen kleinen Clinamina, die die Möglichkeit eines Aufeinandertreffens, eines Zusammenseins, in unseren Weg geworfen haben, sind so absichtslos wie Atome. Das Kollektiv schlingert. Die Dinge, die wir machen, schlingern ebenso, in ihrer Interpretierbarkeit, ihrem Willkommen, ihrer Ausdauer. Immer entgeht der Intention etwas Entscheidendes. In dieser Hinsicht ähneln Kunstwerke Subjekten: ziemlich unberechenbar sind sie, fast glitschig. Sie haben Anteil daran zu deklinieren, was Gemeinschaft bedeutet. Nicht indem sie Gemeinschaft erzeugen oder bestimmen, sondern indem sie die Art, wie Menschen zusammenkommen, durch Kunst verändern. So lautet unsere Grundannahme. Streitsüchtig, befangen in Scheitern und Zusammenbruch, sind wir willige Fehldeuter*innen der arrhythmischen Charakteristika, die solche Unruhe in unsere Wahrnehmung, unsere schlecht skalierten Wünsche und unseren erlernten Ablauf von Tauschvorgängen bringen: Manche Beziehungen werden uns nicht gegeben, sondern wir wursteln uns durch, und ihr

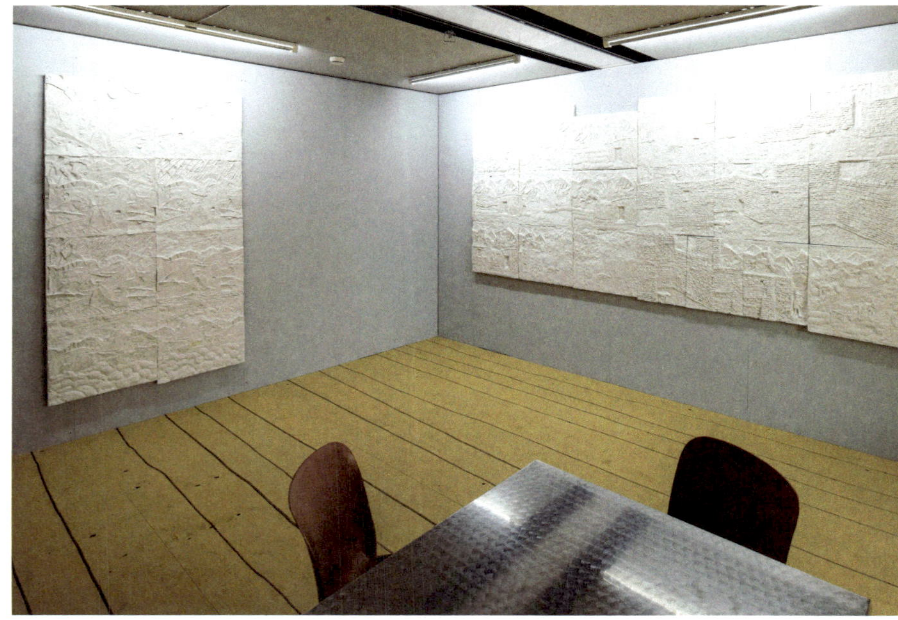

91 “Do not waste your feelings of discontent on society. When you feel discontented ask yourself ‘what do I want,’ ‘what do I really want.’ As soon as you ask yourself this question you will realize that discontent arises out of it. Your unwillingness to function may be so strong that you cannot even ask yourself this question, in which case you will seek help from others. But there will be no help for you anywhere. You will find your vision for yourself at some time when you are alone.” Agnes Martin, *Writings*. ZUR SACKGASSE 4. STOCK, exhibition view, Kunstmuseum Luzern, photo: Marc Latzel

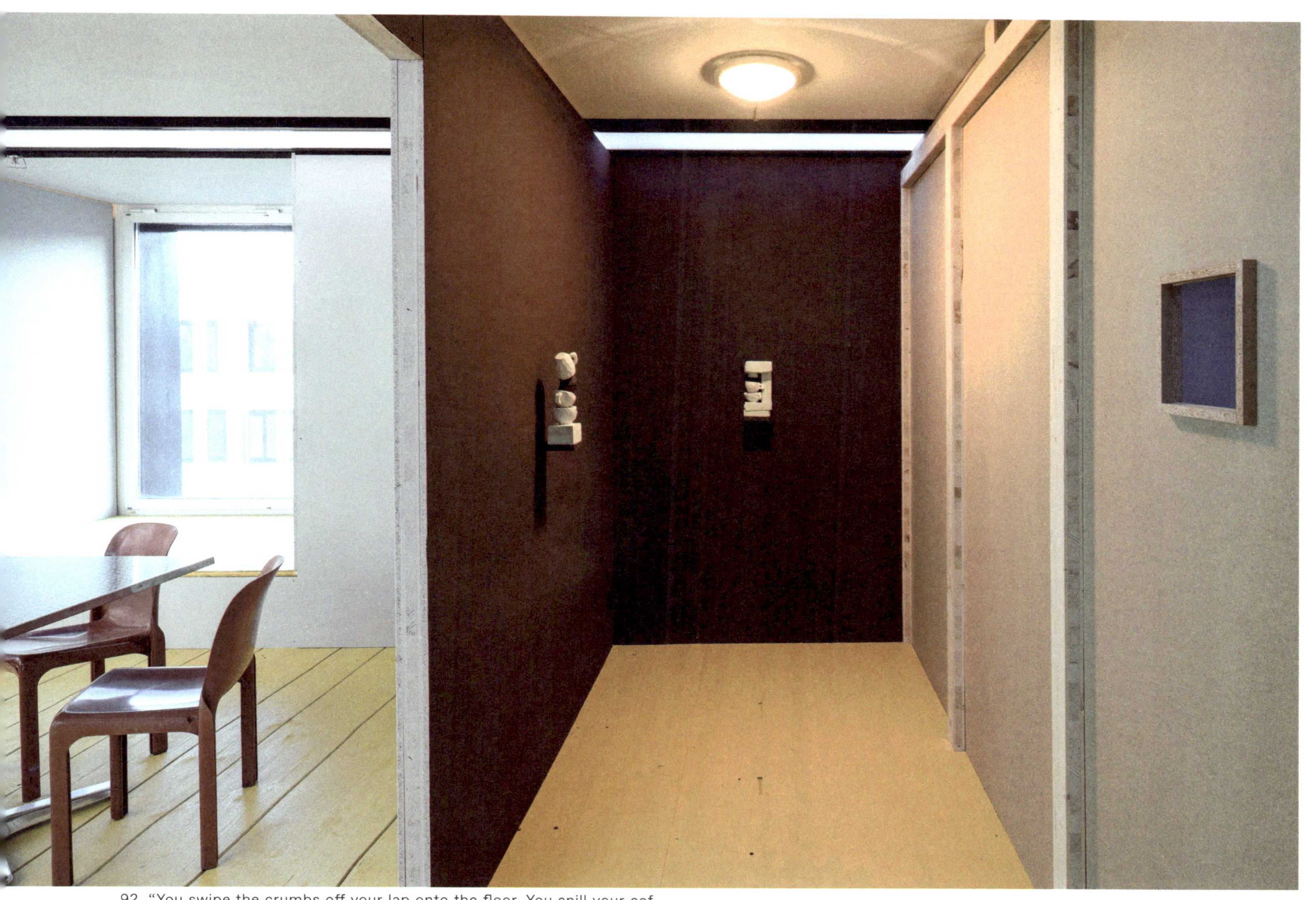

92 “You swipe the crumbs off your lap onto the floor. You spill your coffee, a milky puddle of coffee and crumbs surrounds your shoes and you sit there. Agog.” Eileen Myles, *Afterglow (a dog memoir)*. ZUR SACKGASSE 4. STOCK, exhibition view Kunstmuseum Luzern, photo: Marc Latzel

offenbarer Mangel an institutioneller Rahmung lockert oder hebt ihre Komplexität nicht auf. Manchmal ist das Liebe. Welch schwierige Gunst! Wir verweisen auch auf die gedämpft schmerzende Empfindung eines Ortes der Abwesenheit, wo ganz einfach jemand oder etwas Unbenanntes fehlt. Es gibt Kollektive, die sich noch nicht zu Kollektiven erklärt haben; sie werden sich erst in der Rückschau erkennen und ihre Überlieferung ästhetisieren. Manche Kollektive teilen keine Zeit, manche werden nur Gleichgesinnte ihrer Ahn*innen oder künftiger Gemeinschaften sein. Reibung, wie bei ungeschliffenem Holz, das kleine entzündliche Splitter unter unserer Haut hinterlässt und dadurch unser Verständnis des Begriffs Oberfläche kritisch verstrickt und befragt: dem neigen wir zu. Die Motivation ist hier, mit dem Material zu denken.

Die Jahreszeit hat gewechselt. Wir haben sie Jahreszeit genannt, aber das ist Überlieferung seit alters her. Sie wird von einer erlernten Empfindung aufrechterhalten. Es gibt Winterstimmungen, die lange andauern. Zeit ist nicht viergeteilt, auch die Elemente nicht. An manchen Orten gibt es keinen Frühling oder Herbst. Aber vielleicht drei verschiedene Sommer von variierender Feuchtigkeit. Doch hier sind wir, in unseren betont nonchalanten Schichten von Kleidung, mit unseren Herbstgefühlen und präzisen Gelüsten. Der Himmel hat gewechselt. Wir sind darin, darunter, daneben, essen die überreifen Früchte des Herbstes, lassen diese unsere Zähne und Handflächen dunkel färben, spucken Fäule aus, metabolisieren das schräg einfallende Licht, schneiden und grillen formschöne Kürbisse. Vielleicht hängen wir der vorigen Jahreszeit nach oder sehnen eine kommende herbei. Wir sind Zeug*innen dieser

Nostalgie, ohne sie zu werten. Später werden wir uns ihrer Analyse widmen. Jetzt wollen wir eine vollkommen neue Jahreszeit, eine unkartierte Erfahrung von Zeit. Wir brennen auf eine Zeitlichkeit, die noch nicht beschrieben wurde und von niemandem je erlebt. Wir werden es sein, die die Kosmologie ergänzen, die ein neues Element synthetisieren. Was bedeuten uns Kalender? Unsere Haut ist trocken und wir wollen Wurzeln essen. Wir erklimmen die nonchalanten Stufen zu einem metaphysischen Zwischengeschoss, erblinzeln die überlieferte Jahreszeit, mit ihrer mythisierten Nomenklatur, unten durch die Lücken zwischen den Bohlen. Das lässt uns leicht schwindeln, ein Schwindel, der weniger Symptom einer banalen Pathologie ist als ein Duft in Erwartung einer vorzüglichen Sättigung. Wir schauen wieder nach oben, gehen weiter aufwärts, neugierig, darauf bedacht, auf den leicht unregelmäßigen Oberflächen nicht auszurutschen. Wir erreichen das nächste, spontane, horizontale Restaurant.

Das ist die verflucht elegante Zukunft. Hier ist eine satte Pause im Bedürfniswerden. Hier wird Philosophie zum Superfood, das unsere Synapsen akzentuiert. Unser Hunger ist eine Uhr. Wonach hungern wir? Wir hungern nach Zeit; Zeit ist das Medium der Gastlichkeit. Wir wollen sie kosten, genießen, verschlingen, reiben, in ihr baden, gemeinsam und einzeln. Dieser Hunger verbindet uns miteinander und mit den Dingen, die jemand macht. Indem wir in das vorläufige Zwischengeschoss treten, erreichen wir diese robuste und doch kontemplative Synthese. Unvermutete Ausblicke auf eine bis dahin vertraute Landschaft eröffnen sich. Ein Fries, der eine Mischung aus archaischen und erfundenen Bräuchen darstellt, lädt uns zum Verweilen ein. Es ist ein Restaurant, weil es uns in Bezug auf die sinnliche Mannigfaltigkeit etwas neu Geteiltes und Wertvolles anträgt, um uns damit zu unterhalten. (Zu unterhalten, so Samuel Johnson's Wörterbuch, bedeutet den Tisch zu bereiten und den Geist zu nähren.) Geboten wird, für eine neu anbrechende, kritische Lust und durch die Gnade einer Alltagsmystik eine veränderte Art von Dauer. Sie folgt keinem Ablauf und ist deutlich geformt. Was soll das Restaurant wiederbeleben? Am gewandtesten und schönsten in ihrer anarchischen Fülle, ihrer schlenkernden Anmut, ihrem unermesslichen Glück, ihrem spärlichen Bau und ihrer Unbarmherzigkeit: die Zeit, die wir ersehnen. Eine Zeit außerhalb von Regulierung und Maß, die aus unseren Körpern strömt und unsere Gedanken weitet. Kant nennt Zeit ein synthetisches a priori. Was so viel heißt wie, dass Zeit ein Medium aller Erfahrung und Erkenntnis ist, sowohl konstruiert als auch gegeben, und notwendig unverlangt. Was verbindet Begriffe, wenn nicht Erfahrung? Eine synthetische, aktive Immerkeit, auf der Erkenntnis beruht. Zeit ist unserer Wahrnehmung immanent, und wir haben sie zu uns selbst gemacht, wie wir sie übertragen haben, indem wir nicht aufhörten zu sprechen und miteinander zu essen, indem wir über unsere Beobachtungen nachdachten und Fehler begingen. Aber unser Anteil an der Synthese von Zeit vollzieht sich nicht willentlich. Das ist äußerst frustrierend und stimulierend zugleich. Weil wir störrisch und unersättlich sind, wollen wir eine Möglichkeit finden, einen flüchtigen Eindruck der Matrix dieses a priori zu erhaschen. Mit welchen Mitteln soll das Gasthaus Zeit wiederbeleben? Wie treten wir aus den Metriken aus und retten das Empfindungsvermögen? Hier ist die Annäherung an den Begriff eines zeitlichen Extrems architektonisch wie auch gustativ. Architektonisch ist

93 "How often have you told someone they look fabulous and they say thanks cause I feel terrible. And you can see it right behind their eyes. Terrible puts a candle in there. Terrible turns on the light. You wonder if people are just empty when they're moving forward with the plan." Eileen Myles, *Afterglow (a dog memoir)*. STOFFEL, 2019, carved stone pine, tooth brush, ONONO Rotterdam

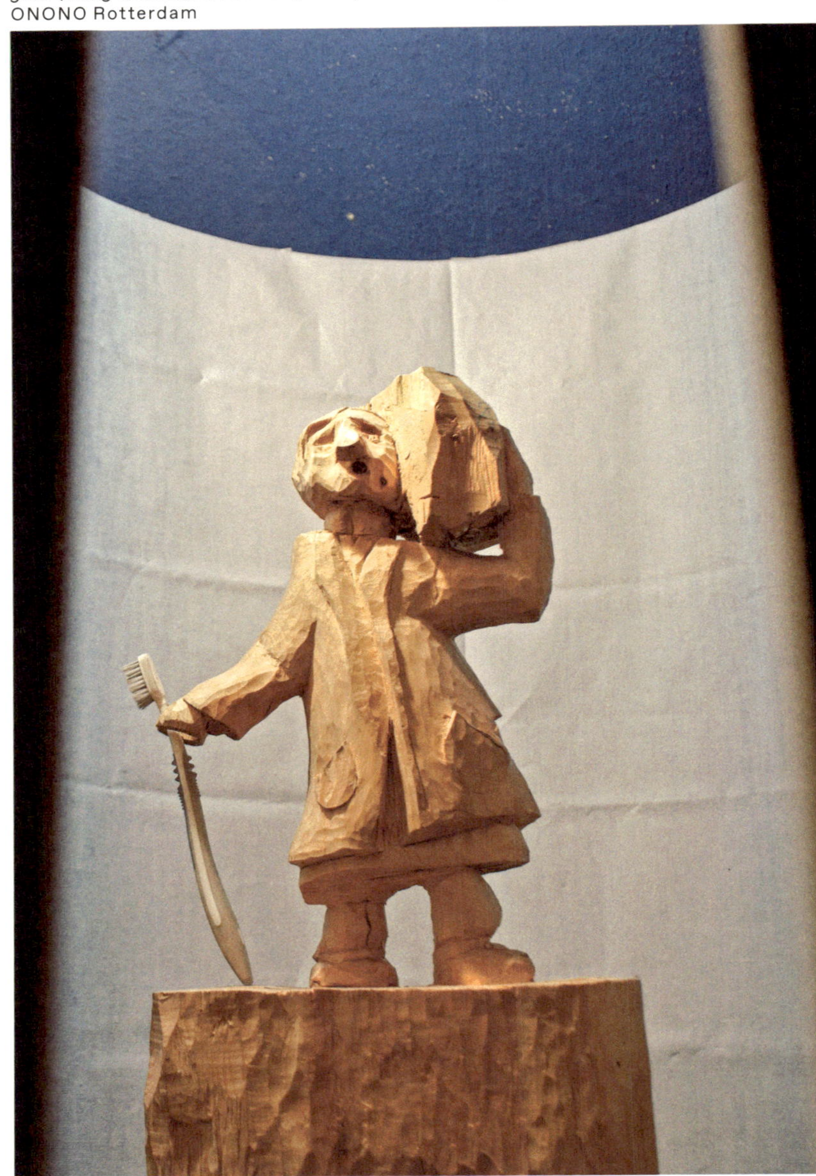

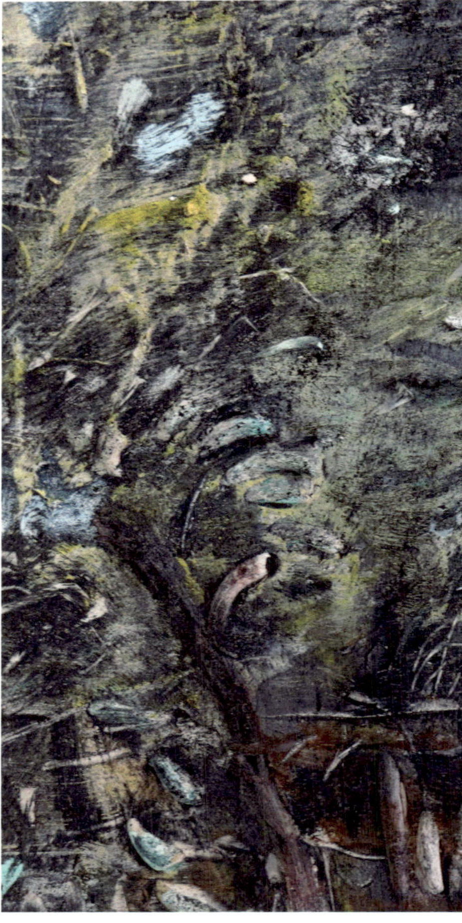

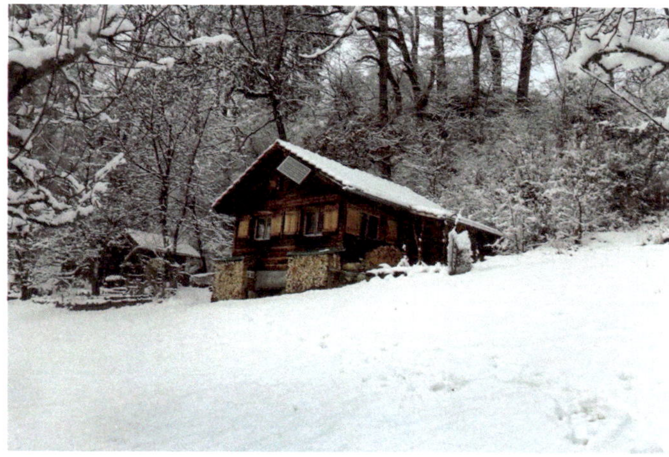

94 "An art which cannot be specified in detail cannot be transmitted by prescription, since no prescription for it exists. It can be passed on only by example from master to apprentice. This restricts the range of diffusion to that of personal contacts, and we find accordingly that craftsmanship tends to survive in closely circumscribed local traditions." Michael Polanyi, *Personal Knowledge*. Tschoma, 2017

95 "Perhaps the change began when the swallows went silent. The shimmering sky was suddenly empty, and there were no more birds. Sophia waited. The answer to her prayers was in the air. She looked out to sea and saw the horizon turn black." Tove Jansson, *The Summer Book*. OXFORD 2ND OF MAY, 2018 (Detail), plaster, pigments

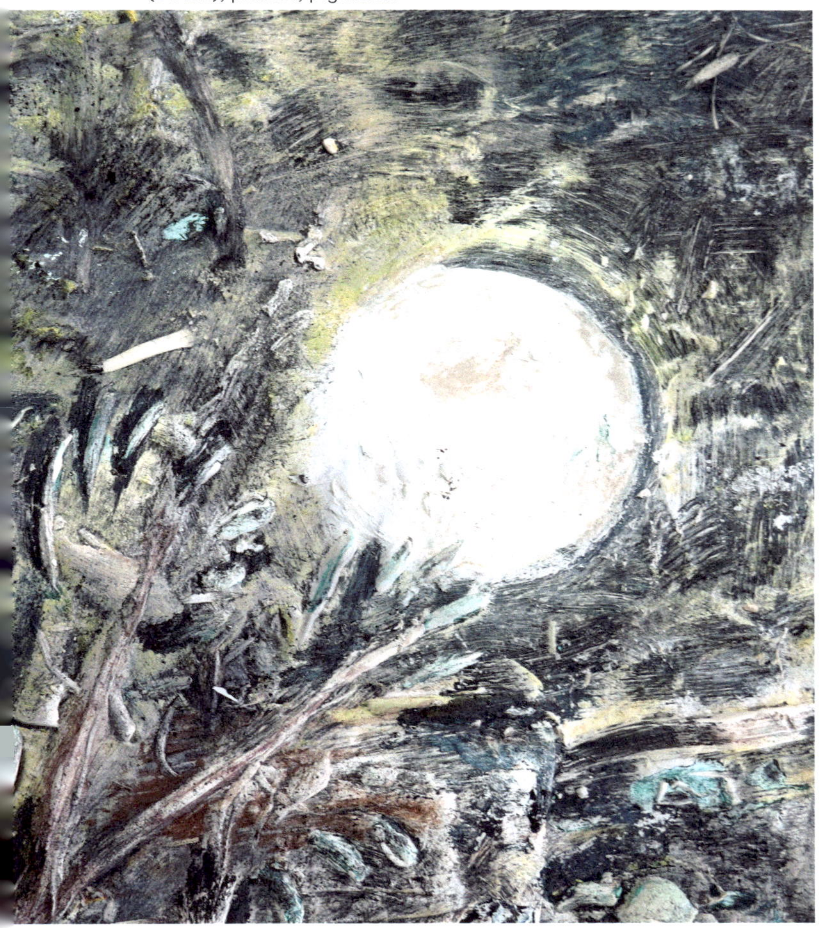

das Restaurant ein Spekulum. Sanft öffnet es die intuitive Wahrnehmung für geduldige Bouillons, Liaisons, Amuse-Bouches, Anregungs- wie Beruhigungsmittel und weitere Geheimtränke, kleine Gedichte, kitschiges Gedenken, leichte Snacks, Mitternachtsimbisse, gemeinsame Frühstücke, O'Hara-eske Lunchs, anarchische Vespern, kontrollierten Zerfall, Gesalzenes und Eingelegtes, strenge Reduktionen und, sehr in Maßen und nur in frühen Forschungsstadien, synthetisierte Schäume: all dies auf einem gezimmerten Podest, von elegant zweckmäßiger Einrichtung, schon zur Demontage geplant. Die wiederbelebende Küche spielt ihre Techniken aus, überlieferte wie erfundene, in eigenwilligen Rhythmen, im synthetisierten Medium der Zeit, indem sie Fragen stellt und Ornamente des Begehrens erlaubt. Geschmack ist teils Erinnerung und teils Synapse, Genuss, wie er behutsam, doch flüchtig einen Raum experimenteller Gastlichkeit spannt.

Es wird eine Jahreszeit von der Dauer eines Ausatmens sein oder ein luzider Traum und sie wird in keine erkennbare Abfolge fixiert. Die Jahreszeit wird kommen, wenn nötig, vielleicht. Sie wird der Notwendigkeit Ornament sein.

»[E]s ist endlich an der Zeit, die Kantische Frage, ›wie sind synthetische Urteile *a priori* möglich?‹ durch eine andre Frage zu ersetzen, warum ist der Glaube an solche Urteile *nötig*?«, forderte Nietzsche eingangs von *Jenseits von Gut und Böse*. Zu Ehren seiner moralischen These synthetisieren wir absichtlich, doch zufällig und träumerisch eine neue Jahreszeit, nicht einfach, weil wir es können, sondern weil auch wir glauben, dass es nötig ist. Unsere Jahreszeit unternimmt die Wiederbelebung einer gastlichen Zeitlichkeit, die jeden Zwang verschmäht. Wir werden ein bebendes Podest errichten zur Dauer von geteiltem Zufall und Ornament. Wir werden diese Jahreszeit ein Gasthaus taufen. Es ist eine Art Gnade; es formt das Experiment der Einwilligung. Es mag wahrnehmbar sein oder nicht. Wir dürfen diese Kunstfertigkeit nach Belieben betreten. Falschheit ist nicht verwerflich – auf falsche Urteile zu verzichten, sagt Nietzsche, wäre »ein Verzichtleisten auf Leben, eine Verneinung des Lebens«. Die fiktive, das heißt die *gemachte* Beschaffenheit des spontanen Restaurants, die utopische Jahreszeit, das Angebot von Einwilligung, verlangt von uns, so zu handeln, als wären unsere Fiktionen nötig für sein Gedeihen. Weil jetzt eine gute Zeit ist, um miteinander zu gedeihen, ungeachtet des totalisierenden Rahmens der allgemeinen Wirtschaft, nicht nur um sie zu umgehen oder zu widerlegen, sondern um die schwierige Zärtlichkeit noch einmal neu schätzen zu lernen, die wir in der flüchtigen Gabe finden, dem spielerischen Vertrag.

Verweile! Rufen wir
Zur Jahreszeit
Die aufblättert
Wie ein Comicstrip

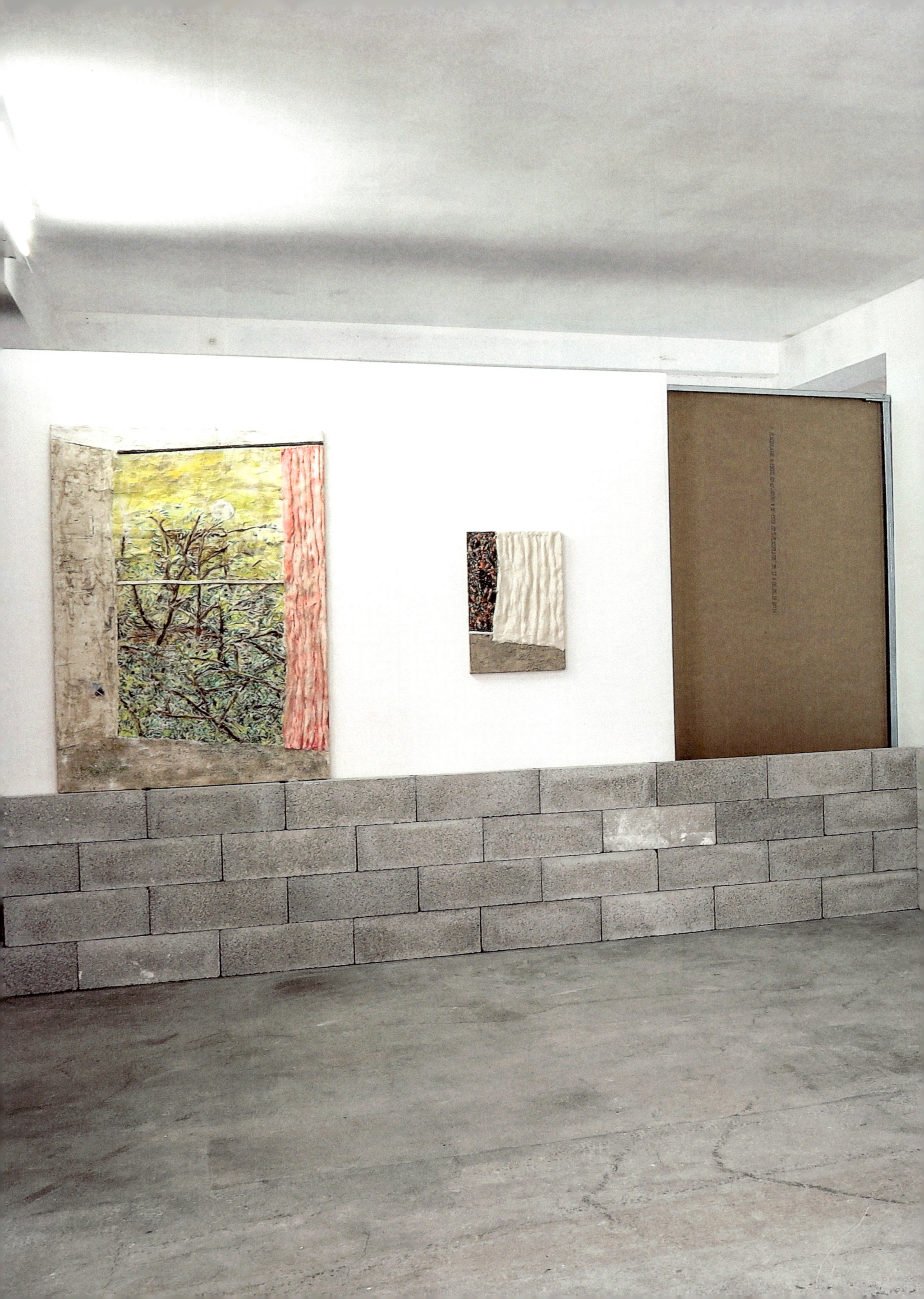

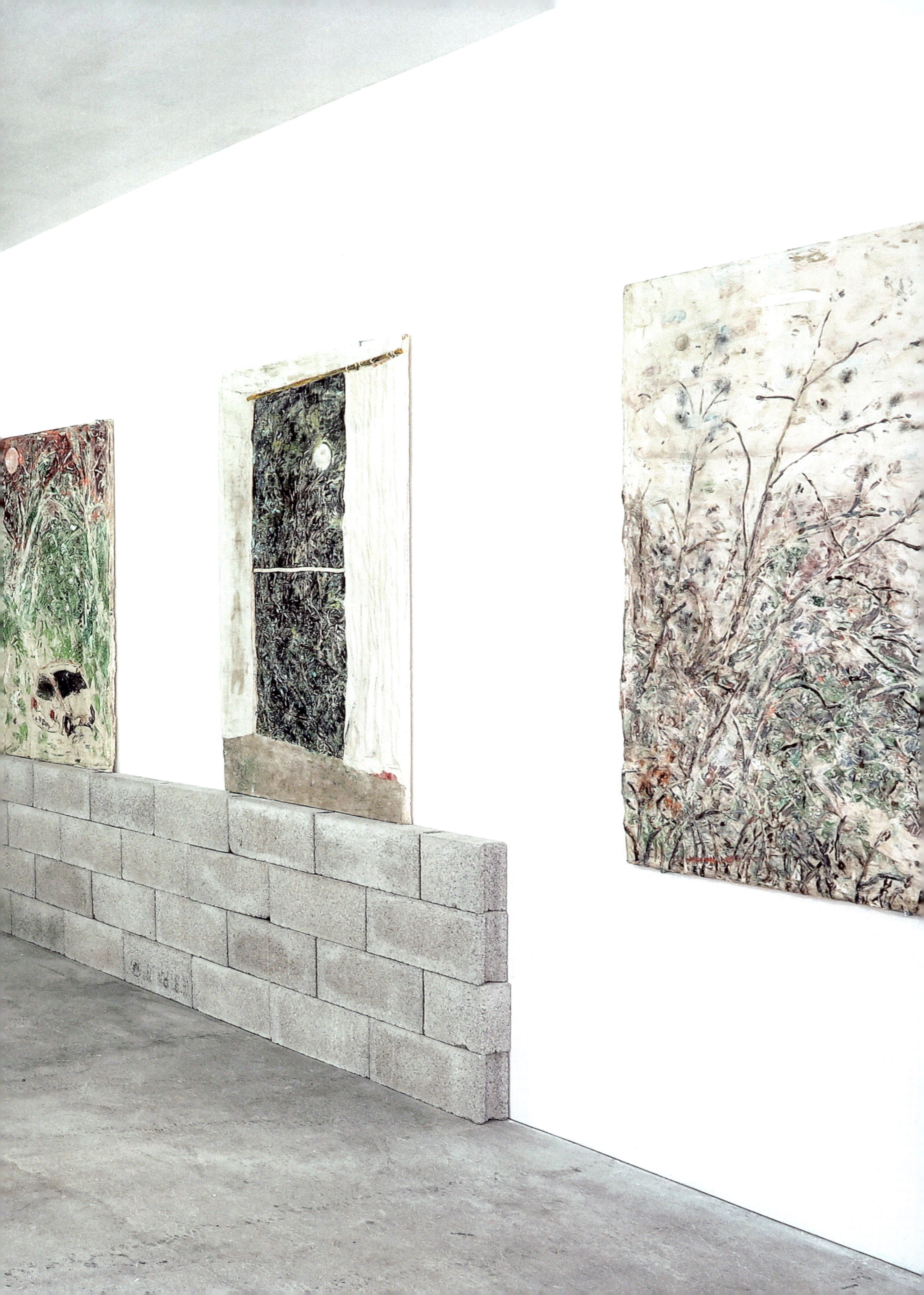

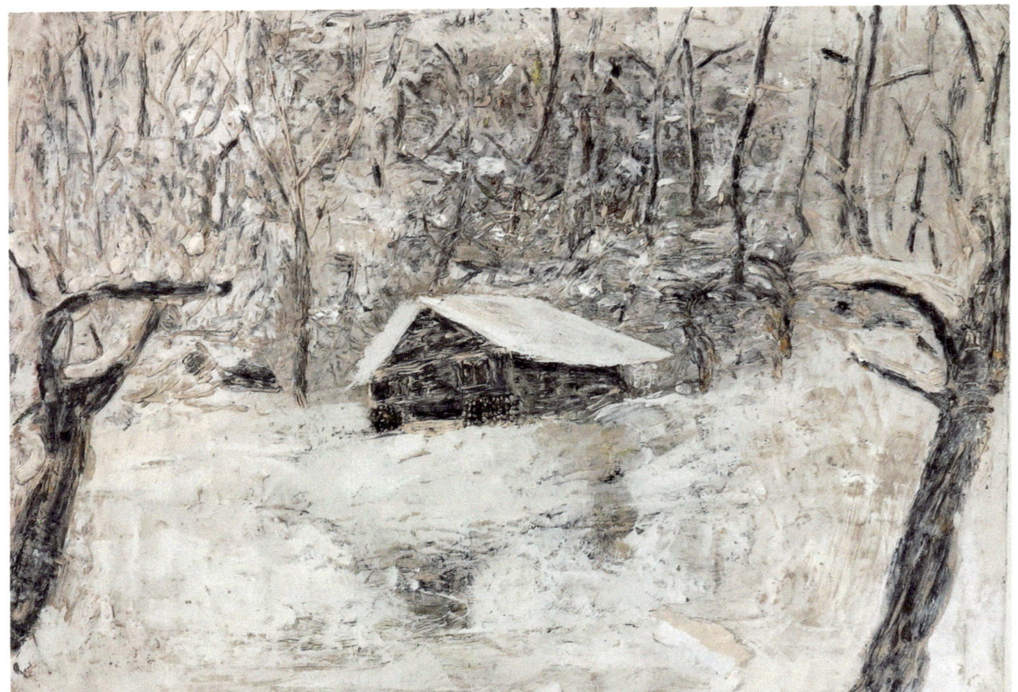

97 "She lay down in her bed and looked at the fire dancing on the ceiling, and all the time the island seemed to be coming closer and closer to the house. They were sleeping by a meadow near the shore, with patches of snow on the covers, and under them the ice darkened and began to glide. A channel opened very slowly in the floor, and all their luggage floated out in the river of moonlight." Tove Jansson, *The Summer Book*. TSCHOMA 28TH OF DECEMBER, 2018, plaster, pigments

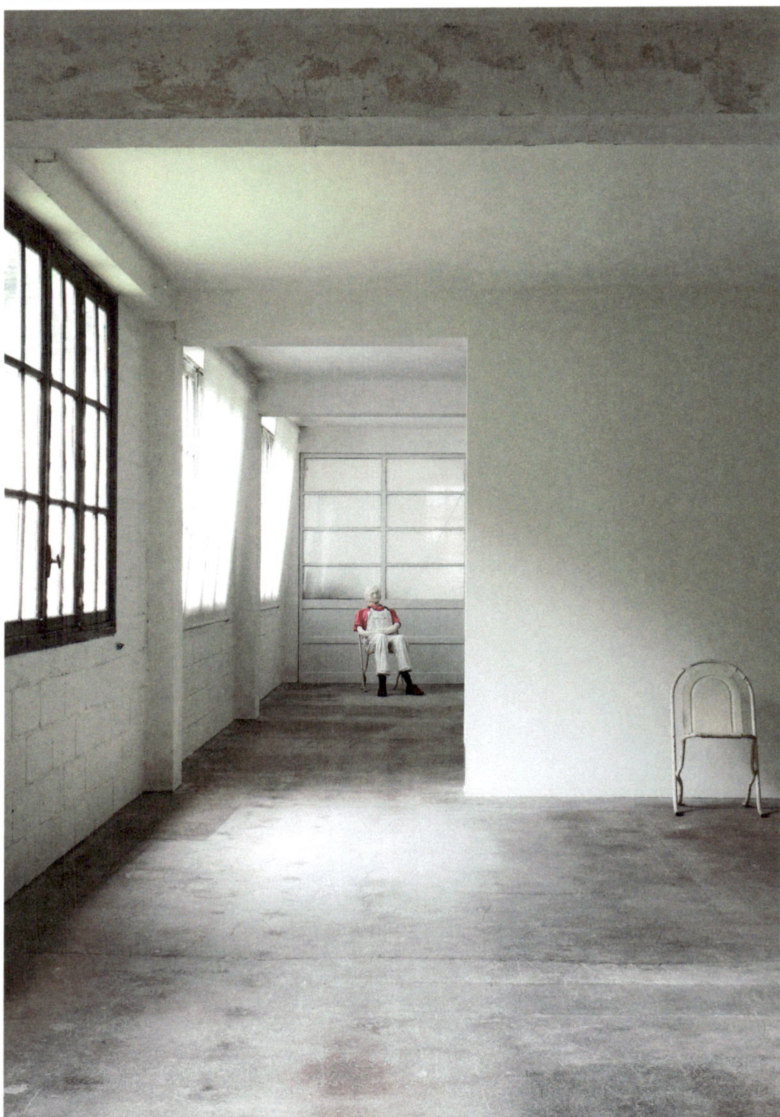

98 "Let us call him the man of letters. His inkpots and pen-holder are still laced delicately to his belt—part of an array of ties and strings that is clearly barely holding together under the pressure of his swollen stomach. He may be specifically a cleric—the book next to him has the look of a Bible—but he could as well be a notary or wandering scribe. The manuscript being crushed by his sleeve has a legal look." T.J. Clark, *Painting at Ground Level*. UNTITLED (SEATED FIGURE), 2018, plaster, clothes, chair, Treignac Projet

99 "We enjoy watching the plants grow and the fruit develop. Imagine a pear tree covered with golden fruit. Suddenly we pick the fruit and eat it and it is entirely destroyed. It is the same with animals. They are beautiful to us and we enjoy them but suddenly we kill them and eat them." Agnes Martin, *Writings*. Sam's car, 2018

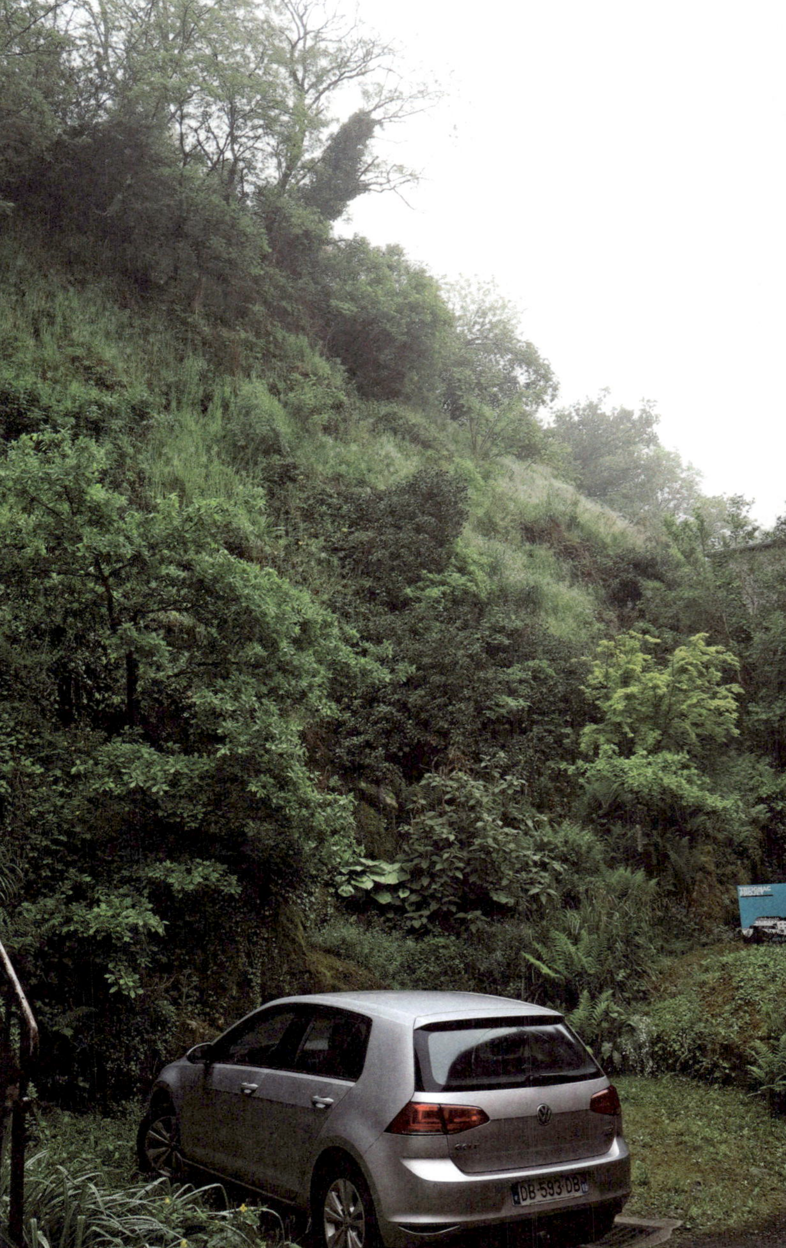

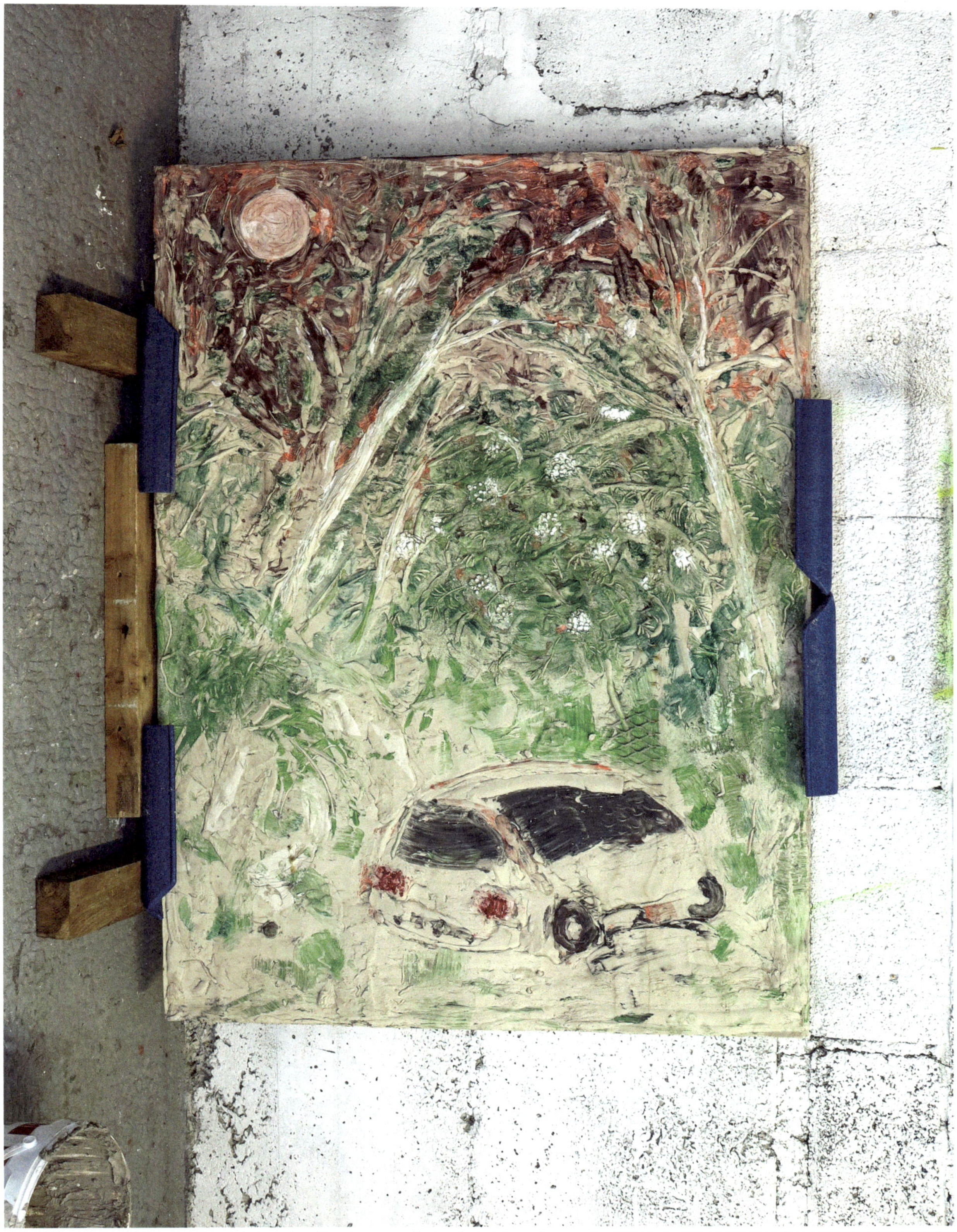

100 “Thoughts collide, objects exist close together in space. A ghostly battle on the sports fields for the souls of the masses. All the more relentless because dreams are at stake.” Siegfried Kracauer, *The Salaried Masses*. TREIGNAC 13TH OF MAY (SAM’S CAR), 2018, plaster, pigments, Treignac Projet

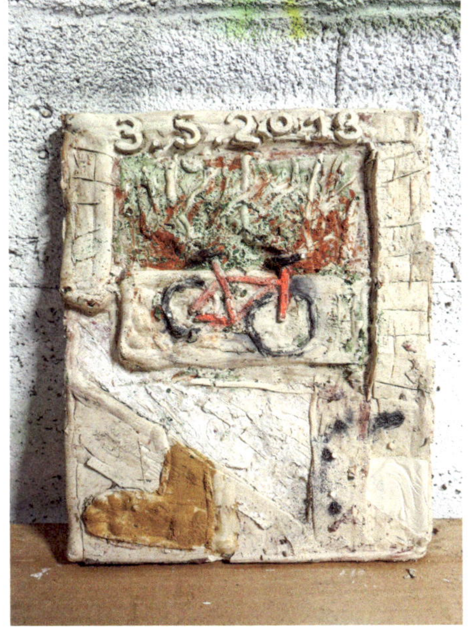

101 “The quotations in my works are like robbers lying in ambush on the highway to attack the passerby with weapons drawn and rob him of his conviction.” Walter Benjamin, *One Way Street* in *Illuminations*. OXFORD BALCONY WITH BIKE, 2018, plaster, pigments

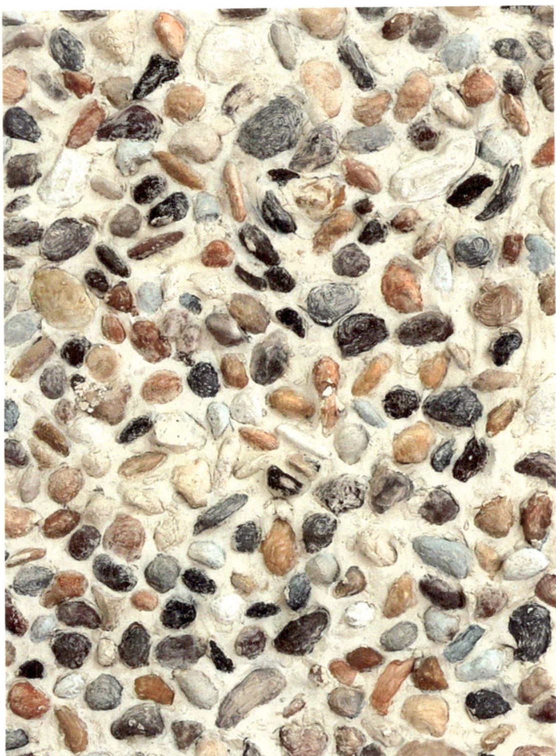

102 "All the suitcases were open and full of darkness and moss, and none of them ever came back." Tove Jansson, *The Summer Book*. PEBBLES, 2018, plaster, pigments

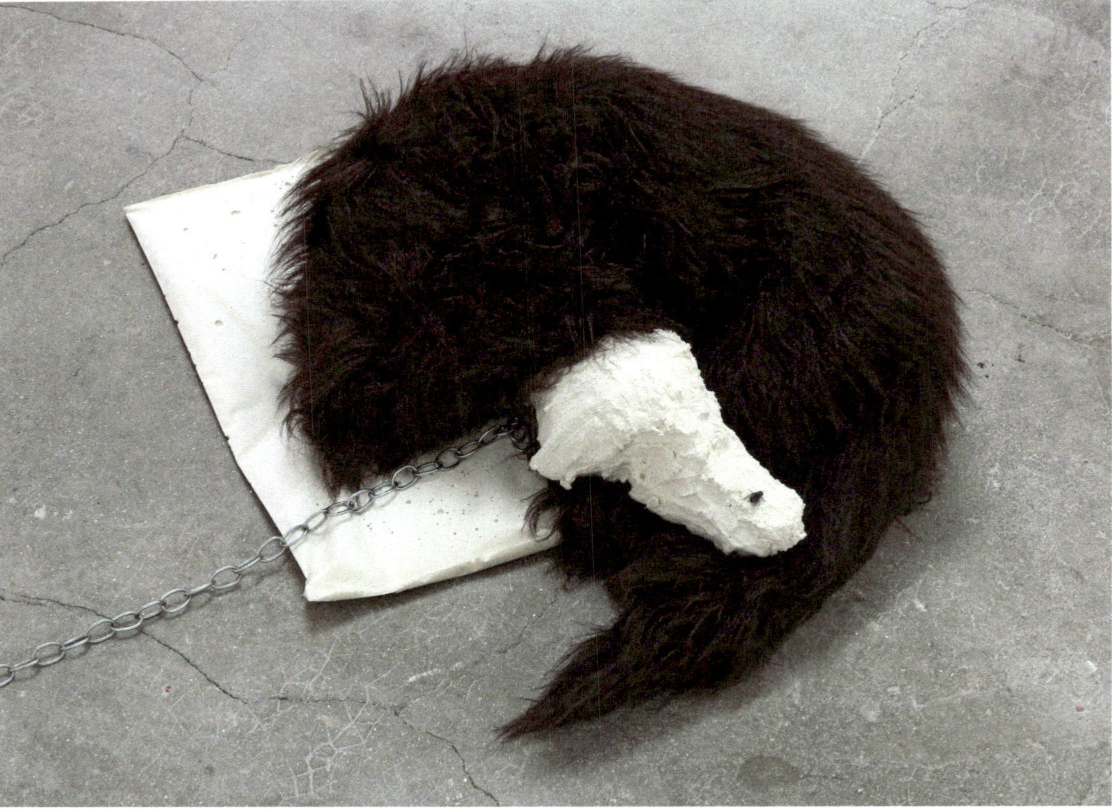

103 "The books in the shop were overseen by a girl whose hair wound over her ears in spirals; like pieces of puff pastry in peacetime. Even though the space was well heated, Elfriede—her name, it turned out—always appeared to be freezing; at any rate, she had wrapped herself in a batik cloth on which grasses ran together. When she stood before the bookshelves and pulled the thin mantle up higher, Ginster had the impression that she retreated into a meadow which had just then come into existence, in order to direct the rays of the sun onto herself." Siegfried Kracauer, *Ginster*. DOG AND FLY, 2018, plaster, faux fur, dead fly, chain

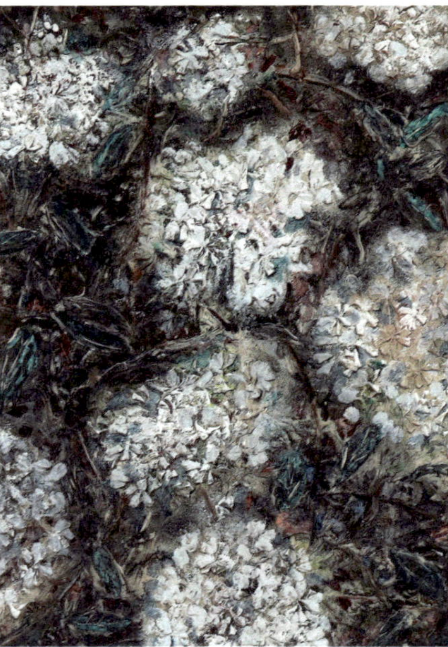

104 "Sometimes people never saw things clearly until it was too late and they no longer had the strength to start again. Or else they forgot their idea along the way and didn't even realize that they had forgotten. As Grandmother rowed home, she gazed at the big house interrupting the horizon, and it seemed to her it looked like a channel marker. If you squinted and thought about something else, it might almost be a channel marker—an objective indicator that here was a change of course." Tove Jansson, *The Summer Book*. OXFORD 25TH OF MAY (BLOSSOMS), 2018, plaster, pigments

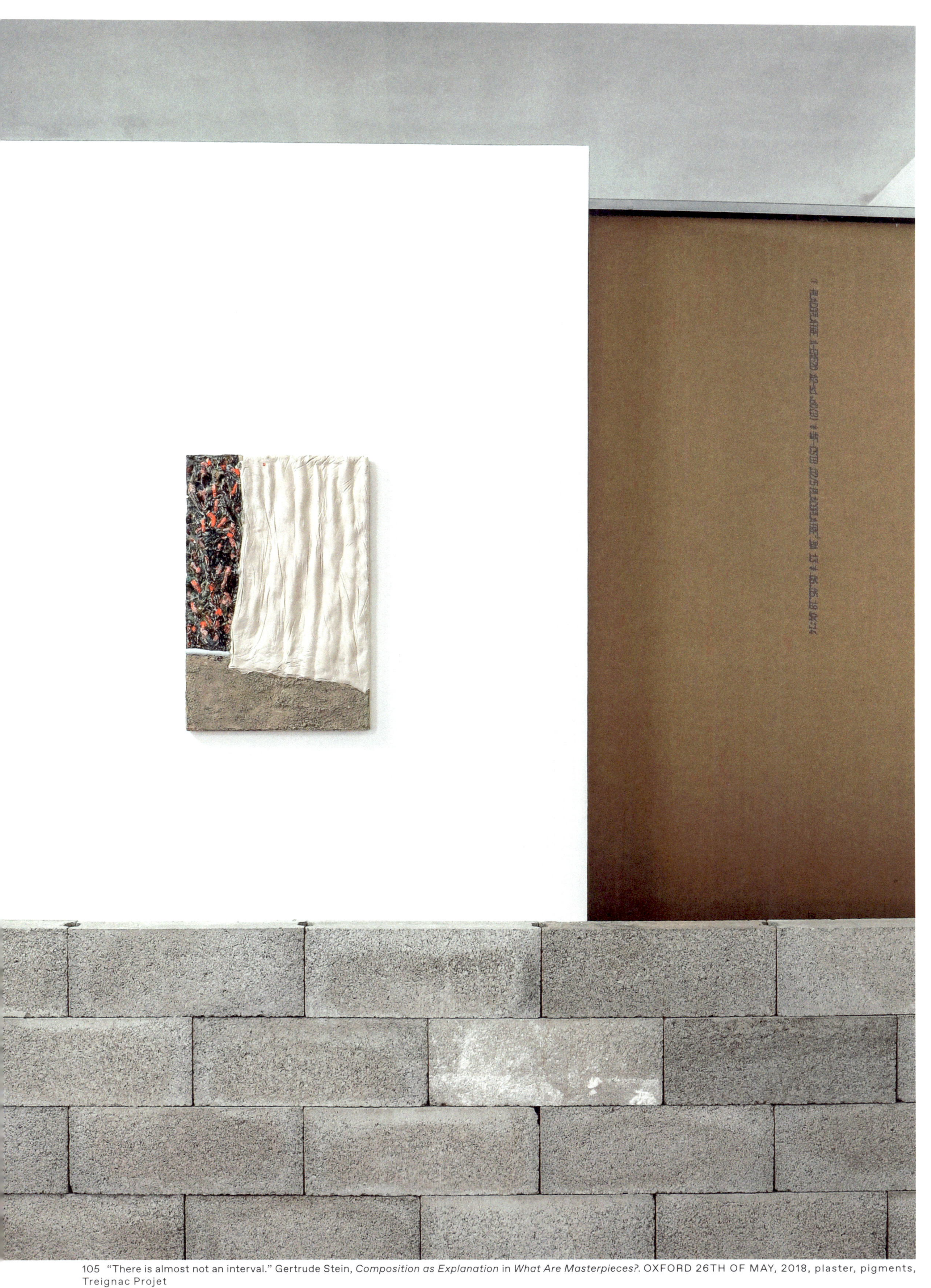

105 "There is almost not an interval." Gertrude Stein, *Composition as Explanation* in *What Are Masterpieces?*. OXFORD 26TH OF MAY, 2018, plaster, pigments, Treignac Projet

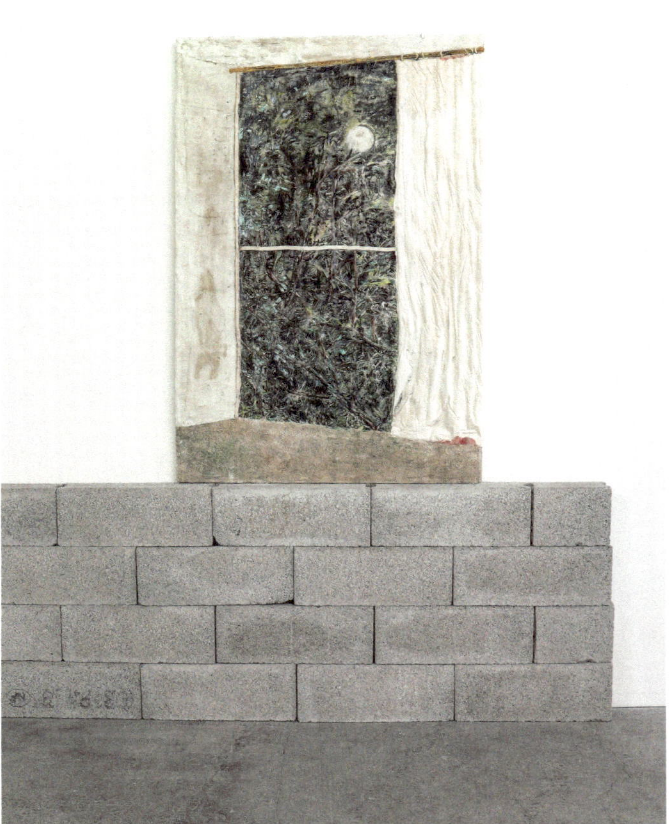

106 "The unfolding of potential in obedience to inspiration is happiness in this life. An arduous happiness in which we move forward." Agnes Martin, *Writings*. OXFORD 2ND OF MAY, 2018, plaster, pigments, Treignac Projet

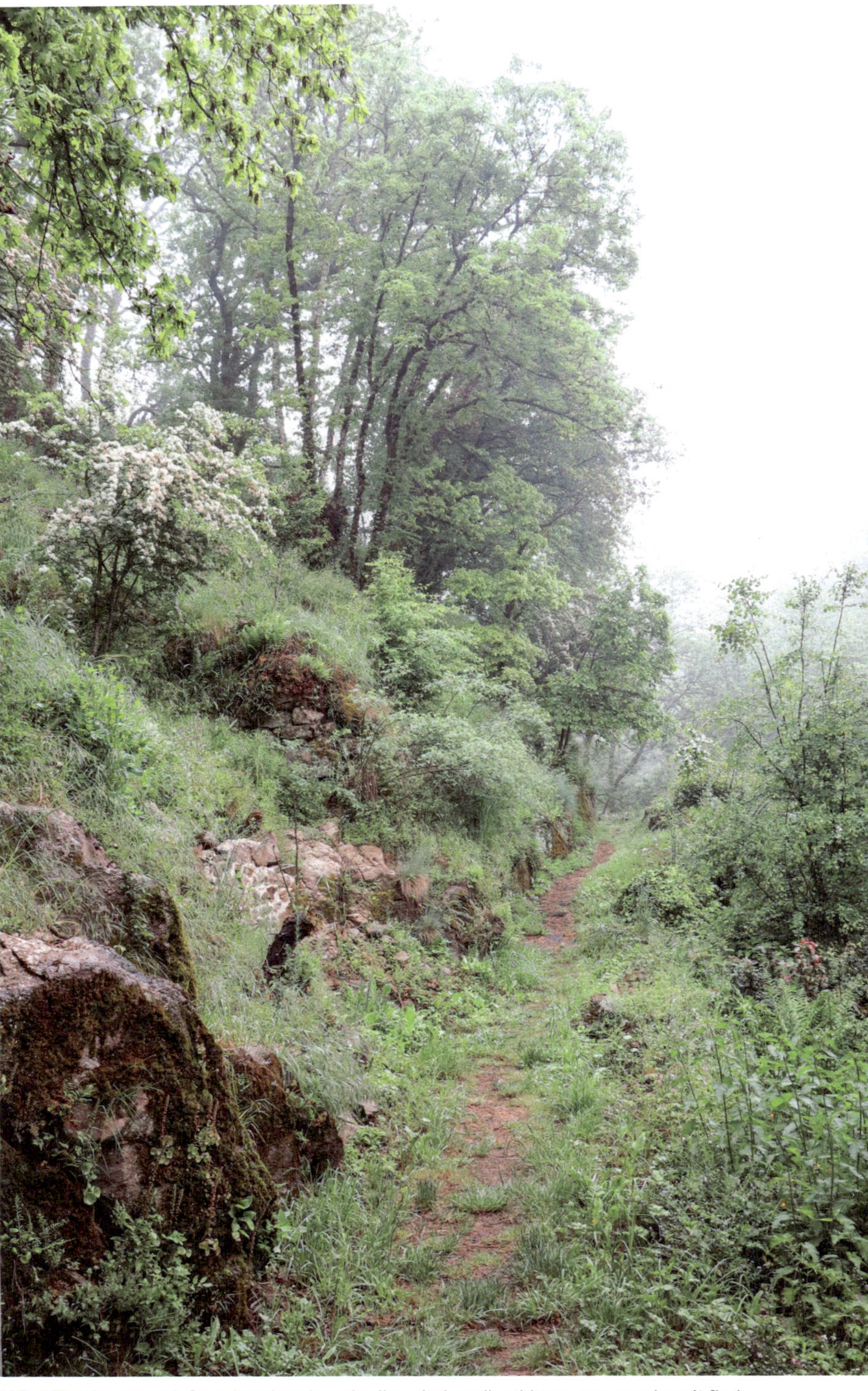

107 "'That's strange', Grandmother thought. 'I can't describe things any more. I can't find the words, or maybe it's just that I'm not trying hard enough.' It was such a long time ago. No one here was even born. And unless I tell it because I want to, it's as if it never happened; it gets closed off and then it's lost. She sat up and said, 'Some days I can't remember very well. But sometime you ought to try and sleep in a tent all night.'" Tove Jansson, *The Summer Book*. Path above Treignac Projet, 2018

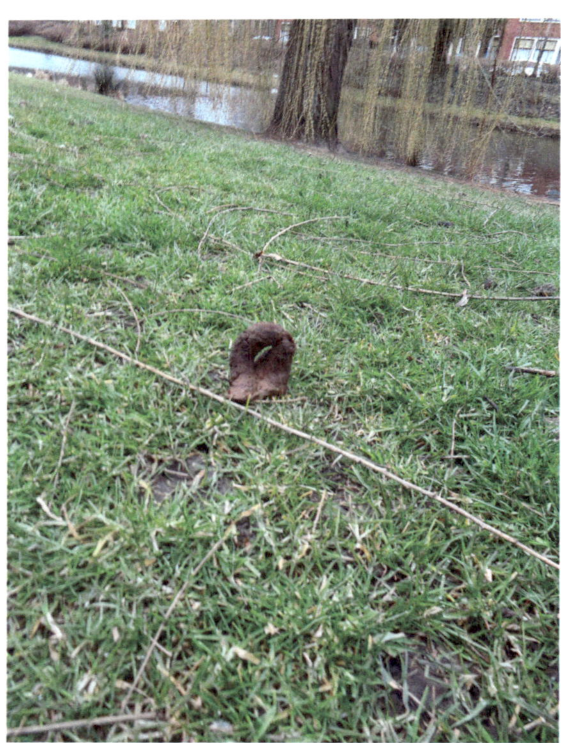

108 "On an even more general level we might think of fecal production as creative power. Just as scholars of the *fabliau* have begun to see excrement-making as a trope of fiction itself, the recirculation of dead matter, these latrines of fecal form swirling at the edges of the page can similarly evoke the artist's power to make forms from the 'clay' of the earth." Michael Camille, *Image on the Edge*. Turd, 2017

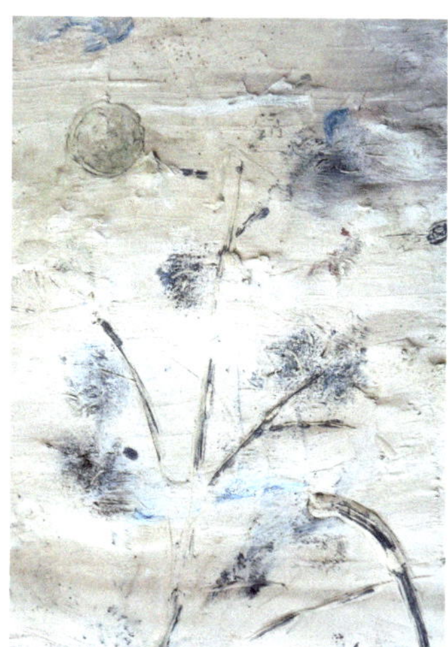

109 "Now let us turn to abstract response, the response that we make in our minds free from concrete environment. We know that it prevails. We know that it is infinite, dimensionless, without form and void. But it is not nothing because when we give our minds to it we are blissfully aware. Being without imperfection it is perfection. And being without parts it is whole." Agnes Martin, *Writings*. TREIGNAC 15TH OF MAY, 2018 (Detail), plaster, pigments

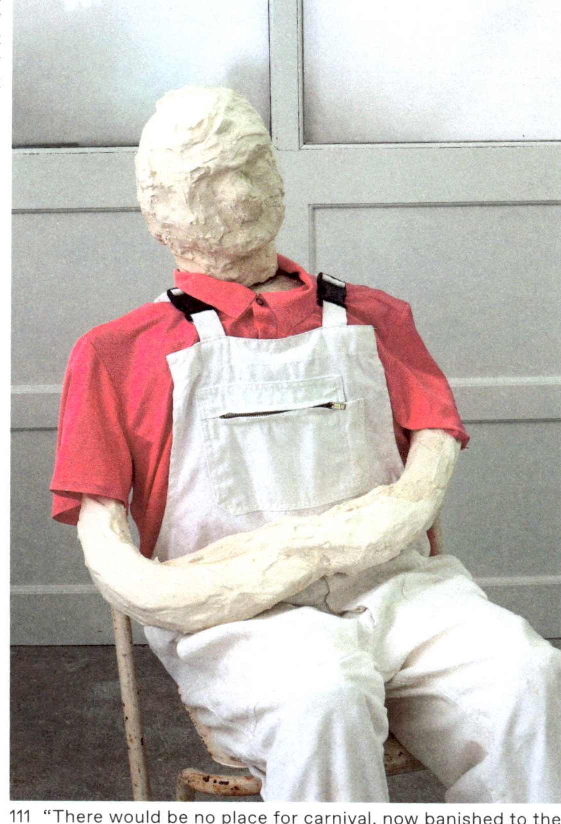

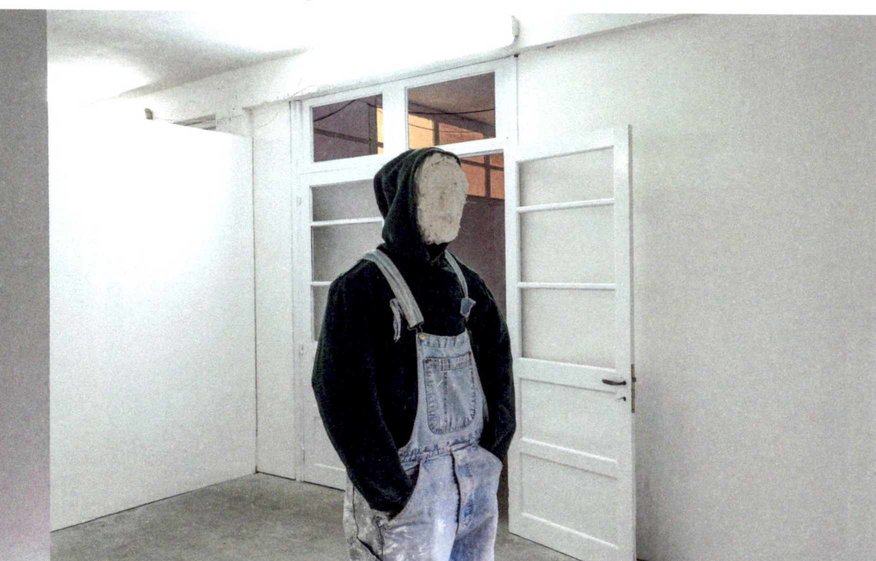

111 "There would be no place for carnival, now banished to the 'popular' end of the market and only of interest to the curious antiquarian of folklore. Unlike the medieval patron or donor, the connoisseur positioned himself (he was usually male) above the tastes of the 'vulgar', and wanted images untainted by any whiff of the lower bodily stratum of the body politic." Michael Camille, *Image on the Edge*. UNTITLED (SEATED FIGURE), 2018, plaster, clothes, chair, Treignac Projet

110 "All clothing is armor or prosthesis. Human beings are not bodies—even when they have eaten their fill, and they lie there like over-enlargements of themselves—they are outfits with bodies in hiding." T.J. Clark, *Painting at Ground Level*. UNTITLED (STANDING FIGURE), 2018, plaster, old clothes, Treignac Projet

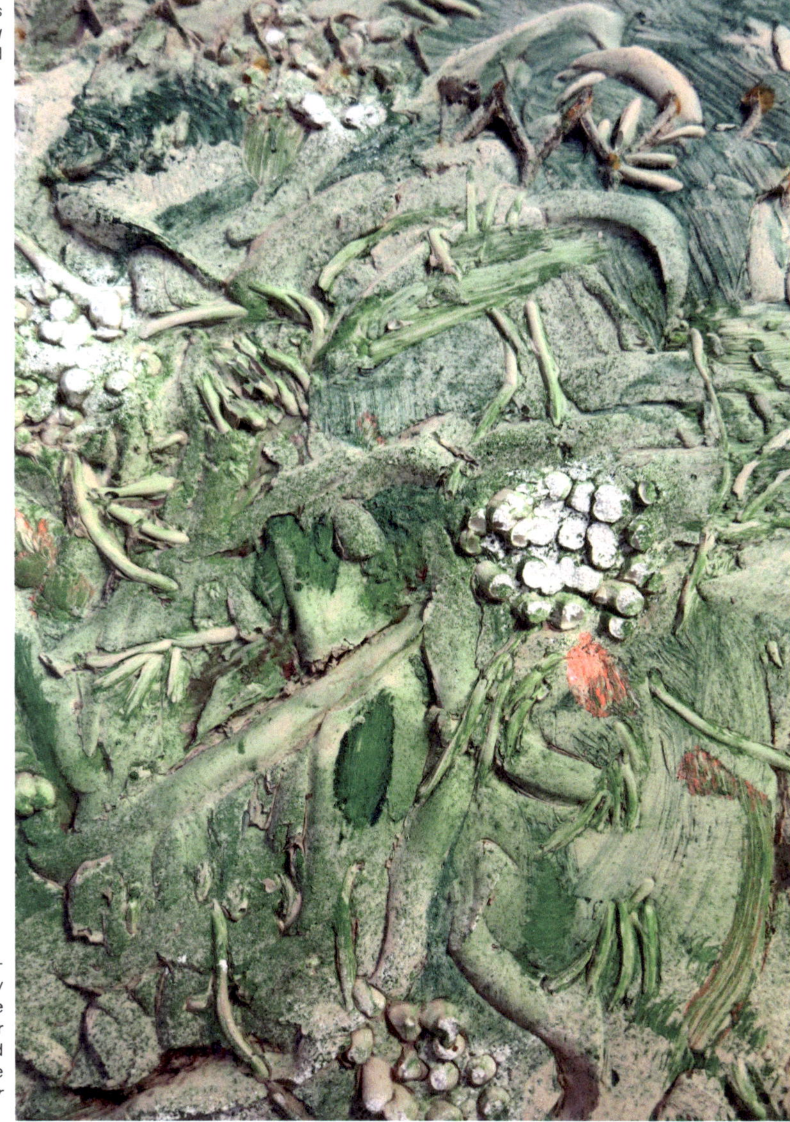

112 "The nights were already long, and when Sophia woke up, there was nothing to see but the dark. A bird flew over the ravine and screamed, first close by and then once more far away. It was a windless night, yet she could hear the sea. And there was no one in the ravine, yet the gravel crunched as if under someone's foot. The sheltering tent had let in the night, as close as if she'd been sleeping on the open ground. More birds cried in various ways, and the darkness was filled with strange movements..." Tove Jansson, *The Summer Book*. TREIGNAC 13TH OF MAY, 2018 (Detail), plaster, pigments

113 “When we use a hammer to drive in a nail, we attend to both nail and hammer, but in a different way. We watch the effect of our strokes on the nail and try to wield the hammer so as to hit the nail most effectively. When we bring down the hammer we do not feel that its handle has struck our palm but that its head has struck the nail. Yet in a sense we are certainly alert to the feelings in our palm and the fingers that hold the hammer. They guide us in handling it effectively, and the degree of attention that we give to the nail is given to the same extent but in a different way to these feelings. The difference may be stated by saying that the latter are not, like the nail, objects of our attention, but instruments of it.” Michael Polanyi, *Personal Knowledge*. HÜNDLI, 2014–2018, Portland cement, pebbles, dish towel, plumbing tubes, leash, photo: Sabrina Chou

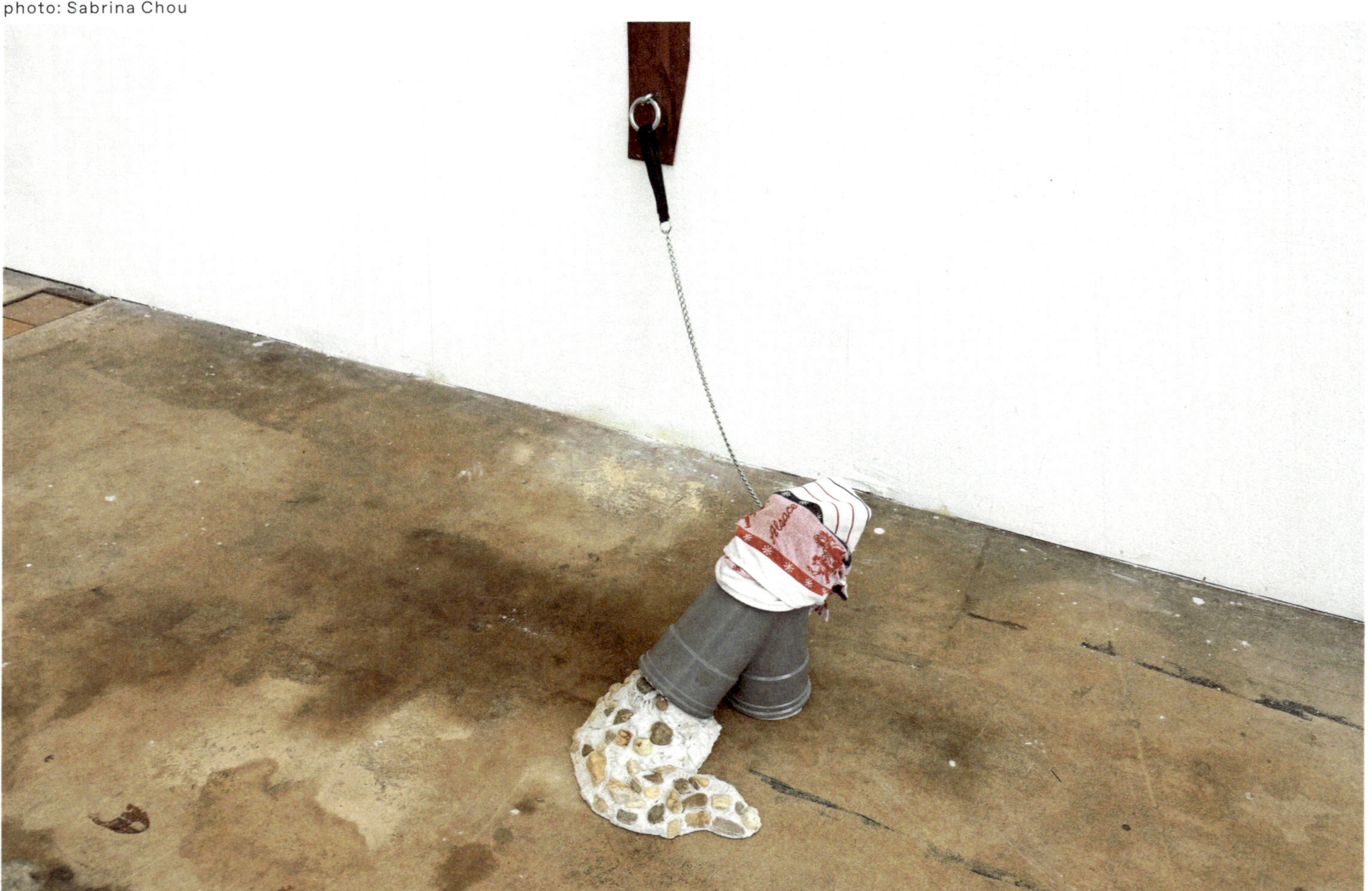

19 May Dear Christoph, Yesterday, without having any particular plan or motif, I worked on linocuts. I cut out letters that can be read in reverse, but make no particular sense. TATATA. What does it mean to work without a specific intention, without filling the activity with meaning in advance? I was reminded of your carved wooden bowls or your walking sticks. Have you ever asked yourself this question? It seems to me that those forms (the bowl or the stick) enable something else. Somehow meaning is elegantly ignored. All the best from Oxford, Micha

19 May Dear Micha, of course, I know the question well. It has plagued me often since I retired. Now that Daniela is working again, the order in my life has been upset. I enjoyed it when we two were at home, drinking coffee at 10am after our morning walk, simply sitting there talking. In this way we gave ourselves a bit of meaning and were of significance for one another. I love the sticks, as companions, I speak to them, ask the bushes if I may saw off a branch, and ultimately I always have a bit of a bad conscience because I have wounded the plant. I watch myself taking that action and sometimes have to laugh at myself. I actually like carving those objects very much and find it satisfying. I don't need to earn money with it. Now that I spend the day alone, the question of meaning shifts more to the foreground: What will I do now? I don't ignore meaning, it is simply losing its importance for me. I understand how you feel and hope that now and then you can elegantly ignore meaning. Best wishes from Thusis, Christoph

20 May Dear Christoph, Yes I can well imagine that. Every change always demands adaptation. Unvarying forms in particular, like the bowl or the stick, grant a formal stability, free up our attention for other things: a composition made up of question and answer, critique, associations, tactile things. These decisions made while working are difficult to legitimize or defend. They are practically defenseless. I like how you describe the walking sticks as your companions, as having character. I wish you a pleasant Wednesday! Micha

28 May Dear Micha, How are you both? I will be better able to write when my mood is sunnier again. But cordial greetings from Thusis as a sign of life from me. Tomorrow I want to go up to the Glaspass, where I hope to find lots of mountain flowers. Greetings to you both, Christoph

4 June Dear Micha, As the world of work is gone, the focus is now on me. And for me, relationships have become very important. It is fundamental for me to feel that I am in conversation with others, related to others. If these relationships don't come about or I can't feel them, I don't feel well. Such a situatedness also plays a big part in your working environment: How and where do I stand in the art world? How do I justify my work, how can I explain it? This kind of meaning is still very important for me. Is it not a balancing act between doing-justice-to-yourself and doing-justice-to-a-task, a work? I believe experience always takes place in this field of tension. Happy the person who can reconcile these. Greetings to you and Sabrina. Christoph

11 June Dear Micha, I came across this text by Rilke yesterday. Since then it has preoccupied and inspired me and I would like to share it with you: "For whether something

can become a life depends not on great ideas, but on whether you can develop a craft from them, something every day that abides with you till the end." Does this text also inspire you? Life as a craft? Heartfelt greetings from Thusis, where it has been quite foggy and rainy lately. Christoph

29 Aug Dear Christoph, I'm picking up where we left off last time. We spoke about structure and substances, action and thinking. We are greatly influenced by such dualist, dialectical thought patterns, the either-or. When we begin to work, these categories dissolve. Often one hesitates to make decisions because one wants to avoid failure, or because one overestimates meaning. But failure must be included somehow, must be inherent in the thing or the work. Someone once said that a banal idea well developed or radically pursued is often more exciting than an interesting idea carried out in a rudimentary fashion. I like the idiotic, the not-reaching-beyond-yourself. Banal motifs interest me more than complex ones as they draw attention to problems related to production, composition, and relations. This is why Rilke's poem appeals to me. Seen that way, the craft is also the moment when the material meets the idea. And the material always has it peculiarities, its contrariness. It rained here last night, and the river Sitter is carrying a lot of water again and is quite green. Cordial greetings, Micha

1 Sept Dear Micha, Many thanks for your lovely photographs of the Sitter. In them I see the river's sedimentations, the gravel, the gashes in the mud walls. The sedimentations, the stones, the river also provide a nice image for our conversation. You write that the simple and the idiotic appeal to you. But then what is simple and idiotic? Under the gravel and the mud are numerous layers that say something, that can also be worked on, and that are altogether complex, depending on your viewpoint. I like simple things not so much because of the problem of production and composition, but because of their beauty, their poetry, their subtlety. They leave me more scope for my own thoughts. Yet over and over again I find it hard to accept the simple, to live and create simply. Just like the "everyday craft". The "everyday craft" frequently permits failure, but there will be many other days of more successful work. Last weekend the river Nolla worked on its bed again with lots of power and energy, shifting stones and filling the gaps with gravel and sand. Best wishes, Christoph

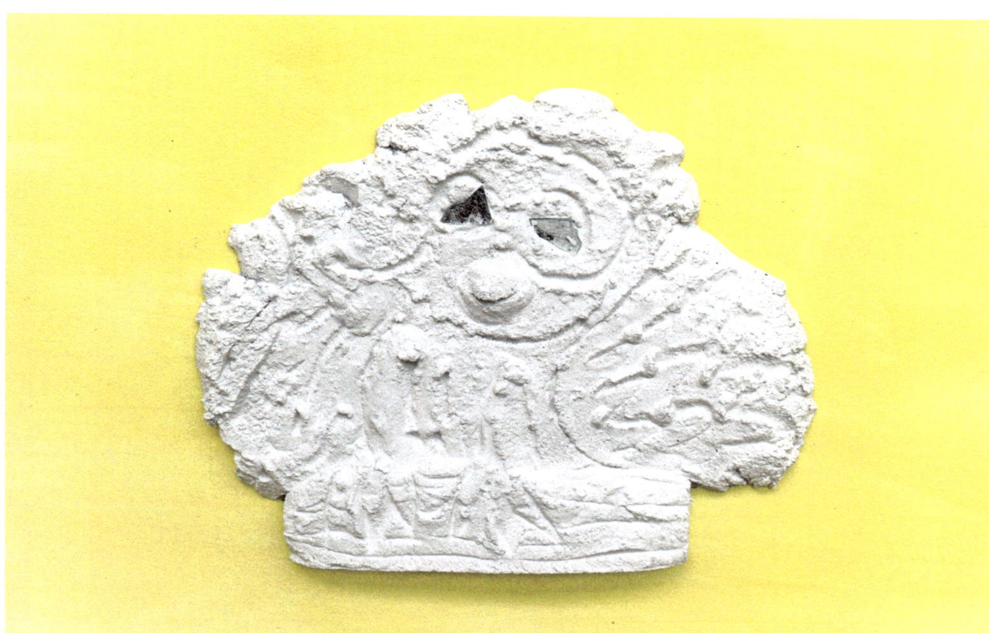

114 "History decays into images, not into stories." Walter Benjamin, *Arcades Project*. OWL, 2013, Portland cement, glass, photo: Sabrina Chou

115 "Money, like shit, is everywhere in the margins, being passed to beggars, between lovers, between buyer and merchant, between client and prostitute. Jangling in the beggar's cup like the bells that are rung on this page, coin was the 'new song'—the *canticum novum* to which everyone had to dance, even the patron of this book who bought these very images and paid the urban artist, just as he paid the prostitute, with these sullied signs of the city." Michael Camille, *Image on the Edge*. AGIP, 2013, Portland cement, spray paint, photo: Sabrina Chou

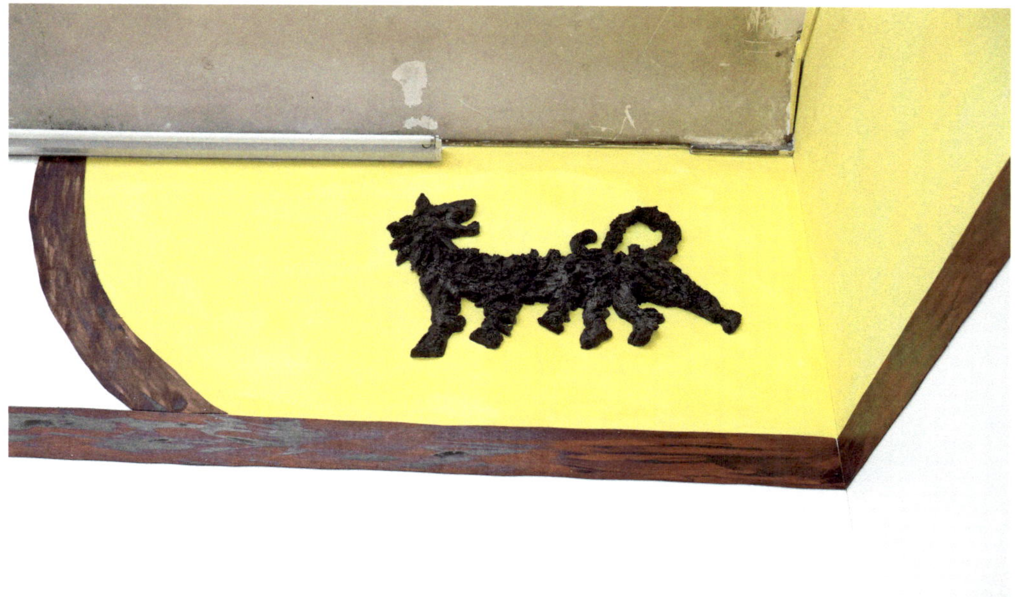

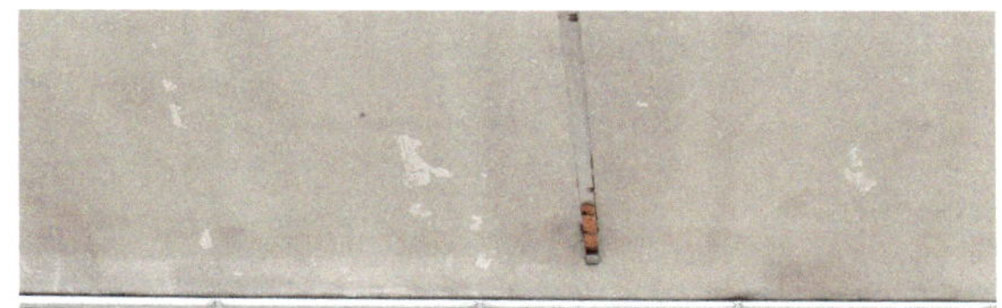

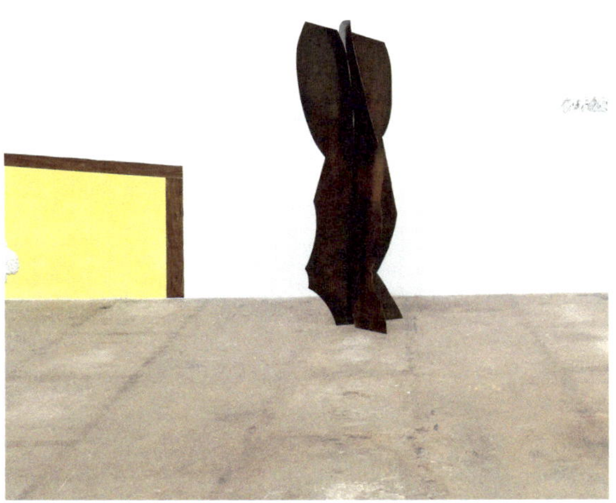

116 "It was hot and quiet and lonely. The house was crouched like a long, squat animal, and the black swallows circled above it with piercing shrieks, like knives in the air. Sophia walked all around the shoreline until she was back where she started. On the whole island, there was nothing but rock and juniper and smooth round stones and sand and tufts of dry grass. The sky and the sea were veiled by the yellow haze, which was stronger than sunshine and hurt the eyes. The waves heaved in toward land like hills and curled into breakers at the shore. It was a very heavy swell. 'Dear God, let something happen,' Sophia prayed. 'God, if You love me. I'm bored to death. Amen.'" Tove Jansson, *The Summer Book*. UNTITLED (FIGURE), 2014, stained plywood, photo: Sabrina Chou

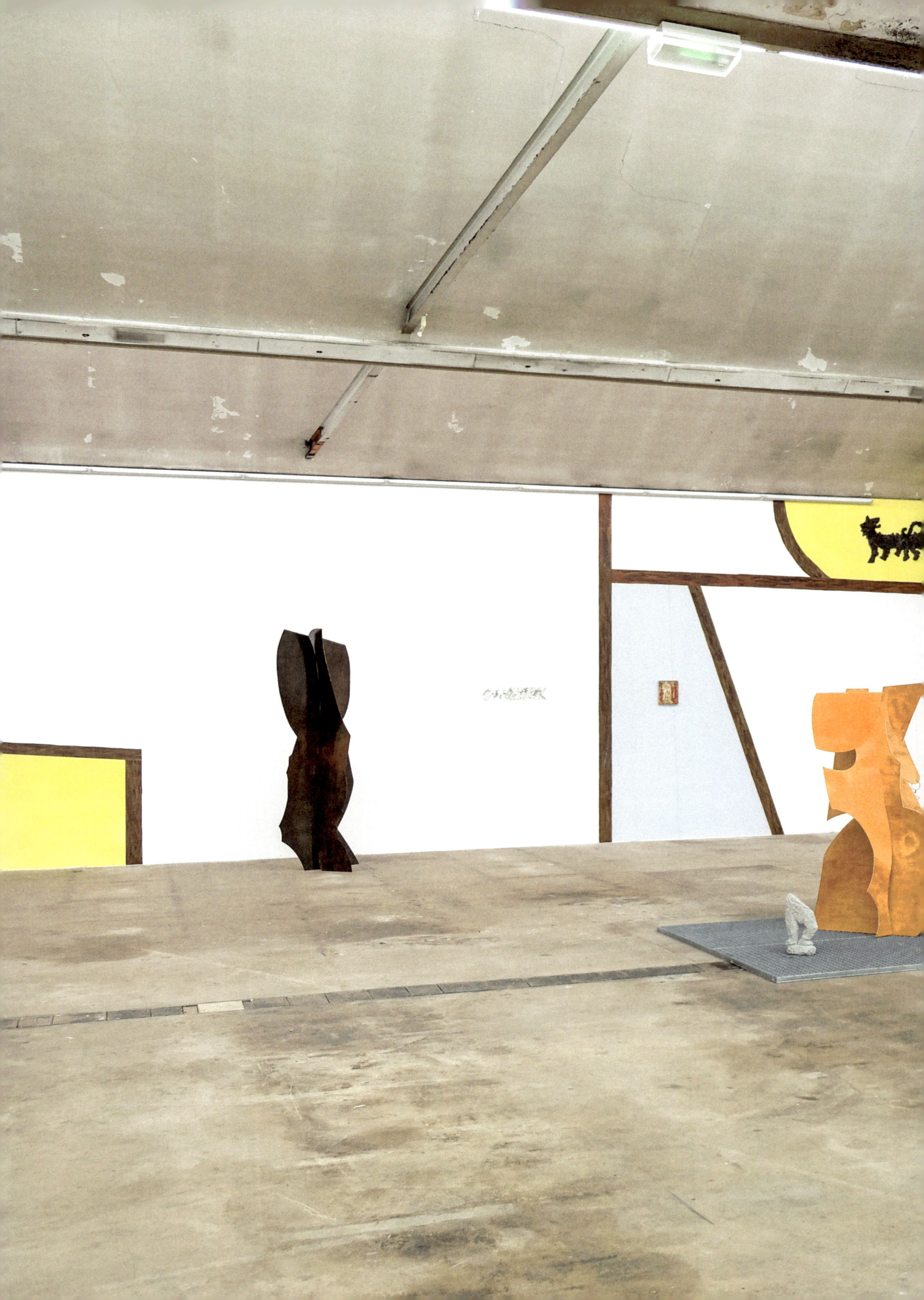

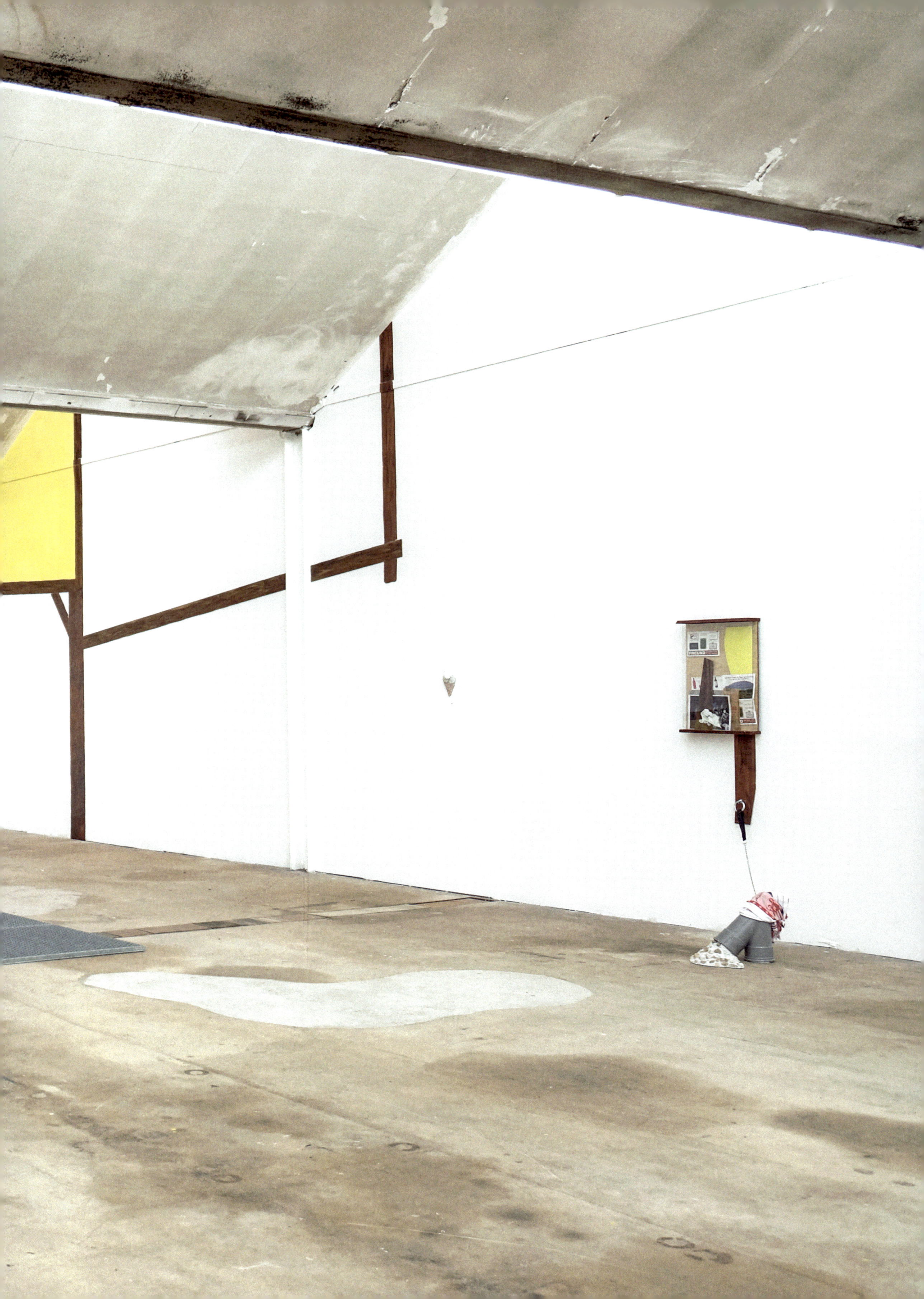

19. Mai Lieber Christoph, gestern habe ich ohne bestimmten Plan oder Motiv an Linolschnitten gearbeitet. Ich habe Buchstaben geschnitten, die spiegelverkehrt zwar noch lesbar sind, aber keinen eindeutigen Sinn ergeben. TATATA. Was bedeutet es ohne bestimmte Absicht zu arbeiten, ohne die Tätigkeit bereits mit Bedeutung zu füllen? Ich habe an deine geschnitzten Holzschalen oder deine Spazierstöcke gedacht. Hast du dir diese Frage auch schon gestellt? Es scheint mir, dass diese Formen (die Schale oder der Stock) etwas Anderes ermöglichen. Bedeutung wird da irgendwie elegant ignoriert. Alles Liebe aus Oxford, Micha

19. Mai Lieber Micha, und ob ich diese Frage kenne. Gerade als Pensionierter plagt sie mich oft. Jetzt, wo Daniela wieder arbeitet, ist die Ordnung durcheinandergeraten. Ich genoss es, wir beide zu Hause, der Kaffee um 10 Uhr nach dem Morgenspaziergang, einfach dazusitzen und uns auszutauschen. So haben wir einander ein Stück Sinn gegeben und waren füreinander bedeutungsvoll. Ich liebe die Stöcke als Begleiter, spreche mit ihnen, frage die Sträucher, ob ich ihnen ein Ast absägen darf und habe anschließend immer ein wenig ein schlechtes Gewissen, weil ich diese Pflanze verletzt habe. Ich schaue mir bei dieser Tätigkeit zu und muss manchmal über mich lachen. Eigentlich mag ich es sehr, diese Objekte zu schnitzen und empfinde es als sehr befriedigend. Ich muss ja kein Geld damit verdienen. Nun, da ich alleine durch den Tag gehe, drängt sich die Frage nach der Bedeutung wieder mehr in den Vordergrund: Was mache ich jetzt? Ich ignoriere die Bedeutung nicht, sie verliert für mich einfach an Wichtigkeit. Ich kann dir nachfühlen und wünsche dir, dass du ab und zu die Bedeutung elegant ignorieren kannst. Herzliche Grüße aus Thusis, Christoph

20. Mai Lieber Christoph, ja, ich kann mir das gut vorstellen. Jede Veränderung erfordert immer auch Anpassungen. Gerade gleichbleibende Formen wie die Schale oder der Stock geben eine formale Stabilität, so dass Aufmerksamkeit für anderes frei wird: Eine Komposition von Frage und Antwort, Kritik, Assoziationen, Taktiles. Diese Entscheidungen, die während der Arbeit getroffen werden, können nur schwierig legitimiert oder verteidigt werden. Sie sind praktisch wehrlos. Mir gefällt, wie du beschreibst, dass die Spazierstöcke zum Begleiter werden, einen Charakter haben. Wünsche noch einen schönen Mittwoch! Micha

28. Mai Lieber Micha, wie geht es euch? Wenn mein Gemüt wieder sonniger ist, kann ich besser schreiben. Aber als Lebenszeichen von mir herzliche Grüße aus Thusis. Morgen möchte ich in die Höhe auf den Glaspass und hoffe viele Bergblumen anzutreffen. Liebe Grüße an euch, Christoph

4. Juni Lieber Micha, da die Arbeitswelt weg ist, liegt der Fokus auf mir selber. Für mich sind Beziehungen sehr wichtig geworden. Mich im Gespräch und in einer Bezogenheit zu anderen zu fühlen, ist grundlegend. Wenn sich diese Beziehungen nicht einstellen oder ich sie nicht fühlen kann, geht es mir nicht gut. Eine solche Verortung spielt doch auch in deinem Arbeitsumfeld eine große Rolle: Wie und wo stehe ich in dieser Kunstwelt? Wie legitimiere ich meine Arbeit, wie kann ich sie begründen? Für mich ist diese Art von Bedeutung immer noch sehr wichtig. Ist es nicht ein Balanceakt zwischen dem Sich-selber-Gerecht-werden und dem Gerecht-werden

einer Aufgabe, einer Arbeit gegenüber? Ich glaube die Erfahrung liegt immer in diesem Spannungsfeld. Glücklich der Mensch, der das unter einen Hut kriegt. Liebe Grüße an dich und Sabrina. Christoph

11. Juni Lieber Micha, gestern ist mir dieser Text von Rilke über den Weg gelaufen. Seither beschäftigt und begeistert er mich und ich möchte ihn gerne mit dir teilen: »Denn ob etwas ein Leben werden kann, das hängt nicht von den großen Ideen ab, sondern davon, ob man sich aus ihnen ein Handwerk schafft, ein Tägliches, das bei einem aushält bis ans Ende.« Regt dich dieser Text auch an? Das Leben als Handwerk? Herzliche Grüße aus Thusis, wo es in letzter Zeit eher neblig und regnerisch ist. Christoph

29. Aug Lieber Christoph, ich knüpfe an unser Gespräch von letzter Woche an. Wir haben über Struktur und Eingeweide, das Handeln und das Denken gesprochen. Wir sind stark geprägt von solchen dualistischen, dialektischen Denkmustern, vom Entweder-oder. Im Anfangen lösen sich diese Kategorien auf. Oft zögert man, Entscheidungen zu treffen, weil man ein Versagen ausschließen will, oder weil man die Bedeutung überschätzt. Versagen muss aber irgendwie mit rein, muss im Ding oder in der Arbeit angelegt werden. Jemand hat mal gesagt, dass eine banale Idee die gut ausgearbeitet oder radikal verfolgt wird, oft spannender ist als eine interessante Idee, die rudimentär ausgeführt ist. Mir gefällt das Idiotische, das Nicht-über-sich-hinausgreifende. Banale Motive interessieren mich mehr als komplexe, da sie die Aufmerksamkeit auf Probleme des Herstellens, der Komposition und der Verhältnisse richten. Insofern spricht mich Rilkes Gedicht an. Das Handwerk ist, so gesehen, auch der Moment, in dem eine Idee auf ein Material trifft. Und das Material hat immer seine Eigenheiten, seine Widerständigkeit. Hier hat's über Nacht geregnet und die Sitter führt wieder mehr Wasser und ist ganz grün. Herzliche Grüße, Micha

1. Sept Lieber Micha, herzlichen Dank für deine schönen Sitter-Bilder. Ich sehe in den Fotos die Ablagerungen des Baches, das Geröll, die angeschnittenen Lehmwände. Die Ablagerungen, die Gesteine, der Bach geben doch ein schönes Bild für unser Gespräch. Du schreibst, dass dir das Einfache oder Idiotische gefällt. Was ist schon einfach und idiotisch? Unter dem Geröll und dem Lehm liegen viele Schichten, die etwas erzählen, die man auch bearbeiten kann und die je nach Betrachtungsweise ganz schön komplex sind. Ich liebe die einfachen Dinge, weniger wegen des Problems des Machens und der Komposition, aber wegen ihrer Schönheit, ihrer Poesie, ihrer Hintergründigkeit. Sie lassen mir Raum für meine eigenen Gedanken. Und doch finde ich es immer wieder schwierig, das Einfache zu akzeptieren, zu leben und zu erschaffen. Wie eben das »tägliche Handwerk«. Das »tägliche Handwerk« lässt auch immer wieder das Scheitern zu, es kommen ja noch viele andere gelungenere Tageswerke. Der Nolla hat das vergangene Wochenende auch wieder mit viel Kraft und Energie an seinem Bachbett gearbeitet, Steine umgelagert und die Zwischenräume mit Kies und Sand schön ausgefüllt. Mit lieben Grüßen, Christoph

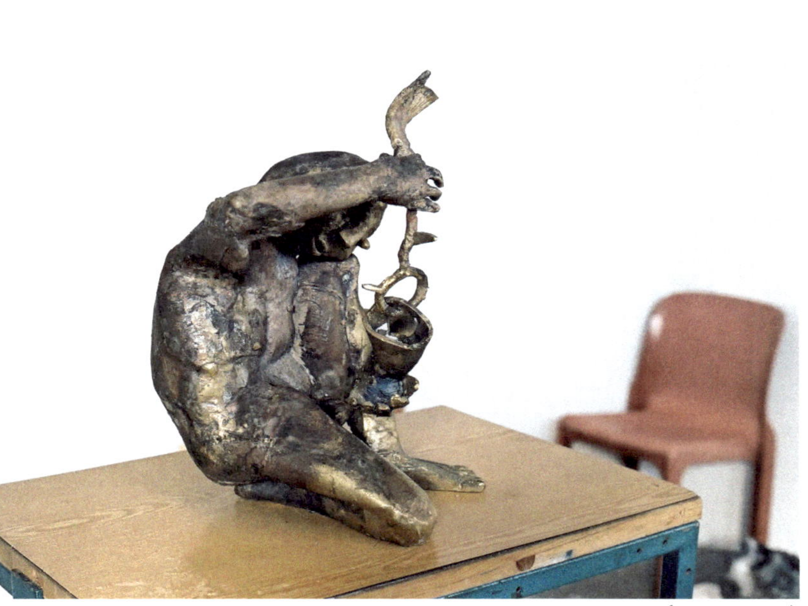

118 "Watching you is so much yoga." Eileen Myles, *Afterglow (a dog memoir)*. UNTITLED, 2020, Brass, studio view at Sitterwerk Foundation, photo: Katalin Deér

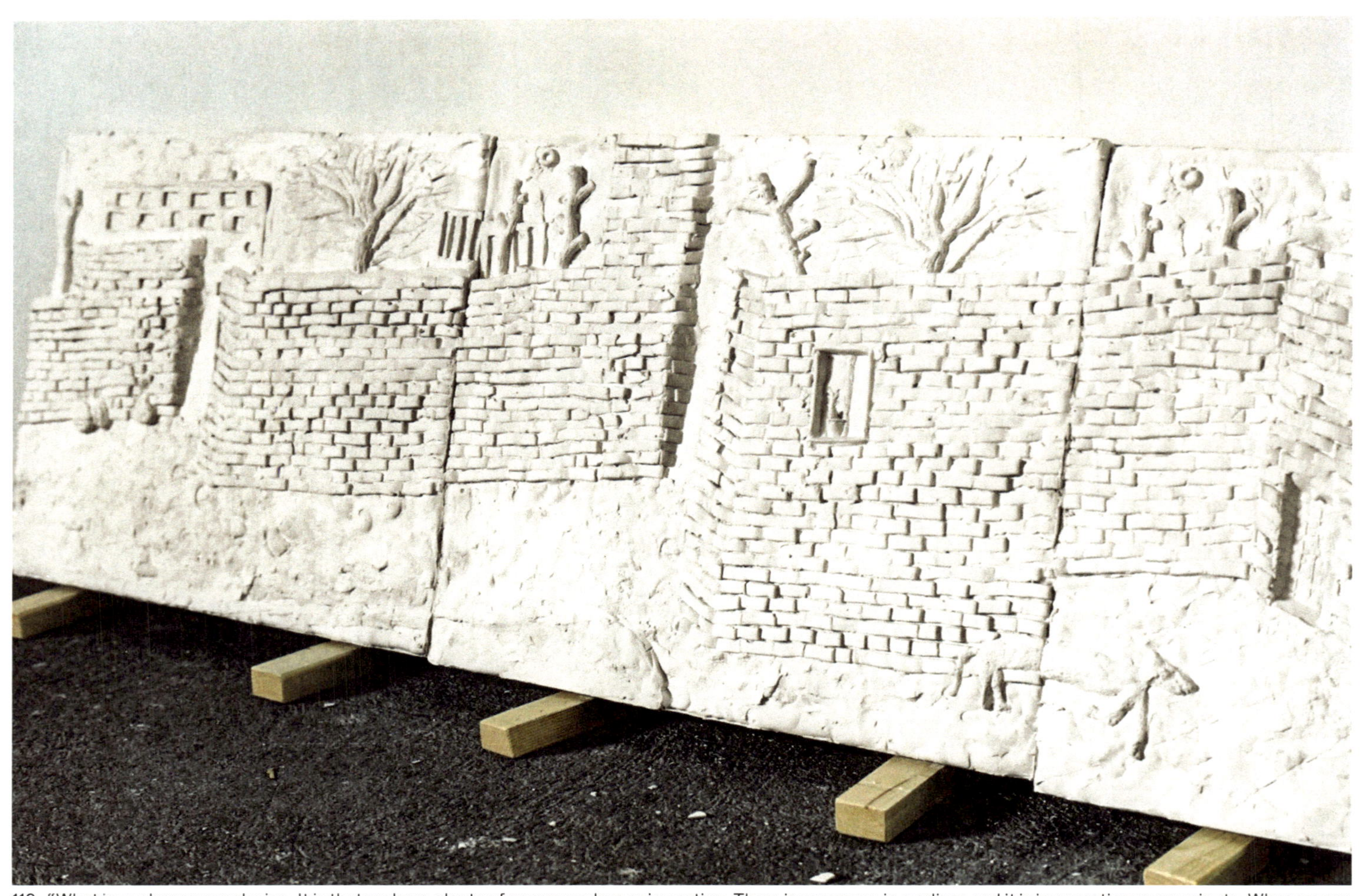

119 “What is our happy conclusion. It is that we have plenty of energy and we enjoy action. There is a purpose in our lives and it is in operation every minute. When we are right on the track we are rewarded with joy. We can know the whole truth with a request to our minds. If we are completely without direction we can withdraw and our minds will tell us the next step to take.” Agnes Martin, *Writings*. CALENDAR, 2020, plaster, studio view Sitterwerk Foundation, photo: Katalin Deér

1 »Sophia hatte keine Taschenlampe dabei, es war dunkel, der Gang lag wie eine verlassene Straße zwischen spitzgiebligen Häusern im Mondschein, unendlich lang. Am Ende der Straße schaute der mondweiße Himmel durchs Fenster, und unterhalb des Fensters lag der Schlafrock, eine Gestalt aus starren Falten voller kohlschwarzer Schatten. Sophia hatte die Luke so laut zugeschmettert, dass sie keinen Rückzieher machen konnte. Daher kroch sie weiter und kauerte sich in ihre Pappschachtel.« Tove Jansson, *Das Sommerbuch*. THE TALK, 2014, Ausstellungsansicht, TENT Rotterdam, Foto: Ghislain Amar

2 »Die Beine waren allein auf der Welt. Sie rissen den Fußboden in Fetzen und bewegten sich ohne Unterlage fort. Oft marschierten sie über den Wolkenhimmel, dessen blaue Löcher sie durchwateten.« Siegfried Kracauer, *Ginster*. FAIRE DES COMMISSIONS, 2014, Sperrholz, Sprayfarbe, Beize, Styropor, Foie gras, TENT Rotterdam, Foto: Ghislain Amar

3 »Was Kinder vorgeben sind keine Träume. Sie spielen und Sie wissen es.« Agnes Martin, *Schriften*. BAIGNEUR, 2014, gebeiztes Sperrholz, Ohrring, Badetücher, Foto: Ghislain Amar

4 »Denn sogar hier, im Land der Gefallenen, lebt die Erinnerung an die Bipedie (Zweifüßigkeit) weiter. Das Ei ist der evolutionäre Zyklus, der aufs Neue beginnt. Der ersten Zelle sprießen Beine, sie stabilisiert sich und macht sich auf den Weg den Darwin-Hügel hoch.« T.J. Clark, *Painting at Ground Level*. Schaufenster, Biel / Bienne, 2016

5 »Die Bauern schwelgen im Luxus der temporären Stadt.« T.J. Clark, *Painting at Ground Level*. THE TALK, 2014, Ausstellungsansicht, TENT Rotterdam, Foto: Ghislain Amar

6 »Gewalt, Zerstörung und Besitzanspruch sind ein wichtiger Bestandteil der Reaktion auf das Konkrete. Dies bekümmert manche Leute sehr stark, und sie möchten der Reaktion auf das Konkrete entgehen, um all diesem auszuweichen. Doch es gibt kein Entrinnen.« Agnes Martin, *Schriften*. THE TALK, 2014, Ausstellungsansicht, TENT Rotterdam, Foto: Ghislain Amar

7 »Er war lang und ausdruckslos wie ein Interpunktionszeichen, das nichts trennt. Nach dem Krieg wollte er noch weiter wachsen; in das Geschäft seines Vaters hinein.« Siegfried Kracauer, *Ginster*. LEANING FIGURE, 2016, beschichte Spanplatte, Glasbausteine, Rib Rotterdam, Foto: Sabrina Chou

8 »Ground Level (Grundebene) bedeutet demnach unter anderem Regression. Es ist der Ort, wo Körper in den Schlaf oder in den Tod oder in die Zersetzung zurücksinken; der Ort, wo fette Babys träumen.« T.J. Clark, *Painting at Ground Level*. Konsole aus Kalkstein, Aquitanien, ca. 1150-1200, 2018, The Metropolitan Museum of Art, New York

9 MEUBELS, CHARLOIS?, 2016, Ausstellungsansicht, (OHR: Gemeinschaftsarbeit mit Sabrina Chou) Rib Rotterdam, Foto: Job Willems

10 »Gegen Morgen löste sich die Flotte fast gleichzeitig auf und trieb auseinander, jedes Boot fuhr in seine jeweilige Richtung davon, immer weiter fort. Im Morgengrauen war das Meer leer. Der Wind legte sich. Der Regen hörte auf. Ein schöner, klarer Mittsommermorgen ordnete seine Farben am Himmel. Es war sehr kalt.« Tove Jansson, *Das Sommerbuch*. Unbekannter Künstler, Tulpen mit Rollator, Schulpweg, Rotterdam, 2016

11 »Die Art und Weise, wie wir einen Hammer oder ein Blinder seinen Stock benutzt, zeigt letztlich, dass wir in beiden Fällen die Punkte, an denen wir mit den Dingen in Berührung kommen, die wir als Objekte außerhalb unseres Selbst beobachten, nach außen verlagern. Während wir uns auf ein Werkzeug oder eine Sonde verlassen, werden diese jedoch nicht als äußere Objekte behandelt. Wir können das Werkzeug auf seine Wirksamkeit oder die Sonde auf ihre Eignung prüfen, z.B. bei der Entdeckung der verborgenen Details eines Hohlraums, aber das Werkzeug und die Sonde können niemals im Bereich dieser Arbeitsgänge liegen. Sie bleiben notwendigerweise auf unserer Seite dieser Tätigkeiten und bilden einen Teil von uns, dem Bedienpersonal. Wir ergießen uns in sie hinein und nehmen sie als Teile unserer eigenen Existenz auf. Wir nehmen sie existentiell an, indem wir in ihnen verweilen.« Michael Polanyi, *Personal Knowledge*. BUTLER (A SERVING SCULPTURE), 2016, Sperrholz, Farbe, Filzstift, Ringgummimatte, Schnürsenkel, Rib Rotterdam, Foto: Sabrina Chou

12 »Sophia und die Großmutter setzten sich ans Ufer, um sich weiter darüber zu unterhalten. Es war ein schöner, windstiller Tag mit langer Dünung. Genau an solchen Tagen, in den Hundstagen, kommt es vor, dass Boote sich allein von ihren Ufern aufmachen. Große, fremde Gegenstände lassen sich vom Meer herantragen, manches sinkt und manches steigt nach oben, die Milch wird sauer, und die Libellen tanzen wie verzweifelt. Die Eidechsen sind nicht mehr ängstlich.« Tove Jansson, *Das Sommerbuch*. DACKEL, 2016, gebeiztes Sperrholz, Rib Rotterdam, Foto: Sabrina Chou

13 »Vor der Widerwertigkeit eines verschwommenen Genres fühlt sich der Anhänger der Tradition schwach. Wie wenn der Tod das Leben infiziert, wenn die Poesie die Fiktion, die Identität, das System, die Ordnung stört. Der Rest streckt sich vor uns aus, krampfend und blutend.« Dodie Bellamy, *Crimes Against Genre*, in *Academonia*. SKULPTUR FÜR TASCHEN, JACKEN UND SCHLÜSSEL (AN DER WAND LEHNEND), 2016, laminierte Spanplatte, Doppelhaken, Filzstift, Rib Rotterdam, Foto: Job Willems

14 »Man erfährt, dass der Quälgeist das Opfer öfters zwang, nach seinen falschen Angaben zu arbeiten; dass er den schon ohnedies Erniedrigten als einen Simulanten bezeichnete; dass er ihn gegen den Abteilungsleiter und den Abteilungsleiter gegen ihn aufhetzte. Wie aus dem Aktenstück zu ersehen ist, hat das Büromonstrum auch die Kollegen des Klägers gepeinigt. Machte einer von ihnen Anstalten, sich zu beschweren, so erklärte er von vornherein: ›Ich bestreite alles‹, und die Leute schwiegen vor Angst. Der Kläger begann dann in seiner Verzweiflung zu trinken und kam unregelmäßig zum Dienst.« Siegfried Kracauer, *Die Angestellten*. MEUBELS, CHARLOIS?, 2016, Ausstellungsansicht, Rib Rotterdam, Foto: Job Willems

15 »Inmitten der Wirklichkeit reagieren wir mit Freude. Es ist eine völlig zufriedenstellende Erfahrung, aber ganz unfassbar. Sie ist unfassbar, weil wir gleichzeitig so viele andere Dinge erkennen müssen.« Agnes Martin, *Schriften*. Jupiterfab, *Community Human Identity*, 2010, Wandmalerei an der Verboomstraat, Rotterdam, 2016

16 »In Zaubersprüchen und Rätseln besaßen Dinge, die weder dies noch das waren, durch ihre Renitenz gegen Klassifizierung eine starke Magie. Öffnungen, Eingänge und Tore, sowohl von Gebäuden als auch vom menschlichen Körper (in einem mittelenglischen medizinischen Text wird ein Medikament erwähnt, das ›the margynes of the skynne‹, ›die Ränder der Haut‹, angreift), waren besonders wichtige Schwellenbereiche, die geschützt werden mussten.« Michael Camille, *Image on the Edge*. OHNE TITEL / PISTAZIENBODEN, 2016, Schaumstoffkissen mit Vinylüberzug (Gemeinschaftsarbeit mit Sabrina Chou) / Zement und Pistazienschalen, Rib Rotterdam, Foto: Job Willems

17 »Drachen, Menschen, Meerjungfrauen und Fische essen alles Mögliche. Gemüse und Tiere werden nicht einfach bunt zusammengemischt, sondern beißen und verdauen sich gegenseitig, manchmal sogar sich selbst, in aus dem Ruder laufenden Selbstfresser-Orgien. « Michael Camille, *Image on the Edge*. LEVEL (OBJET TROUVÉ), 2016, gerahmter Farbdruck, Rib Rotterdam, Foto: Job Willems

18 »Wie sähe eine Welt aus – diese Frage scheint sich Bruegel gestellt zu haben –, in der alle menschlichen Aktivitäten auf die Geschwindigkeit des Dickdarms verlangsamt wären?« T.J. Clark, *Painting at Ground Level*. OHNE TITEL, 2015, Gips, Pigmente, Foto: Vivian Sky Rehberg

19 »Im Inneren erinnerte es mich an etwas anderes, an die ganze Luft. Ist es notwendig, dass es eine erste Luft gibt – eine Luft, die einfach deine ist? Einen Ort, der im höchsten Maße jung und alt ist, an dem man sein ganzes Leben verbracht hat. Aufwachsen, Sterben, an den Strand gehen, trinken, küssen. Gibt es Menschen, die nie in ihrer Luft gelebt haben? Ist dies meine? Ich bin nie Teil eines jungen Liebespaares gewesen, eines jungen Paars – aber diese Luft ist meine. Ich kenne meine Luft.« Eileen Myles, *Afterglow (a dog memoir)*. DIE ZWEI FREUNDE, 2020, Arvenholz, Acrylfarbe, Nagellack, Hundeleinen, Kunstmuseum Luzern, Foto: Marc Latzel

20 »Bei Spaziergängen fielen ihm fast nie spannende Themen ein.« Siegfried Kracauer, *Ginster*. SPIEGEL OHNE TITEL, 2016, Spiegel und Zement, Robin Hood Second Hand Shop, Rotterdam, Foto: Sabrina Chou

21 »›Gibt es im Himmel Ameisen?‹, fragte Sophia. ›Nein‹, sagte die Großmutter und legte sich vorsichtig auf den Rücken, zog sich den Hut über die Nase und versuchte heimlich zu schlafen. In weiter Ferne war das unermüdliche, friedliche Brummen irgendeiner Landmaschine zu hören.« Tove Jansson, *Das Sommerbuch*. OHNE TITEL (OXFORD MYSTERY SERIES), 2019, Öl auf Holzbrett

22 »Methode dieser Arbeit: literarische Montage. Ich habe nichts zu sagen. Nur zu zeigen. Ich werde nichts Wertvolles entwenden und mir keine geistvollen Formulierungen aneignen. Aber die Lumpen, den Abfall: die will ich nicht inventarisieren sondern sie auf die einzig mögliche Weise zu ihrem Rechte kommen lassen: sie verwenden.« Walter Benjamin, *Das Passagen-Werk*. Michiel Brink, Mosaik, 2016, Clemensstraat, Charlois, Rotterdam

23 »Das junge Volk, das in den breiten Schichten zwischen dem Proletariat und dem Bürgertum aufwächst, passt sich mehr oder weniger leicht dem Betrieb an. Viele lassen sich unwissend treiben und machen mit, ohne noch zu ahnen, dass sie eigentlich gar nicht dazugehören.« Siegfried Kracauer, *Die Angestellten*. PASSAGIER, 2018, Schaumstoff, Kleider, Kabelbinder

24 »Ginster sah zum Fenster hinaus, die Straße war leer, nichts verändert. Er dachte, dass er kein Auftreten habe. Der Assessor trat auf. Man dürfe Untergebene nicht vertraulich grüßen, hatte ihm ein Bekannter gesagt. Wenn der Bekannte in eine Bank oder ein Verwaltungsgebäude kam, ging er einfach am Portier vorbei und wurde sofort vom Generaldirektor empfangen. Niemals würde er, Ginster, zum Generaldirektor gelangen. Sollte er noch in die Stadt?« Siegfried Kracauer, *Ginster*. PASSAGIER, 2018, Schaumstoff, Kleider, Kabelbinder,

25 »Der Körper war im Grunde genommen das erste menschliche Gebäude. Der Leichnam wurde buchstäblich zu der Behausung, aus der die Geister des Bösen vertrieben werden konnten.« Michael Camille, *Image on the Edge*. Wachsmodell für LIFT, 2019

26 »Daraus folgt, dass eine Kunst, die für die Dauer einer Generation in Vergessenheit geraten ist, gänzlich verloren ist. Dafür gibt es Hunderte von Beispielen, zu denen durch den Prozess der Mechanisierung ständig neue hinzukommen. Diese Verluste sind für gewöhnlich unwiederbringlich. Es ist erbärmlich, die endlosen Anstrengungen zu beobachten, ausgestattet mit Mikroskopie und Chemie, mit Mathematik und Elektronik, eine einzige Geige zu reproduzieren, wie sie der über eine unvollkommene Bildung verfügende Stradivarius vor mehr als 200 Jahren regelmäßig hergestellt hat.« Michael Polanyi, *Personal Knowledge*. Tschoma, 2016, Foto: Sabrina Chou

27 »Das langsame Surren der Zahnräder, das fette Geräusch des Glockenspiels, das immer zur Mittagszeit ertönt, die Ruhe und der Stillstand, die den aufgeblasenen Körper spüren lässt, wie sich die Welt unter ihm dreht – ich spüre diese Dinge innerlich, wie sicher viele Zuschauer, und will darüber nachdenken, warum sie uns so tief berühren.« T.J. Clark, *Painting at Ground Level*. LIFT, 2019, MDF, Sperrholz, Bronze, Vinylboden, Lampe, ONONO Rotterdam

28 »Zum Beispiel die Gleichsetzung eines Dinges mit einem Werkzeug: Dies impliziert, dass ein nützlicher Zweck erreicht werden kann, indem man das Ding als ein Instrument für diesen Zweck behandelt. Ich kann das Ding nicht als Werkzeug bezeichnen, wenn ich nicht weiss, wozu es dient – bzw., wenn ich seinen vermeintlichen Zweck kenne, dann glaube ich, dass es für diesen Zweck nutzlos ist.« Michael Polanyi, *Personal Knowledge*. PAPADADA, 2016, Arvenholz, Feige, Pracownia Portretu, Łódź, Foto: Maciek Łuczak

29 »Als die Großmutter aufwachte, blieb sie lange liegen und überlegte, ob sie hinausgehen sollte oder nicht. Ihr war, als sei die Nacht ganz nah ans Haus herangerückt und warte jetzt dort draußen. Außerdem taten ihr die Beine weh. Die Treppe war falsch gebaut, die Stufen waren zu hoch und zu schmal, dann kam gleich der Fels, der bis zum Holzplatz hinunter rutschig war. Und dann der ganze Weg wieder zurück. Kein Licht machen, weil man dadurch Richtung und Abstand verliert und die Dunkelheit näher heranlässt. Die Beine über die Bettkante schwingen und warten, bis das Gleichgewicht wieder stimmt.« Tove Jansson, *Das Sommerbuch*. LIFT, 2019, MDF, Sperrholz, Bronze, Vinyl, Lampe, ONONO Rotterdam

30 »Nach einer Weile fragte Sophia: ›Bist du sicher, dass die Tür geschlossen ist?‹ ›Die Tür ist offen‹, antwortete ihre Großmutter. ›Sie ist immer offen, du kannst ganz beruhigt schlafen.‹ Sophia wickelte sich in ihre Decke. Sie ließ die ganze Insel aufs Eis hinaustreiben und immer weiter, bis zum Horizont. Kurz bevor sie einschlief, stand der Vater auf und legte noch Holz in den Herd.« Tove Jansson, *Das Sommerbuch*. LIFT, 2019, MDF, Sperrholz, Bronze, Vinyl, Lampe, ONONO Rotterdam

31 »Ein Problem, das ich irgendwann einmal gelöst habe, kann mir kein Kopfzerbrechen mehr bereiten: Ich kann nicht erraten, was ich bereits weiss. Nachdem ich eine Entdeckung gemacht habe, werde ich die Welt nie wieder so sehen wie zuvor. Meine Augen haben sich verändert. Ich habe mich zu einem Menschen gemacht, der anders sieht und anders denkt. Ich habe eine Kluft überquert, die heuristische Kluft, die zwischen Problem und Entdeckung liegt.« Michael Polanyi, *Personal Knowledge*. Hauswand, Treignac Projet, 2018

32 »Gegenüber den Hafenbassins erstrecken sich die Depots, gleichgültige, gelbe Speichergebäude, die niemand bemerkt. Zwischen ihnen und den Kais schleppen die Hafenarbeiter Waren hin und her. Mich ziehen die Speicher an, sie sind am helllichten Tag so verborgen, und nichts bleibt in ihnen. Sämtliche Arbeiter tragen übrigens blaue Blusen. Früh hängen sie in dicken blauen Klumpen an den Trambahnen, die zum Hafen fahren. Das Blau spritzt überall hin.« Siegfried Kracauer, *Ginster*. Atelier, Charlois, Rotterdam

33 »Ich entsinne mich der Mobilmachungstage, in denen es hieß, dass der Kriegsminister dank dem Organisationswunder der fertigen Aufmarschpläne unbeschäftigt in seinem friedlichen Arbeitsraum säße, während draußen die Truppen marschierten. Der Krieg selbst ging dann freilich verloren...« Siegfried Kracauer, *Die Angestellten*. Hauseingang, Rotterdam, 2016, Micha Zweifel

34 »Wir erkennen die Angst, sobald wir allein sind. Manche von uns sind so kleinmütig, dass sie sich aus diesem Grund nie erlauben, allein zu sein. Doch Künstler müssen notwendigerweise allein sein, und deshalb müssen sie Ängste erkennen und überwinden. Das ist ein sehr langwieriger Vorgang.« Agnes Martin, *Schriften*. LIFT, 2019, MDF, Sperrholz, Bronze, Vinyl, Lampe, ONONO Rotterdam

35 Zur Sackgasse 4. Stock, Ausstellungsansicht Kunstmuseum Luzern, Foto: Marc Latzel

36 »Nur Kinder wollen sie keine haben.« Siegfried Kracauer, *Die Angestellten*. TASSENBAUM, 2020, Polyurethan, Acrylfarbe, Kunstmuseum Luzern, Foto: Marc Latzel

37 »Tiere können Fehler machen. Kaninchen geraten in Fallen. Fische beißen bei der Fliege des Anglers an, und solche Fehler können tödlich sein. Aber Tiere sind ausgenommen von Fehlern, die aufgrund ausgeklügelter Systeme der Fehlinterpretation basieren, wie sie nur durch sprachliche Ausdrücke entstehen.« Michael Polanyi, *Personal Knowledge*. OHNE TITEL, 2020, Bronze, Kunstmuseum Luzern, Foto: Katalin Deér

38 »Sie sitzt an einer Imbisstheke und taucht fettige Churros in ihren Kaffee. Öl, das im Morgenlicht auf der Oberfläche ihres Kaffees tanzt. Sie öffnet ihr Notizbuch, aber sie hat nichts zu sagen. Es ist lediglich ein schimmerndes Loch im Tag. « Eileen Myles, *Afterglow (a dog memoir)*. DOPPIO, 2020, Polyurethan, Acrylfarbe, Kunstmuseum Luzern, Foto: Marc Latzel

39 »Eine junge Verkäuferin hat mir von ihrer Freundschaft mit einem tüchtigen Metallarbeiter erzählt, der auf das Drängen ihres Vaters hin seinen Beruf gewechselt habe. Der Vater ist nichts Geringeres als ein Justizwachtmeister und duldet daher keinen Arbeiter in der Familie. Nun muss sich der Erwählte mit dem subalternen Posten eines Kassenboten begnügen, ist aber dafür zum Bräutigam avanciert.« Siegfried Kracauer, *Die Angestellten*. OHNE TITEL, 2020, Bronze, Kunstmuseum Luzern, Foto: Marc Latzel

40 »Technologie lehrt Handeln. Das wird deutlich, wenn sie sich in Imperativen ausdrückt, wie sie es oft in Kochbüchern oder Gebrauchsanweisungen für Maschinen tut.« Michael Polanyi, *Personal Knowledge*. ZUR SACKGASSE 4. STOCK, Ausstellungsansicht Kunstmuseum Luzern, Foto: Marc Latzel

41 »Kein Hund wird allein geboren.« Eileen Myles, *Afterglow (a dog memoir)*. DIE ZWEI FREUNDE, 2020, Arvenholz, Acrylfarbe, Nagellack, Hundeleinen

42 »Wenn du die Wahrheit wissen willst, wirst du sie wissen.« Agnes Martin, *Schriften*. ZUR SACKGASSE 4. STOCK, Ausstellungsansicht Kunstmuseum Luzern, Foto: Marc Latzel

43 »Licht trifft auf alles und ist dort, wo die Farbe hingeht. Es ist das, was übrigbleibt, wenn es weg ist.« Eileen Myles, *Afterglow (a dog memoir)*. ZUR SACKGASSE 4. STOCK, Ausstellungsansicht Kunstmuseum Luzern, Foto: Marc Latzel

44 »Er zitterte selbst und vermochte in dem Fernrohr nichts zu erkennen, die Tränen rannen auch über das Blickfeld, alles verwischt. Wäre es wenigstens wärmer gewesen, aber wo er nur hin griff, stachen Nadeln nach ihm, und auf der Scheibe hatten sich lauter Körnchen gehäuft.« Siegfried Kracauer, *Ginster*. FEUERWERK, 2017, Gips, Pigmente, Foto: Marc Latzel

45 »Sie lebten in jenem Winter zu dritt, und auch Ginster wurde der Geheimsprache mächtig.« Siegfried Kracauer, *Ginster*. Rheinländerstrasse, Basel, 2020

46 »Die Arbeitsnachweise erinnern an Rangierbahnhöfe mit unzähligen Gleisen, auf denen die Stellenlosen wie Waggons hin- und hergeschoben werden.« Siegfried Kracauer, *Die Angestellten*. REFILL, 2020, Polyurethan, Acrylfarbe, Kunstmuseum Luzern, Foto: Marc Latzel

47 »Bis Mai haben alle vergessen, wie schnell ich war. Ich sprang auf den Tisch und aß das ganze Essen auf. Es lag direkt auf den Tellern. Ihr wart im Nebenraum und hasstet euch gegenseitig.« Eileen Myles, *Afterglow (a dog memoir)*. Canapés, Luzern, 2020

48 »Klagen reihen sich ununterbrochen an Klagen. Sie sind schon gesiebt, ehe sie vorgebracht werden. Entweder durch einen Gerichtsbeamten in der Anmeldestube oder, was die Regel ist, durch die Organisationen.« Siegfried Kracauer, *Die Angestellten*. REFILL, 2020, Polyurethan, Acrylfarbe, Kunstmuseum Luzern, Foto: Marc Latzel

49 »Die Grenzen zwischen Genres nicht nur verschwimmen zu lassen, sondern völlig außerhalb von ihnen zu schreiben–das klingt nach einer wunderbaren Utopie, aber ist das überhaupt möglich? Was für eine Grenzsituation ist das, freischwebend außerhalb der sozialen Ordnung wie David Bowies Major Tom? Steckt Genre nicht alles an, was wir schreiben oder denken?« Dodie Bellamy, *Crimes Against Genre*, in *Academonia*. DOOR MAT 1, 2017, Gips, Pigmente, Kunstmuseum Luzern, Foto: Marc Latzel

50 »Tausende junge Angestellte träumen vom Paddeln.« Siegfried Kracauer, *Die Angestellten*. Charlois, Rotterdam, 2018

51 »In einem Sommer besorgte Sophias Vater ein Zelt und schlug es in der Schlucht auf, um sich dort verstecken zu können, falls zu viele Leute kommen sollten. Das Zelt war so klein, dass man auf allen vieren kriechen musste, um hineinzugelangen. Wenn man ganz eng nebeneinander lag, war Platz für zwei.« Tove Jansson, *Das Sommerbuch*. Schnitzen, Tschoma, 2018

52 »Viele Arbeitgeber haben höchst subjektive Vorstellungen von einer Gemeinschaft. ›Mein Kind‹, so reden die Aufsichtsdamen eines bekannten Warenhauses ihre Untergebenen an. Ein Familienleben, das vielleicht den Eifer der Kinder beflügelt, im Übrigen aber nicht weiter rührend ist, da es von Kontrollen durchsetzt wird, die nur ein geringes Vertrauen zu seiner Herzlichkeit bekunden.« Siegfried Kracauer, *Die Angestellten*. OHNE TITEL, 2018, Sperrholz, Farbe

53 »Der Mund ist ein ambivalenter Teil des Körpers, da er sowohl der Ort des Sprechens als auch des Kauens ist. Der Mönch sollte sich nicht vom Fleisch der Tiere ernähren, sondern vom Wort Gottes mit einer Bewegung des Kaumuskels–einer so genannten *Ruminatio (Wiederkäuen)*, die den vollen Geschmack bzw. Sinn des Textes freisetzt. Der Geschmack des Textes, das Kauen auf seinen saftigen Bedeutungen, ist eine Metapher, die sich bis zum heiligen Augustinus zurückverfolgen lässt.« Michael Camille, *Image on the Edge*. STOFFEL, 2018, geschnitztes Arvenholz, Zahnbürste, I am not your Guru, Arnhem

54 »Man darf hier weiter ausgreifen und sich darauf besinnen, dass das Unterbrechen eines der fundamentalen Verfahren aller Formgebung ist. Es reicht über den Bezirk der Kunst weit hinaus. Es liegt, um nur eines herauszugreifen, dem Zitat zugrunde. Einen Text zitieren, schließt ein: seinen Zusammenhang unterbrechen.« Walter Benjamin, *Was ist episches Theater?*. CONTRAPPOSTO, 2014, Zement, Foto: Sabrina Chou

55 »Eine ernste und manchmal unheilbare Form davon ist das ›Lampenfieber‹, das darin zu bestehen scheint, dass man ängstlich die Aufmerksamkeit auf das nächste Wort oder die nächste Note oder Geste lenkt, die man finden oder sich merken muss. Dadurch wird der Sinn für den Kontext zerstört, der allein die richtige Abfolge von Worten, Notizen oder Gesten reibungslos hervorrufen kann.« Michael Polanyi, *Personal Knowledge*. LIFT, 2019, MDF, Sperrholz, Bronze, Vinyl, Lampe, ONONO Rotterdam

56 »...mit anderen Worten: Wir, die wir den Begriff der modernen Komposition geschaffen haben, erhielten die Anerkennung dafür, bevor wir tot waren; einige von uns sogar ziemlich lange, bevor sie tot waren. Und so kann man sagen, dass der Krieg eine allgemeine Anerkennung des Begriffs der zeitgenössischen Komposition um fast dreißig Jahre beschleunigt hat.« Gertrude Stein, *Composition as Explanation*, in *What Are Masterpieces?*. Miniatur der Skulptur *Die zerstörte Stadt von Ossip Zadkine*, Warenhaus Bijenkorf, Rotterdam, 2019

57 »In der Nacht fällt Eingebung wie Regen auf die Welt und durchdringt unseren Geist, wenn wir schlafen. Deshalb sind wir so gierig, so wild nach Schlaf.« Agnes Martin, *Schriften*. Hafen Rotterdam, 2017

58 »Herr Allinger hatte Ginster für einen Schwimmbadentwurf verpflichtet, den er mit ihm gemeinsam im Interesse einer keramischen Firma ausarbeiten wollte, zu der er geschäftliche Beziehungen unterhielt. Er war ein Kunstgewerbler, den es zur gemächlichen Erzeugung von Landschaftsbildern hinzog. Auf die gemalten Wiesen passte er selber. Meist ging die Sonne unter.« Siegfried Kracauer, *Ginster*. OHNE TITEL (RENÉ DANIËLS SCHWÄNE), 2017, Gips, Pigmente

59 »Unter den Tannen war es angenehm kühl, und niemand hatte es eilig, darum machten sie ein kurzes Nickerchen. Als sie aufwachten, krochen sie bis an den Eingang der Höhle, aber die Großmutter war zu dick und kam nicht hinein. ›Du musst mir erzählen, wie es drin aussieht‹, sagte sie.« Tove Jansson, *Das Sommerbuch*. OHNE TITEL, 2017, Gips, Pigmente,

60 KURZE LÜFTUNGSPAUSE, 2017, Ausstellungsansicht, Swiss Art Awards, Foto: Guadalupe Ruiz

61 »Wir wissen intuitiv, dass der Alltag nicht den einfachen Umrissen gut gemachter Genres gehorcht. Tatsächlich kommt jedes Ereignis (und ich schließe die Handlungen des Schreibens, Lesens, Aufführens auf oder neben der Buchseite in diese Kategorie ein) weitgehend überraschend, und zwar vor allem in dem Masse, wie es seine eigenen typischen Erwartungen übertrifft. Wenn es dies wirklich tut, wenn es über die kalkulierte Überraschung einer kunstvollen Handlung oder eines auffallend tadelnswerten Themas hinausgeht, wird es von denjenigen, die die ästhetischen Erwartungen überwachen, sofort als Verbrechen bezeichnet.« Joan Retallack, zitiert von Dodie Bellamy, *Crimes Against Genre*, in *Academonia*. STREET VIEW, 2017, Gips, Pigmente

62 »Es ist kein Hund, sondern lediglich dessen Wiederholung.« Eileen Myles, *Afterglow (a dog memoir)*. STREET VIEW, 2017, Gips, Pigmente, Studioansicht

63 »Lampenfieber verfliegt und fließendes Sprechen wird wiederhergestellt, wenn es uns gelingt, unsere Gedanken nach vorne zu lenken und sie mit einem klaren Blick auf die umfassende Tätigkeit wirken zu lassen, an der wir in erster Linie interessiert sind.« Michael Polanyi, *Personal Knowledge*. STREET VIEW, 2017, Gips, Pigmente, Swiss Art Awards, Foto: Sabrina Chou

64 »Er hatte oft Pech und ärgerte sich über schlechtes Wetter oder Probleme mit dem Motor. Die Netze rissen oder blieben am Propeller hängen, und die Fische und die Vögel waren nicht da, wo man sie erwartet hätte. Kaum hatte man einen guten Fang gemacht, fielen die Preise, und es war gehupft wie gesprungen.« Tove Jansson, *Das Sommerbuch*. VERBOOMSTRAAT 182–184, Rotterdam, 2017, Gips, Pigmente

65 »Am Rand des Wassers offenbarte sich die Weisheit; Geister wurden an die raumlosen Orte ›zwischen Schaum und Wasser‹ oder ›zwischen Baum und Rinde‹ verbannt. Auch die zeitlichen Übergänge zwischen Winter und Sommer oder zwischen Nacht und Tag waren gefährliche Momente der Überschneidung mit dem Jenseits.« Michael Camille, *Image on the Edge.* Schwan im Hafenbecken, Rotterdam, 2017

66 »Wir gehen immer abends aus. Manchmal nimmt er mich schon nachmittags ins Café mit, dann kommen wir nicht mehr zurück. Sehen Sie sich meine Schuhe an, ich vertanze alle paar Monate die Schuhe.« Siegfried Kracauer, *Die Angestellten.* Wohnblock, Charlois, Rotterdam, 2016

67 »Auf der rosa Grundfläche der Schinkenscheiben schuf Ginster eine sternartige Komposition, die aus Einheiten von Essiggürkchen bestand. Kleinobst und Keks ließen sich zu ähnlichen Gebilden verwenden. Die Tatsache, dass man als Gast und Gastgeber zusammen aß, erforderte eine kurze Eingewöhnungszeit.« Siegfried Kracauer, *Ginster.* Ringgummimatte, 2017

68 »Für private Auftraggeber ersann er Porzellanteller und Kaffeekannen, die sich mit Vorbedacht wölbten. Sie glichen englischen Damen, die allein Italien bereisen und auf einer Bank an einem abgelegenen Zypressenörtchen Romane lesen.« Siegfried Kracauer, *Ginster.* KURZE LÜFTUNGSPAUSE, 2017, Ausstellungsansicht, Swiss Art Awards, Foto: Sabrina Chou

69 »So etwas wie ›zeitgenössische‹ Kunst gibt es nicht. Jedes Material kann verwendet werden, aber das Thema ist dasselbe, und sie Reaktion ist dieselbe für jedes Kunstwerk.« Agnes Martin, *Schriften.* Eingang Verboomstraat 182-184, Rotterdam, 2017

70 »Wissenschaftler, besser gesagt: kreative Wissenschaftler, verbringen ihr Leben damit, richtig zu raten. Dabei werden sie von ihrer heuristischen Leidenschaft unterstützt und geleitet. Wir nennen ihre Arbeit kreativ, weil sie die Welt, wie wir sie sehen, verändert, indem sie unser Verständnis davon vertieft. Die Veränderung ist unwiderruflich.« Michael Polanyi, *Personal Knowledge.* KURZE LÜFTUNGSPAUSE, 2017, Ausstellungsansicht, Swiss Art Awards, Foto: Sabrina Chou

71 »Hinter dem Felsen, zum offenen Meer hin, erstreckte sich ein Waldgürtel mit abgestorbenen Bäumen, der ständig dem Wind ausgesetzt war. Seit vielen hundert Jahren versuchte der Wald, gegen die Stürme anzuwachsen, dadurch hatte er ein ganz eigenes Gesicht erhalten. Im Vorbeirudern sah man deutlich, dass die Bäume sich vom Wind wegstreckten, sie duckten und verknoteten sich, ja, viele von ihnen krochen geradezu. Nach und nach brachen die Stämme, oder sie vermoderten und versanken, das abgestorbene Holz stützte oder erdrückte jenes, das noch grüne Spitzen hatte, und alles zusammen bildete eine verfilzte Masse aus hartnäckiger Ergebenheit.« Tove Jansson, *Das Sommerbuch.* Wandmalerei, Charlois, Rotterdam, 2017

72 »Weil wir die Fäkalien so säuberlich von allem anderen in unserem Leben getrennt haben, ruft ihr mittelalterlicher Status, verwoben mit dem heiligen Text, Unbehagen bei uns hervor. Fäkalien sind nicht einfach nur das, was sie sind, nämlich Materie, sondern sie werden zu mysteriösen Zeichen, die wir nicht mit der gleichen Begeisterung wie unsere Vorfahren deuten, würdigen und genießen können.« Michael Camille, *Image on the Edge.* Kleingarten, Rotterdam, 2017

73 »Die Zeit der Komposition ist die Zeit der Komposition. Sie war manchmal ein gegenwärtiges Ding, manchmal ein vergangenes Ding, manchmal ein zukünftiges Ding, manchmal ein Streben nach Teilen oder nach der Ganzheit dieser Dinge. In meiner Anfangszeit war sie eine kontinuierliche Gegenwart, wieder und wieder und wieder und wieder ein Anfang, sie war eine Serie, sie war eine Liste, sie war eine Ähnlichkeit und alles andere, sie war eine Verteilung und ein Gleichgewicht. Das ist die ganze Zeit, ein Teil der Zeit, das Wesen der Komposition. Gertrude Stein, *Composition as Explanation,* in *What Are Masterpieces?.* Pferd und Esel, Treignac, 2018

74 »Die Verdoppelung war Herrn Valentin zu üppig. Lieber weniger und nicht so leichtfertig abgerundete Ziffern. Er ärgerte sich, dass die Soldaten nach und nach fielen, statt schon jetzt fertig für den Friedhof zu sein.« Siegfried Kracauer, *Ginster.* DOOR MAT 1 & 2, 2017, Gips, Pigmente

75 »Vor dem Einschlafen pflegte sich im Bett regelmäßig das Folgende mit mir zu ereignen: ich legte zuerst den Kopf für eine gewisse Zeit auf die eine Seite, und zwar auf die Seite, auf der ich gewöhnlich schlief. Dann wandte ich mich um und kehrte mich der anderen Seite zu; wobei ich darauf achtete, dass ich in der mir unbequemeren Lage ungefähr ebenso lang wie in der früheren verharrte. Erst nach Erledigung dieses täglichen Bettpensums schien mir zu schlafen erlaubt. Wenn meine Mutter, die mich abends fast immer besuchte, nach dem Grund des ihr unerklärlichen Verhaltens fragte, antwortete ich lakonisch: ›Von wegen schief.‹« Siegfried Kracauer, *Ginster.* BÜSI, 2013, Kunstharz, Bouillonwürfel, Zigarettenstummel, Swiss Art Awards, Foto: Sabrina Chou

76 »Mein Traum ist, dass sich die Geschichte rückwärts bewegt. Was, wenn ich von ihm geboren worden wäre, von Kronos – von seinem Zorn und seiner Trunkenheit und der reifen Zerstörung der Waffen seines Vaters. Ich bin dafür. Und ich kenne diese Männer.« Eileen Myles, *Afterglow (a dog memoir).* KURZE LÜFTUNGSPAUSE, 2017, Swiss Art Awards, Foto: Guadalupe Ruiz

77 »Herren bedienen die schweren Ungetüme, deren Radau das eintönige Geklapper der lochenden Mädchen gewaltig übertrifft. Ich erkundige mich bei dem Bürovorsteher nach der Arbeitsweise der Maschinistinnen. ›Die Mädchen‹, erwidert er, ›lochen nur sechs Stunden und sind während der übrigen zwei Stunden als Kontoristinnen beschäftigt. So wird jede Überanstrengung vermieden. Das vollzieht sich in einem bestimmten Turnus, so dass jede Angestellte an alle Arbeiten kommt. Aus hygienischen Gründen schalten wir überdies von Zeit zu Zeit kurze Lüftungspausen ein.‹« Siegfried Kracauer, *Die Angestellten.* KURZE LÜFTUNGSPAUSE, 2017, Lüftungsschacht mit versteckten Lautsprecher, Swiss Art Awards, Foto: Sabrina Chou

78 »Vielleicht ist das die Erklärung dafür, warum die Dinge auf der Grundebene so bewegend sind. Es geht nicht so sehr darum, dass sie für das stehen, was verworfen werden muss, damit Ekstase entstehen kann. Vielmehr geht es darum, dass wir sie letztlich spüren, dass sie für den Zustand stehen, auf den die Ekstase ausgerichtet ist.« T.J. Clark, *Painting at Ground Level.* ON / OFF, 2017, Gips, Pigmente, Swiss Art Awards, Foto: Guadalupe Ruiz

79 »Der Außenbereich von Aulnay ist ein giftiger Knorpel – verseucht, befallen von unzähligen schleimigen und pelzigen Ungeziefern an seinen tragenden Wandvorsprüngen, Fensterbänken und Ecken, und diese Schädlinge sprießen aus diesen schattigen Wandvorsprüngen. Diese Idee, grinsende Dämonen und andere Formen, zumeist Köpfe, als Stütze für andere Bauelemente entlang der oberen Wände zu platzieren, ist in der antiken Geschichte tief verwurzelt. Im Norden hängt sie mit dem keltischen Brauch zusammen, enthauptete Köpfe zu verehren.« Michael Camille, *Image on the Edge.* Snackbar, St. Louis, 2017

80 »Mit besonderer Zärtlichkeit nahm sie die Namensschilder von längst zerfallenen Booten wahr, las die ersten Untersuchungen über ›Wahrscheinlichkeit von Sturm‹, Berichte über einen erschossenen Nerz, tote Seehunde und anderes mehr, und vor allem blieb ihr Blick an dem schönen Bild hängen, dem Bild mit dem Eremiten in seinem offenen Zelt vor einem Meer aus Wüstensand, mit einem beschützenden Löwen im Hintergrund.« Tove Jansson, *Das Sommerbuch.* KURZE LÜFTUNGSPAUSE, 2017, Ausstellungsansicht, Swiss Art Awards, Foto: Guadalupe Ruiz

81 »Genres sind von Natur aus verschieden, jedes einzelne bildet sich um den entsprechenden Gegenstand herum. Daher ist es ganz natürlich, dass Fiktion fiktional, d.h. erfunden ist; dass kreative Non-Fiction-Literatur auf Fakten beruht (obwohl ihr ein wenig Spielraum eingeräumt wird, so wie man von Hollywood-Starlets erwartet, dass sie über ihr Alter lügen); dass Poesie auf einer Erleuchtung basiert. Und all diese Formen besitzen eine Art von generischem Teflon, das sie vor offensichtlichen sexuellen Inhalten schützt. Sex – wenn er überhaupt irgendwo hingehört – wird in die gering geschätzten Schauplätze von Schundromanen und Pornos verstoßen.« Dodie Bellamy, *Crimes Against Genre,* in *Academonia.* LUILEKKERLAND 1-8 (NACH PIETER BRUEGEL DER ÄLTERE), 2018, Ausstellungsansicht, I am not your Guru, Arnhem

82 »Diese Adelsfamilie suhlt sich jedoch in Exkrementen, und der Sohn, Audiger, nimmt es mit einer inkontinenten alten Frau als einem seiner Gegner auf. Sie zwingt ihn, dreieinhalb ihrer Scheißhaufen zum Frühstück zu essen, und sagt zu ihm: ›Anschließend wirst du meine Fotze und meine Arschritze küssen‹. Sie isst, verdaut und recycelt ihn immer wieder, vergleichbar mit den Allesfresser-Orgien, die in der gotischen Marginalkunst abgebildet sind.« Michael Camille, *Image on the Edge.* Hühner beim Bouwmaat, Rotterdam, 2018

83 »Wir sind am meisten betroffen, weil wir wissen, wenn wir die Erfahrung der Freude besitzen, dass sie ausschlaggebend ist und wir denken, dass wir mit Gewalt, Zerstörung und Besitzanspruch auf dem falschen Geleise sind. Die transzendente Reaktion, die frei von der konkreten Umgebung und nicht auf sie bezogen ist, ist so glückselig und erscheint so viel unschuldiger, dass wir wünschen, sie auf Kosten einer konkreten Reaktion zu behalten suchen. Aber dies ist nicht möglich und es ist nicht wünschbar.« Agnes Martin, *Schriften.* Atelier, Treignac Projet, 2018

84 »Hatten Mäzene im Mittelalter noch die Gewinnmargen mit Affen, Jongleuren und Bauern geteilt, über die sie in Wirklichkeit jedoch herrschten, so spalteten sich in späteren Jahrhunderten die Repräsentationsformen auf, um auf diese Weise eindeutige Klassenpositionen auszuweisen. Das ›Groteske‹ wurde zu einer Kategorie, in die alles Barbarische und ›Mittelalterliche‹ einzuordnen war, bis es dazu kam, dass solche Dinge im 19. Jahrhundert das Empfinden der Romantik erregten.« Michael Camille, *Image on the Edge.* KALENDER, 2020 (Detail), Gipsrelief

85 »Dies ist das Schlaraffenland bzw. Luilekkerland, wie die Niederländer es nannten, während die Franzosen und Engländer es als ›The Land of Cockaigne‹ bezeichneten. Es ist das Königreich, in dem es überall vorzügliche Speisen gibt, die frisch gebraten aus der Luft in den Mund des Müßiggängers fallen, die auf Tischen liegen, die an sämtlichen Bäumen befestigt sind, oder die die Landschaft auf der Suche nach Essern durchstreifen – Schweine mit Tranchiermessern, die in Halfter gesteckt werden, die aus ihrer eigenen Kruste hergestellt sind. Niemand hier wird jemals wieder sein Brot im Schweiße seines Angesichts essen.« T.J. Clark, *Painting at Ground Level.* Pieter Bruegel der Ältere, Schlaraffenland, 1567, Alte Pinakothek, München

86 »Sie dachte an Zugvögel und an den Gesang der Drossel an einem Sommerabend und an den Kuckuck, ja, auch an den Kuckuck, und an die großen, kalten Vögel, die segeln und spähen, und an die ganz kleinen, die im Spätsommer in hektischen Schwärmen kurz zu Besuch kommen, kugelrund, dumm und unerschrocken, und an die Schwalben, die nur das Haus, in dem man glücklich ist, beehren. Seltsam, dass die unpersönlichen Vögel zu so starken Symbolen geworden sind.« Tove Jansson, *Das Sommerbuch.* Gänse, Waal, Rotterdam, 2018

87 »Was das Schlaraffenland damals über die Religion aussagte (und mit Sicherheit sprach aus ihm dabei die bäuerliche Kultur selbst, in einer ihrer unauslöschlichen Formen), war, dass alle Vorstellungen von Flucht und Vollkommenheit von den weltlichen Realitäten heimgesucht werden, die sie vorgeben zu verändern. Jeder Garten Eden ist die Erde, die perfektioniert ist; Unsterblichkeit ist fortgesetzte Sterblichkeit; jegliche Vorstellung von Glückseligkeit ist durch und durch körperlich und begehrend.« T.J. Clark, *Painting at Ground Level.* LUILEKKERLAND 6 (NACH PIETER BRUEGEL DER ÄLTERE), 2018, Gips, Pigmente

88 »Ein Problem... ist eine Vorstellung von etwas, nach dem wir streben. Es ist der intellektuelle Wunsch, eine logische Kluft zu überbrücken, auf deren anderer Seite das Unbekannte liegt, das durch unsere Vorstellung von ihm vollständig abgegrenzt, das aber bisher noch nie in sich selbst gesehen wurde. Die Suche nach einer Lösung besteht darin, mit diesem Ziel vor Augen zu suchen.« Michael Polanyi, *Personal Knowledge.* LUILEKKERLAND 5 (NACH PIETER BRUEGEL DER ÄLTERE), 2018, Gips, Pigmente

89 »Hin und wieder erschiene in weiter, weiter Ferne ein äffender Höhenzug, dünn wie die Kante eines Taschenmessers, eine Art Wald. Und da würden wir wissen, dass jenseits dieses Waldes, an dessen Rand wir nach vielen Stunden anlangten, sich weitere endlose Ebenen ausdehnten. Von Zeit zu Zeit fielen Schüsse.« Robert Walser, Jakob von Gunten. Karl Walser, *Blick vom Weissenstein,* 1899

90 »Beine und Karabinerläufe schlugen so unwiderstehlich auf die Landschaft los, dass sie zersprang. Ein Stück Fluss splitterte ab und fiel in den Himmel hinein, Felder wurden durchschnitten, aus den Pfützen flog Wasser hoch. Vor ihnen tauchte

ein Regiment Hopfenstangen auf, das den Weitermarsch verhindern wollte. Die Hopfenstangen vergrößerten sich schnell, lange, hagere Dinger, um die sich gefährliche Spiralen wanden, aber die Beine fuhren mitten unter sie und warfen sie in den Fluss.« Siegfried Kracauer, *Ginster*. OHNE TITEL (OXFORD MYSTERY SERIES), 2019, Öl auf Holzbrett

91 »Vergeude deine Gefühle von Unzufriedenheit nicht an der Gesellschaft. Wenn du dich unzufrieden fühlst, frage dich: ›Was will ich?‹, ›Was will ich wirklich?‹ Sobald du dir diese Frage stellst, wirst du erkennen, dass daraus Unzufriedenheit entsteht. Dein Unwillen, eine Aufgabe zu übernehmen, kann so stark sein, dass du dir diese Frage nicht einmal stellen kannst; in diesem Fall wirst du Hilfe bei anderen suchen. Doch es wird nirgendwo Hilfe für dich geben. Du wirst deine Vision für dich selber zu einem Zeitpunkt finden, da du allein bist.« Agnes Martin, *Writings*. ZUR SACKGASSE 4. STOCK, Ausstellungsansicht, Kunstmuseum Luzern, Foto: Marc Latzel

92 »Du schnippst die Krümel von seinem Schoß auf den Boden. Du verschüttest deinen Kaffee, eine milchige Pfütze aus Kaffee und Krümeln umgibt deine Schuhe, und du sitzt einfach da. Voller Erwartung.« Eileen Myles, *Afterglow (a dog memoir)*. ZUR SACKGASSE 4. STOCK, Ausstellungsansicht, Kunstmuseum Luzern, Foto: Marc Latzel

93 »Wie oft haben Sie jemandem gesagt, er sehe fabelhaft aus, und er oder sie sagte danke, ich fühle mich nämlich schrecklich. Und man kann es direkt hinter ihren Augen sehen. Das Schreckliche stellt eine Kerze dort hinein. Das Schreckliche macht dort das Licht an. Man fragt sich, ob die Leute einfach nur leer sind, wenn sie einfach so weitermachen mit dem Plan.« Eileen Myles, *Afterglow (a dog memoir)*. STOFFEL, 2019, geschnitztes Arvenholz, Zahnbürste, ONONO Rotterdam

94 »Eine Kunst, die nicht im Detail näher beschrieben werden kann, kann nicht per Vorschrift übermittelt werden, da für sie keine Vorschrift existiert. Sie kann nur anhand eines Beispiels vom Meister an den Lehrling weitergegeben werden. Das schränkt die Reichweite der Verbreitung auf persönliche Kontakte ein, und dementsprechend ist festzustellen, dass die Kunstfertigkeit in der Regel in eng begrenzten lokalen Traditionen überlebt.« Michael Polanyi, *Personal Knowledge*. Tschoma, 2017

95 »Die Veränderung trat vielleicht in dem Moment ein, als die Schwalben verstummten. Plötzlich war der flimmernde Himmel leer, ohne Vögel. Sophia wartete. Erhörung lag in der Luft. Sie ließ das Meer nicht aus den Augen und sah, dass der Horizont schwarz wurde.« Tove Jansson, *Das Sommerbuch*. OXFORD 2. MAI, 2018 (Detail), Gips, Pigmente

96 INEINANDER UND NACHEINANDER, 2018, Ausstellungsansicht, Treignac Projet

97 »Sie legte sich wieder ins Bett und sah dem Feuerschein zu, der über die Zimmerdecke tanzte, und unterdessen rückte die Insel näher an das Haus heran. Die Insel kam immer näher und näher. Die beiden Kinder schliefen auf einer Wiese am Ufer, auf der Bettdecke waren Schneeflecken, und unter ihnen verdunkelte sich das Eis und begann auseinanderzugleiten, ganz sachte öffnete sich eine Fahrrinne im Fußboden, und alle Koffer schwammen ins mondhelle Wasser hinaus.« Tove Jansson, *Das Sommerbuch*. TSCHOMA 28. DEZEMBER, 2018, Gips, Pigmente

98 »Nennen wir ihn einen Gelehrten. Seine Tintenfässer und sein Federhalter sind immer noch behutsam an seinen Gürtel geschnürt – sie sind Teil einer ganzen Reihe von Bändern und Bindfäden, die unter dem Druck seines dicken Bauches eindeutig kaum noch zusammengehalten werden. Vielleicht ist er doch eher ein Geistlicher (das Buch neben ihm sieht aus wie eine Bibel), aber er könnte ebenso gut ein Notar oder ein Wander-Schriftgelehrter sein. Das Manuskript, das von seinem Ärmel zerquetscht wird, sieht aus wie ein juristisches Schriftstück.« T.J. Clark, *Painting at Ground Level*. OHNE TITEL (SITZENDE FIGUR), 2018, Gips, Kleider, Stuhl, Treignac Projet

99 »Wir genießen es, das Wachsen der Pflanzen und das Reifen der Früchte zu beobachten. Stell dir einen Birnbaum voll goldener Früchte vor. Plötzlich pflücken wir eine Frucht und essen sie, und sie wird gänzlich zerstört. Es ist dasselbe mit den Tieren. Sie erscheinen uns schön, und wir genießen sie, aber plötzlich töten wir sie und essen sie.« Agnes Martin, *Schriften*. Sams Auto, 2018

100 »Hart stossen sich die Gedanken, nah beieinander wohnen die Sachen im Raum. Ein Geisterkampf um die Massenseele auf den Sportterrains. Er ist umso unerbittlicher, als er Wunschträumen gilt.« Siegfried Kracauer, *Die Angestellten*. TREIGNAC 13. MAI (SAMS AUTO), 2018, Gips, Pigmente, Treignac Projet

101 »Zitate in meiner Arbeit sind wie Räuber am Weg, die bewaffnet hervorbrechen und dem Müßiggänger die Überzeugung abnehmen.« Walter Benjamin, *Einbahnstraße*. BALKON MIT FAHRRAD, OXFORD, 2018, Gips, Pigmente

102 »Jeder einzelne Koffer war offen und voller Dunkelheit und Moos und kam nie mehr zurück.« Tove Jansson, *Das Sommerbuch*. KIESELSTEINE, 2018, Gips, Pigmente

103 »Die Bücher im Laden wurden von einem Mädchen bedient, dessen Haare sich schneckenförmig über den Ohren wanden; wie Blätterteigstücke im Frieden. Obwohl der Raum gut erwärmt war, schien Elfriede – so hieß, wie sich später herausstellte, das Mädchen – immer zu frieren, wenigstens hatte sie ein Batiktuch um sich geschlungen, auf dem Gräser zerflossen. Wenn sie, vor den Regalen stehend, die dünne Hülle höher zupfte, hatte Ginster den Eindruck, als zöge sie sich in eine eben erst geschaffene Wiese zurück, um die Sonnenstrahlen auf sich zu lenken.« Siegfried Kracauer, *Ginster*. HUND UND FLIEGE, 2018, Gips, Kunstfell, tote Fliege, Kette

104 »Manches begreift man erst, wenn es zu spät ist, dann mag man nicht mehr wieder von vorn anfangen, oder man vergisst es unterwegs und merkt es nicht einmal. Während die Großmutter nach Hause ruderte, sah sie das große Haus, das den Horizont unterbrach, und fand, dass es an ein Seezeichen erinnerte. Wenn man die Augen zukniff und an etwas anderes dachte, könnte es fast ein Seezeichen sein, einfach ein Zeichen dafür, dass der Kurs sich hier ändert.« Tove Jansson, *Das Sommerbuch*. OXFORD 25. MAI (BLÜTEN), 2018, Gips, Pigmente

105 »Ein Intervall existiert so gut wie nicht.« Gertrude Stein, *Composition as Explanation*, in *What Are Masterpieces?*. OXFORD 26. MAI, 2018, Gips, Pigmente, Treignac Projet

106 »Das Entfalten der Begabung im Gehorsam gegenüber der Eingebung bedeutet Glück in diesem Leben. Ein mühseliges Glück in dem wir vorangehen.« Agnes Martin, *Schriften*. OXFORD 2. MAI, 2018, Gips, Pigmente, Treignac Projet

107 »›Eigenartig‹, dachte die Großmutter, ›ich kann es nicht mehr beschreiben, ich finde keine Worte, oder vielleicht strenge ich mich nur nicht genügend an.‹ Das alles ist schon so lange her. Es geht niemanden etwas an. Wenn ich keine Lust habe, davon zu erzählen, ist das, als ob es nie passiert wäre, es verschließt sich, und damit ist es verloren. Sie setzte sich auf und sagte: ›An manchen Tagen erinnere ich mich nicht mehr so genau. Aber irgendwann musst du versuchen, eine ganze Nacht im Zelt zu schlafen.‹« Tove Jansson, *Das Sommerbuch*. Pfad oberhalb Treignac Projet, 2018

108 »Noch allgemeiner gesprochen, könnte man die Fäkalienproduktion als schöpferische Kraft betrachten. So wie die Gelehrten der *Fabliau* [Verserzählung mit komischem, vorwiegend erotischem Inhalt] begonnen haben, die Fäkalienproduktion selbst als einen bildlichen Ausdruck der Fiktion zu verstehen, die Rückführung toter Materie, so können diese Latrinen aus Fäkalienformen, die an den Rändern der Seite herumwirbeln, in ähnlicher Weise das Vermögen des Künstlers heraufbeschwören, Formen aus dem ›Ton‹ der Erde herzustellen.« Michael Camille, *Image on the Edge*. Kothaufen, 2017

109 »Jetzt wollen wir uns abstrakten Reaktionen zuwenden, der Reaktion, die aus unserem Inneren kommt, frei von unserer konkreten Umgebung. Wir wissen, dass sie maßgeblich ist. Wir wissen dass sie unendlich, ohne Dimension ohne Form und leer ist. Aber sie ist nicht nichts, denn wenn wir ihr unseren Geist übergeben, sind wir glückselig bewusst. Indem sie ohne Unvollkommenheit ist, ist sie Vollkommenheit. Und indem sie ohne Teile ist, ist sie ganz.« Anges Martin, *Schriften*. TREIGNAC 15. MAI, 2018 (Detail), Gips, Pigmente

110 »Alle Kleidungsstücke sind Rüstung bzw. Prothesen. Menschen sind keine Körper, auch wenn sie sich satt gegessen haben und wie übergroße Versionen ihrer selbst daliegen. Sie sind Ausstaffierungen mit Körpern, die sich verstecken.« T.J. Clark, *Painting at Ground Level*. OHNE TITEL (STEHENDE FIGUR), 2018, Gips, Kleider, Treignac Projet

111 »Es gab schließlich keinen Platz mehr für den Karneval, der jetzt an das ›volkstümliche‹ Ende des Marktes verbannt wurde und nur für den neugierigen Antiquar des Volkstümlichen von Interesse war. Im Gegensatz zum mittelalterlichen Mäzen oder Stifter erhob sich der Kenner (er war in der Regel männlich) über den Geschmack der ›Vulgären‹ und wollte Bilder, die von keinem Anflug der Unterschicht des Gemeinwesens beschmutzt waren.« Michael Camille, *Image on the Edge*. OHNE TITEL (SITZENDE FIGUR), 2018, Gips, Kleider, Stuhl, Treignac Projet

112 »Die Nächte waren inzwischen schon lang, und als Sophia aufwachte, sah sie nichts als Dunkelheit. Ein Vogel flog über die Schlucht und schrie, zuerst ganz nah und dann noch einmal in weiter Ferne. Es war eine windstille Nacht, dennoch hörte sie das Meer. Niemand ging durch die Schlucht, aber der Kies bewegte sich wie unter Schritten. Man hätte genauso gut draußen im Freien schlafen können, so nah war die Nacht an das schützende Zelt herangekrochen. Fremde Vögel stießen fremde Schreie aus, und die Dunkelheit war voller unbekannter Bewegungen...« Tove Jansson, *Das Sommerbuch*. TREIGNAC 13. MAI, 2018 (Detail), Gips, Pigmente

113 »Wenn wir einen Hammer benutzen, um einen Nagel hineinzuschlagen, befassen wir uns sowohl mit dem Nagel als auch mit dem Hammer, allerdings auf eine jeweils andere Art und Weise. Wir beobachten die Wirkung unserer Schläge auf den Nagel und versuchen, den Hammer so zu führen, dass wir den Nagel möglichst wirksam treffen. Wenn wir den Hammer hinunter zum Nagel führen, haben wir nicht das Gefühl, dass sein Griff in unserer Handfläche aufprallt, sondern dass sein Kopf den Nagel getroffen hat. In gewissem Sinne sind wir uns jedoch sehr wohl des Gefühls in unserer Handfläche und den Fingern bewusst, die den Hammer halten. Sie steuern die effektive Handhabung des Hammers, und der Grad der Aufmerksamkeit, die wir dem Nagel schenken, wird in gleichem Masse auch diesen Gefühlen, allerdings auf eine andere Art und Weise, entgegengebracht. Man kann den Unterschied so definieren, indem man sagt, dass letztere nicht wie der Nagel Objekte unserer Aufmerksamkeit sind, sondern Instrumente derselben.« Michael Polanyi, *Personal Knowledge*. HÜNDLI, 2014–2018, Zement, Kieselsteine, Plastikrohr, Küchentuch, Hundeleine, Foto: Sabrina Chou

114 »Geschichte zerfällt in Bilder, nicht in Geschichten.« Walter Benjamin, *Das Passagen-Werk*. EULE, 2013, Zement, Glas, Foto: Sabrina Chou

115 »Geld ist, wie Scheiße, überall am Rande der Gesellschaft anzutreffen. Es wird an Bettler weitergegeben, zwischen Liebhabern, zwischen Käufer und Händler, zwischen Kunde und Prostituierter. Wie die Glocken, die auf dieser Seite geläutet werden, klimpert es in der Tasse des Bettlers. Die Münze war das ›neue Lied‹, das *canticum novum*, zu dem alle tanzen mussten, sogar der Mäzen dieses Buches, der genau diese Bilder gekauft und den Künstler aus der Stadt mit diesen besudelten Symbolen der Stadt bezahlt hatte, so wie er die Prostituierte bezahlt hatte.« Michael Camille, *Image on the Edge*. AGIP, 2013, Zement, Sprayfarbe, Foto: Sabrina Chou

116 »Es war heiß, still und einsam. Das Haus duckte sich wie ein langes, plattes Tier, und darüber flogen Schwalben mit schrillen Schreien, wie Messer fuhren sie durch die Luft. Sophia folgte dem Ufer rings um die Insel und kam wieder zurück, auf der ganzen Insel gab es nichts als Felsen, Wacholder, Geröll, Sand und Büschel aus trockenem Gras. Der gelbe Nebel, der stärker als das Sonnenlicht war und in den Augen schmerzte, legte sich wie ein Schleier über Himmel und Meer, die Dünung rollte in hohen Wogen landeinwärts und schlug als Brandung an den Strand. Es war eine sehr große Dünung. ›Lieber Gott, lass etwas passieren‹, betete Sophia. ›Ich bin klein, mein Herz ist rein, ich sterbe vor Langeweile, Amen.‹« Tove Jansson, *Das Sommerbuch*. OHNE TITEL (FIGUR), 2014, Gebeiztes Sperrholz, Foto: Sabrina Chou

117 FÜR WEN ARBEITEN SIE EIGENTLICH?, 2018, Ausstellungsansicht *Doch Bitte Aber* (mit Sabrina Chou und Bernd Krauss), FABRIKculture, Hégenheim, Foto: Sabrina Chou

118 »Dir zuzuschauen ist so viel Yoga« Eileen Myles, *Afterglow (a dog memoir)*. UNTITLED, 2020, Bronze, Studioansicht Stiftung Sitterwerk, Foto: Katalin Deér

119 »Was ziehen wir daraus für einen glücklichen Schluss? Wir schließen, dass wir viel Energie besitzen und das wir das Handeln genießen. Unser Leben

hat einen Zweck, und er ist jede Minute wirksam. Wenn wir auf der richtigen Spur sind, werden wir durch Freude belohnt. Wir können die ganze Wahrheit wissen, wenn wir unser Inneres darum bitten. Wenn wir ganz richtungslos sind, können wir uns zurückzeihen, und unser Inneres wird uns sagen, welchen Schritt wir als nächsten tun sollen.« Agnes Martin, *Schriften.* KALENDER, 2020, Gips, Studioansicht Stiftung Sitterwerk, Foto: Katalin Deér

120 »Nach Geschäftsschluss trinkt sie daheim in ihrem möblierten Zimmer noch rasch einen starken Kaffee, der sie wieder frisch macht, und dann geht es los, mitten ins Leben hinein, zu den Studenten und Künstlern, mit denen geschwatzt, geraucht und gepaddelt wird. Wahrscheinlich geschieht auch noch mehr. Über eine kurze Weile, und man hat sie gesehen. Die Kolleginnen in den Büros aber bleiben.« Siegfried Kracauer, *Die Angestellten.* MEC (BIELER VERSION), 2016, Schaumstoff, Schuhe, Lokal_Int, Biel / Bienne

MICHA ZWEIFEL

1987	born in Lucerne / geboren in Luzern, CH
	lives and works in Rotterdam as artist, editor and cook /
	lebt und arbeitet in Rotterdam als Künstler, Verleger und Koch
2015–2017	Co-direction / Ko-Leitung Publication Studio Rotterdam, NL
2012–2014	Piet Zwart Institute, Master of Fine Arts, Rotterdam, NL
2008–2010	Gerrit Rietveld Academie, Bachelor Fine Arts, Amsterdam, NL
2006–2007	Vorkurs, Schule für Gestaltung, Biel / Bienne, CH

SOLO EXHIBITIONS (SELECTION) / EINZELAUSSTELLUNGEN (AUSWAHL)

2020	*Zur Sackgasse 4. Stock*, Kunstmuseum Luzern, CH
	Zähe Zeiten / Chewy times, Hebel_121, Basel, CH
	(with / mit Sabrina Chou)
2019	*LIFT*, ONONO, Rotterdam, NL
2018	*Ineinander und nacheinander*, Treignac Projet, Treignac, FR
2016	*Dwa*, Pracownia Portretu, Lódź, PL
	Rotterdam Gossip, Lokal_Int, Biel / Bienne, CH
	Meubels, Charlois?, Rib, Rotterdam, NL
2015	*Obituary*, Peach, Rotterdam, NL
2011	*Icônes & noir / blanc*, OLM-Space, Neuchâtel, CH
2010	*untitled (its a yam) + YAM*, Lokal_Int, Biel / Bienne, CH
2008	*SL'HDB*, Lokal_Int, Biel / Bienne, CH
2007	*Prix Fondation Anderfuhren*, Centre PasquArt, Biel / Bienne, CH

GROUP EXHIBITIONS (SELECTION) /
GRUPPENAUSSTELLUNGEN (AUSWAHL)

2018	*I am not your guru*, Studio Omstand, Arnhem, NL
	Raumfahrt II, Museum Langmatt, Baden, CH
	Doch bitte aber, FABRIKculture, Hégenheim, FR
2017	Swiss Art Awards, Basel, CH
	Walgenbach, Isabelle, Faysal, Micha, Robin Hood, Rib, Rotterdam, NL
2014	*Lokal_Int*, Biel / Bienne, CH
	Kairos Time, TENT, Rotterdam, NL
2013	Duende, Rotterdam, NL
2012	*Cosa sono le nuvole?*, joli mois de mai, Biel / Bienne, CH

AWARDS, RESIDENCIES (SELECTION) /
PREISE, ATELIERAUFENTHALTE (AUSWAHL)

2020	Manor Kunstpreis Zentralschweiz, Luzern, CH
	Residency, Foundation / Stiftung Sitterwerk, St. Gallen, CH
2018	A mouth for a stew, Residency Kunsthuis SYB, Beetsterzwaag, NL (with / mit Sabrina Chou)
2017	Laureate Swiss Art Awards 2017, Basel, CH
2014	Summer School, Eikones NCCR Iconic Criticism, Basel, CH
	Promotieprijs Piet Zwart Institute, Rotterdam, NL
2013	Residency, FabrikCulture Hégenheim, FR
2009	Public Art Collection / Kunstkommission Biel, Biel / Bienne, CH
2007	Prix Fondation Anderfuhren, Biel / Bienne, CH

SABRINA CHOU is an artist from Los Angeles, California. She has presented work internationally in exhibitions, broadcasts, and publications. She studied at Harvard University in Cambridge and the Piet Zwart Institute in Rotterdam, and she is currently a PhD candidate at the University of Oxford.

MICHEL REBOSURA is a philosopher, an art critic, and a cultural journalist. He lives in Lucerne, and writes, amongst others, for the Kunstbulletin, Journal of Arts, and 041 — Das Kulturmagazin.

VIVIAN SKY REHBERG is a writer based in Brussels. She works as a Senior Research Lecturer at the Willem de Kooning Academy-Piet Zwart Institute in Rotterdam, associated with the Rotterdam Arts and Sciences Lab.

LISA ROBERTSON, the Canadian writer's books include a novel, *The Baudelaire Fractal*; *Nilling*: Prose Essays; *Occasional Work and Seven Walks from the Office for Soft Architecture*; and with Matthew Stadler, *Revolution, A Reader*, as well as eight books of poetry. She lives in France.

MATTHEW STADLER is a writer and editor. He co-founded the publishing network, Publication Studio, and was literary editor of Nest magazine. He's written and published seven novels, and is now editor of the Polity of Literature project, at www.artseverywhere.ca.

EVELINE SUTER is curator and responsible for communication at the Kunstmuseum Luzern. She studied art history, German Literature and Linguistics in Zurich and Valencia. She specializes in contemporary art.

CHRISTOPH ZWEIFEL has lived in Thusis since he retired. He is a househusband and walker, plays violin in the local string orchestra, carves wooden bowls and takes care of fruit trees. From 1989 to 2015 he worked as a restorer in the Museum der Kulturen in Basel.

SABRINA CHOU ist eine Künstlerin aus Los Angeles, Kalifornien. Sie präsentiert ihre Werke international in Ausstellungen, Rundfunksendungen und Publikationen. Sie studierte an der Harvard University in Cambridge und am Piet Zwart Institute in Rotterdam und ist derzeit Doktorandin an der Universität Oxford.

MICHEL REBOSURA ist Philosoph, Kunstkritiker und Kulturjournalist. Er lebt in Luzern und schreibt unter anderem für das Kunstbulletin, Journal of Arts und 041 – Das Kulturmagazin.

VIVIAN SKY REHBERG ist Autorin und lebt in Brüssel. Sie arbeitet als Senior Research Lecturer an der Willem de Kooning Academy-Piet Zwart Institute in Rotterdam, die zum Rotterdam Arts and Sciences Lab gehört.

LISA ROBERTSON, zu den Büchern der kanadischen Schriftstellerin gehören der Roman *The Baudelaire Fractal* und die Prosa-Essays *Nilling* und *Occasional Work and Seven Walks from the Office for Soft Architecture*. Sie hat acht Gedichtbände verfasst und gemeinsam mit Matthew Stadler *Revolution, A Reader* herausgegeben. Sie lebt in Frankreich.

MATTHEW STADLER ist Autor und Herausgeber. Er ist Mitbegründer des Verlagsnetzwerks Publication Studio und war Literatur-Redakteur der Zeitschrift Nest. Er hat sieben Romane verfasst und veröffentlicht und ist jetzt Herausgeber des Polity of Literature Projekts, siehe www.artseverywhere.ca.

EVELINE SUTER ist Kuratorin und Verantwortliche Kommunikation am Kunstmuseum Luzern. Sie studierte Kunstgeschichte, neue deutsche Literatur und Linguistik in Zürich und Valencia. Ihr Spezialgebiet ist zeitgenössische Kunst.

CHRISTOPH ZWEIFEL lebt seit seiner Pensionierung in Thusis. Er ist Hausmann und Spaziergänger, spielt Geige im lokalen Streichorchester, schnitzt Holzschalen und pflegt Obstbäume. Von 1989 bis 2015 arbeitete er als Restaurator im Museum der Kulturen in Basel.

MICHA ZWEIFEL
RINGGUMMIMATTE

This book is published on the occasion of the exhibition / Die Publikation erscheint zur Ausstellung *Micha Zweifel. Zur Sackgasse 4. Stock*, Kunstmuseum Luzern 05.12.2020–31.01.2021

EXHIBITION / AUSSTELLUNG
Director / Direktorin:
Fanni Fetzer

Curator / Kuratorin:
Eveline Suter

Communication / Kommunikation:
Beni Muhl

Head of Administration / Administrative Leiterin:
Gabriele Froning

Bookkeeping and Administration / Buchhaltung und Administration:
Deborah Morozzi

Events:
Judith Wyrsch

Head of Exhibition and Museum Technology / Leiter Ausstellungs- und Museumstechnik:
Tobias Oehmichen

Museum Technology / Ausstellungstechnik:
Daniel Amhof, Samuli Blatter, Michael Greppi, Raphael Muntwyler, Steven Todd

Kunstvermittlung:
Angela Erni, Ursula Helg, Brigit Meier

Head of Museum Services / Leitung Museumsdienst:
Judith Wartenweiler

Front Desk / Kasse, Empfang:
Fabienne Immoos, Ruth Rigert, Esther Stutz

Museum Services / Aufsicht:
Ursula Ambauen, Gabi Andres, Mariann Angehrn, Carla Crameri, Marisa Crameri-Cerutti, Silvia Embacher, Lucia Ferrari Piazza, Enikö Fülöp, Sandra Harmath-Cerutti, Ivana Janackovic, Elisabeth Kaufmann, Angelika Lemaréchal, Aline Peter, Enkh-Oyuna Pokerschnigg, Sirkka Saviranta, Stephanie Schmid, Katharina Schulik, Anja Sidler, Christian Sterchi, Ursula Ulmi, Yvonne Zorzi

Kunstmuseum Luzern

Kunstmuseum Luzern
Europaplatz 1
CH-6002 Luzern
www.kunstmuseumluzern.ch
info@kunstmuseumluzern.ch

PUBLICATION / PUBLIKATION
Editor / Herausgeber:
Kunstmuseum Luzern

Concept, artwork, images / Konzept, Werke, Bilder:
Micha Zweifel

Texts / Texte:
Sabrina Chou, Michel Rebosura, Vivian Sky Rehberg, Lisa Robertson, Eveline Suter, Matthew Stadler, Christoph Zweifel, Micha Zweifel

Translation / Übersetzung:
Jan-Frederik Bandel (EN-GER, Spector Books)
Pauline Cumbers (GER-EN),
Uli Nickel (EN-GER, Captions / Bildlegenden),
Daniela Seel (EN-GER, Robertson)

Lektorat und Korrektorat / Copyediting and Proofreading:
Pauline Cumbers, Anne König, Beni Muhl, Eveline Suter

Design / Gestaltung:
Studio Krispin Heé (Krispin Heé, Tim Wetter)

Printing and Binding / Druck und Bindung:
DZA Druckerei zu Altenburg GmbH

Paper / Papier:
Munken Lynx Rough, 120 g/m²

Font / Schrift:
Favorit by ABC Dinamo

The artist and the Kunstmuseum Luzern would like to thank the following for their support / Der Künstler und das Kunstmuseum danken herzlich für die Unterstützung

MANOR
Casimir Eigensatz Stiftung
Walter Haefner Stiftung
Hulda und Gustav Zumsteg Stiftung

Micha Zweifel thanks / dankt:
For their enduring support and criticality / Für ihre Unterstützung und Kritik: Sabrina Chou, Bernd Krauss, Gabriele Rudin, Matthew Stadler, Christoph Zweifel.
I would like to thank all the authors for their excitement, generosity and insights / Ich möchte mich herzlich bei allen Autorinnen und Autoren bedanken für ihre Begeisterung, Großzügigkeit und Erkenntnisse: Sabrina Chou, Michel Rebosura, Vivian Sky Rehberg, Lisa Robertson, Eveline Suter, Matthew Stadler, Christoph Zweifel.
Thank you for making this publication possible / Vielen Dank, dass ihr diese Publikation möglich gemacht habt: Eveline Suter, Krispin Heé, Tim Wetter.
Thank you to the teams of / Vielen Dank den Teams von Kunstmuseum Luzern, Stiftung Sitterwerk & Kunstgiesserei St. Gallen.

Published by / Erschienen bei:
Spector Books
Harkortstraße 10
D-04107 Leipzig
www.spectorbooks.com

First Edition / Erste Auflage:

Printed in Germany
ISBN 978-3-95905-426-3

DISTRIBUTION / VERTRIEB
Germany, Austria:
GVA, Gemeinsame Verlagsauslieferung Göttingen GmbH & Co. KG
www.gva-verlage.de

Switzerland:
AVA Verlagsauslieferung AG
www.ava.ch

France, Belgium:
Interart Paris
www.interart.fr

UK:
Central Books Ltd
www.centralbooks.com

USA, Canada, Central and South America, Africa:
ARTBOOK | D.A.P.
www.artbook.com

Japan:
twelvebooks
www.twelve-books.com

South Korea:
The Book Society
www.thebooksociety.org

Australia, New Zealand:
Perimeter Distribution
www.perimeterdistribution.com

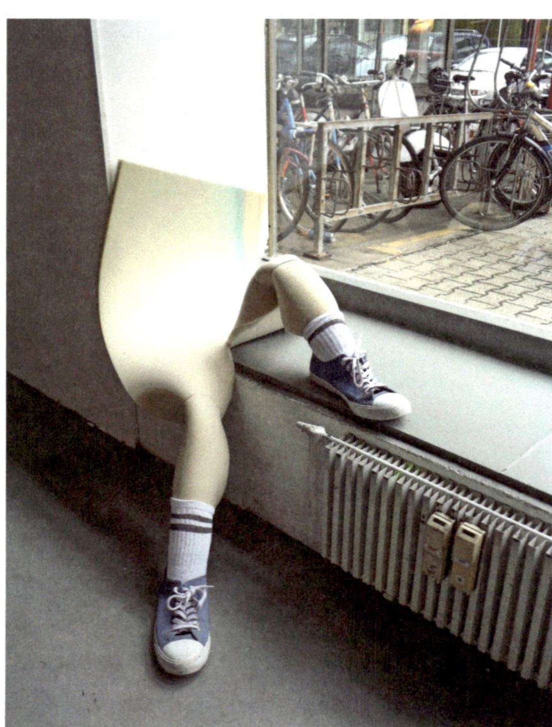

120 "After closing time, at home in her furnished room, she first gulps down a strong coffee to freshen her up again, then it is off and away into the midst of life, to the students and artists with whom there is chatter and smoking and canoeing. More than that probably happens too. After a short while, she will disappear. But in the offices her colleagues remain." Siegfried Kracauer, *The Salaried Masses*. MEC (BIEL VERSION), 2016, foam, shoes, Lokal_Int, Biel/Bienne